Teacher's Resource Book

MATH*thematics*

Book 2

C5 Making Choices

C6 Search and Rescue

The
STEM
Project

✎ **McDougal Littell**
A HOUGHTON MIFFLIN COMPANY
Evanston, Illinois ◆ **Boston** ◆ **Dallas**

McDougal Littell: www.mcdougallittell.com
Middle School Mathematics: www.mlmath.com

Acknowledgments

Writers

The authors of *Middle Grades Math Thematics, Books 1–3,* wish to thank the following writers for their contributions to the Teacher's Resource Books for the *Math Thematics* program: **Mary Buck, Roslyn Denny, Jean Howard, Sallie Morse, Patrick Runkel, Thomas Sanders-Garrett, Christine Tuckerman.**

Photography

Front Cover RMIP/Richard Haynes (t); Per Eide/The Image Bank (b); **1-1** RMIP/Richard Haynes; **2-1** Per Eide/The Image Bank; **Back Cover** Joe McBride/Tony Stone Images.

Illustrations

2-49, 2-50, 2-51 John Sanderson

The STEM Project

Middle Grades Math Thematics is based on the field-test version of the STEM Project curriculum. The STEM Project was supported in part by the

 NATIONAL SCIENCE FOUNDATION

under Grant No. ESI-9150114. Opinions expressed in *Middle Grades Math Thematics* are those of the authors and not necessarily those of the National Science Foundation.

ISBN: 0-395-89469-7
1 2 3 4 5 6 7 8 9 10–B–03 02 01 00 99 98

About the Teacher's Resource Book

This Resource Book contains all of the teaching support that you need to teach *Math Thematics*, Book 2, Modules 1 and 2. This teaching support includes the following material:

Spanish Glossary

A Spanish translation of the Glossary from the pupil textbook in blackline master form. The Spanish Glossary is located at the beginning of the Teacher's Resource Book for Modules 1 and 2.

Teaching Commentary

Planning the Module Contains a Module Overview and charts showing Module Objectives, Topic Spiraling, Topic Integration, Materials needed, and Teacher Support Materials. Also included are a Guide for Assigning Homework for regular and block schedules, Classroom Ideas, and a Home Involvement Math Gazette. For more information on the Guide for Assigning Homework and pacing, see pages vii-viii.

Teaching Suggestions Complete and comprehensive teaching suggestions for each section of the module. These include a Section Planner, a Section Overview, Materials List, Section Objectives, Assessment Options, Classroom Examples, Closure Questions, a Section Quiz, and notes on Customizing Instruction. Each page features a two-page pupil edition reduced facsimile for easy visual reference to the pupil textbook.

Blackline Masters

Labsheets Blackline masters used in conjunction with various Exploration questions to present data and extend the scope of the Exploration. Answers are provided at point of use in the annotated Teacher's Edition.

Extended Exploration Solution Guide A comprehensive discussion of the Extended Exploration in the pupil textbook, including how to assess student responses and performance.

Alternate Extended Exploration An extended exploration that can be substituted for the one in the pupil textbook, including teaching notes and assessment procedures.

Warm-Up Exercises and Quick Quizzes A page featuring the Warm-Up Exercises from the annotated Teacher's Edition and the Section Quizzes from the Teaching Suggestions of this Resource Book. Each page is printed in large easy-to-read type and can be used to create an overhead visual or used as a hand-out. Answers for the exercises and the quiz are provided at the bottom of each page.

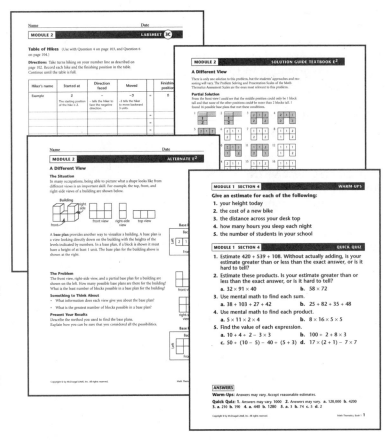

Practice and Applications One to two pages of additional practice for each section of the module. Answers are provided in the Answer section of this Resource Book.

Study Guide Two to three pages of Study Guide for each section of the module. These Study Guide pages feature key concepts, worked-out examples, exercises, and spiral review. They can be used for review and reteaching. Answers are provided in the Answer section of this Resource Book.

Technology Activity A technology activity related to the technology page of each module. Answers are provided in the Answer section of this Resource Book.

Assessment Assessment options include a mid-module quiz and two module tests, Forms A and B. Answers are provided in the Answer section of this Resource Book.

Standardized Assessment A page of standardized multiple-choice questions for each module. Answers are provided in the Answer section of this Resource Book.

Module Performance Assessment A Performance Assessment task for each module. Answers are provided in the Answer section of this Resource Book.

Answers Complete answers to all blackline masters.

Cumulative Test with Answers A cumulative test on both the modules of this Resource Book. Answers to the test follow immediately.

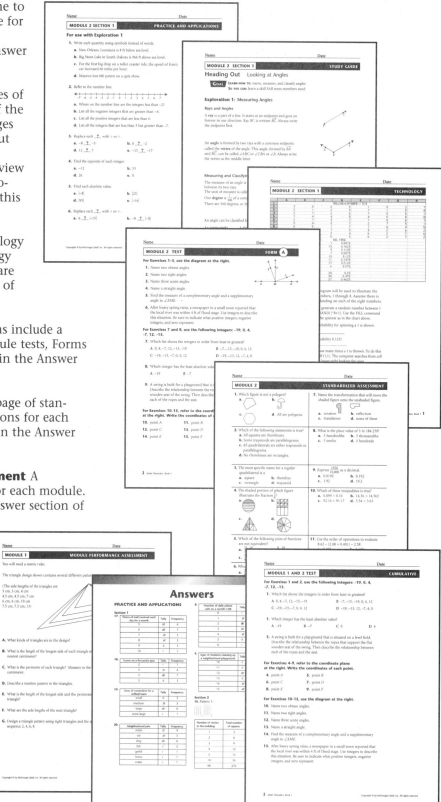

Table of Contents

Pacing and Assigning Homework

Pacing Chart

The Pacing Chart below shows the number of days allotted for each of the three courses: a Core Course, an Extended Course, and a Block Scheduling Course. The Core and Extended Courses require 140 days, and the Block Scheduling Course, 70 days. The time frames include the Module Projects, the Extended Explorations (E^2), and time for review and assessment.

Module	1	2	3	4	5	6	7	8
Core Course	18	16	21	19	17	18	17	14
Extended Course	18	16	21	19	17	18	17	14
Block Scheduling	9	8	11	10	8	9	8	7

Core Course

The Core Course is intended for students who enter with typical, or about average, mathematical skills. The daily assignment provides students with about 20–30 minutes of homework a night taken from appropriate Practice and Application (PA) exercises. Exercises range from straightforward skill practice, to applications that require reasoning, problem solving, and making connections across mathematical strands. The assignments include all the exercises suggested for use as embedded assessment. Each section's Spiral Review (SR) is included, as are all Reflecting on the Section (ROS) problems. Because of all the elements to be covered, assignments for the one-day sections may take more time. Also, sometimes a lengthy Reflecting on the Section problem (or other essential exercise) may cause an assignment to run longer. These problems have been denoted with a star (*). In such cases, teachers may want to spread the assignment out over more than one day, or may wish to provide class time for students to complete the work.

Extended Course

The Extended Course is designed for students who enter with strong or above average mathematical skills. Daily assignments cover all the essential material in the Core Course, including the embedded assessment exercises, the Spiral Review (SR), and the Reflecting on the Section (ROS) problems. Assignments also contain more difficult problems, including all the Challenge (Chal) and Extension (Ext) exercises. As in the Core Course, each assignment is designed to be completed in about 20–30 minutes. Some Extension or Reflecting on the Section problems may cause assignments to run long. These longer problems are denoted by a star (*).

Block Scheduling Course

The Block Scheduling course is intended for schools that use longer periods, typically 90-minute classes, for instruction. The course covers all eight modules. The assignments range from straightforward application of the material to exercises involving higher-order thinking skills. Daily assignments are designed to provide about 40–50 minutes of homework, and to cover all the essential material in the Core Course, including the embedded assessment exercises, the Spiral Review (SR), and Reflecting on the Section (ROS).

Guide for Assigning Homework

The Guide for Assigning Homework appears on each module's opening pages. The first chart suggests Core and Extended Assignments. The second chart offers assignments and pacing for Block Scheduling.

Regular Scheduling (45 min class period)

Section/ P&A Pages	Core Assignment	Extended Assignment	exercises to note		
			Additional Practice/Review	Open-ended Problems	Special Problems
1 pp. 465–470	**Day 1:** 1–3, 5–8, SR 23–25	1–3, Chal 4, 5–8, SR 23–25	EP, p. 470		
	Day 2: 9–11, 14–17	9–11, 14–17	PA 12, 13, 18–20		
	Day 3: 21, *ROS 22, SR 26–32	21, *ROS 22, SR 26–32, Ext 33		ROS 22; Mod Proj 3; St Sk, p. 470	Mod Proj 1–3
2 pp. 480–484	**Day 1:** 1–9, SR 25–32	1–9, SR 25–32	EP, p. 483		
	Day 2: 10–14, 18–20, ROS 24	10–14, 18–20, Chal 23, ROS 24	PA 15–17, 21, 22	Std Test, p. 483; E², p. 484	PA 19; E², p. 484

Additional Practice/Review
Each section contains additional support and practice for the objectives:
• **Extra Skill Practice (EP)** A page for each section, including exercises for each day and a set of Standardized Testing or Study Skills exercises.
• **Practice and Application (PA)** Exercises beyond the 20–30 minute homework period, covering the same skills and concepts as the Core Assignment.
• **Toolbox (TB)** Teaching and practice for pre-book skills applied in this section or in upcoming sections.

Open-ended Problems
Included in this category are exercises where students generate examples, create designs, or use original ideas. The Extended Exploration (E^2) from each module appears here. It is designed to provide a rich problem solving experience, with multiple approaches or solutions. The listing may include Reflecting on the Section (ROS), Career Connection (Career), Module Project (Mod Proj), Study Skills (St Sk), or Standardized Testing (Std Test) exercises, as well as other Practice and Application (PA) exercises where appropriate.

Special Problems Exercises in this category require extra time or additional materials, such as a calculator or a newspaper. All Extended Exploration (E^2) and Module Project (Mod Proj) activities are listed, as well as many Practice and Application (PA) exercises labeled Research, Create Your Own, or Home Involvement. (The E^2 and the final Module Project questions are listed with the sections they follow.) Although Special Problems are not included in the Core Assignment, they are accessible to all students. Teachers may allot class time or extra days for students to complete them.

Block Scheduling (90 min class period)

	Day 1	Day 2	Day 3	Day 4	Day 5	Day 6	
Teach	Sec 1 Expl 1–2	Sec 1 Expl 3; Sec 2 Expl 1	Sec 2 Expl 2; Sec 3 Expl 1	Sec 3 Expl 2–3	Sec. 4	Sec. 5	**Allow 2 days** review/assess/projects
Apply/ Assess (P&A)	Sec 1: 1–3, 5–11, 14–17, SR 23–25	Sec 1: 21, *ROS 22, SR 26–32 Sec 2: 1–9, SR 25–32	Sec 2: 10–14, 18–20, *ROS 24 Sec 3: 1–8, SR 23–26	Sec 3: 9–13, 17–20, ROS 22, SR 27–32	Sec 4: 1–6, 10–14, ROS 16, SR 17–26	Sec 5: 1–4, 6–8, 10–12, 16–18, ROS 20, SR 21–29	
Yearly Pacing	**Mod 7:** 8 days		**Mods 1–7:** 63 days		**Remaining:** 7 days	**Total:** 70 days	

Glossary/Glosario

A ►►►►►►►►►►►►►►►►►►►►►►►►►►

absolute value/valor absoluto (pág. 91) La distancia entre un número y cero en una recta numérica.

acute angle/ángulo agudo (pág. 83) Un ángulo cuya medida es mayor que 0° y menor que 90°. *Véase también* angle/ángulo.

acute triangle/triángulo acutángulo (pág. 415) Un triángulo con tres ángulos agudos.

alternate exterior angles/ángulos externos alternos (pág. 425) Cuando dos rectas son cortadas por una transversal, estos ángulos quedan afuera de las dos rectas y en lados opuestos de la transversal.

Los ángulos 1 y 2 son ángulos externos alternos.

alternate interior angles/ángulos internos alternos (pág. 424) Un par de ángulos externos situados dentro de dos rectas cortadas por una transversal y en lados diferentes de la transversal.

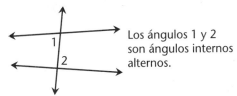

Los ángulos 1 y 2 son ángulos internos alternos.

angle/ángulo (pág. 78) Una figura formada por dos rayos que tienen un extremo en común, llamado *vértice*.

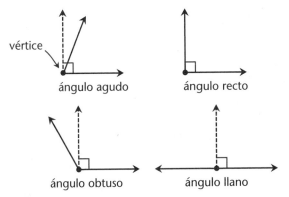

vértice

ángulo agudo — ángulo recto

ángulo obtuso — ángulo llano

arc/arco (pág. 218) Una parte de un círculo.

arco

arc of a network/arco de una red (pág. 442) Una curva o segmento que une vértices de una red. *Véase también* network/red.

associative property of addition/propiedad asociativa de la suma (pág. 105) Cambiar el orden de los números en un problema de suma no afecta el resultado.

associative property of multiplication/propiedad asociativa de la multiplicación (pág. 281) Cambiar el orden de los factores en un problema de multiplicación no afecta el producto.

axis (plural: axes)/eje (pág. 8) *Véase* coordinate plane/plano de coordenadas.

B ►►►►►►►►►►►►►►►►►►►►►►►►►►

bar graph/gráfica de barras (pág. 3) Una muestra visual de datos agrupados bajo distintas categorías.

base/base (pág. 17) *Véase* exponential form/forma exponencial.

base of a polygon/base de un polígono (pág. 383, 514) *Véase* parallelogram/paralelogramo y trapezoid/trapecio.

base of a space figure/base de un cuerpo geométrico (pág. 398, 457, 547 y 568) *Véase* prism/prisma, cylinder/cilindro, pyramid/pirámide y cone/cono.

benchmark/punto de referencia (pág. 208) Un elemento cuya medida es sabida y se puede usar para estimar otras medidas.

box-and-whisker plot/gráfica de frecuencias acumuladas (334, 492) Un diagrama que muestra la mediana, los otros cuartiles y los extremos de un conjunto numérico de datos. La caja contiene aproximadamente el 50% de los valores de los datos y los extremos el 25%.

Temperatura promedio en enero en 50 ciudades de EE.UU.

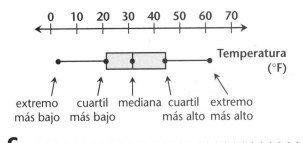

Temperatura (°F)

extremo más bajo — cuartil más bajo — mediana — cuartil más alto — extremo más alto

C ►►►►►►►►►►►►►►►►►►►►►►►►►►

capacity/capacidad (pág. 440) La cantidad de líquido que puede contener un recipiente.

center/centro (pág. 218) *Véase* circle/círculo.

central angle/ángulo central (pág. 500) Un ángulo con su vértice en el centro de un círculo.

certain event/suceso seguro (pág. 33) Un suceso que tiene una probabilidad de 1.

chord/cuerda (pág. 218) Un segmento que conecta dos puntos de un círculo. *Véase también* circle/círculo.

circle/círculo (pág. 218) El conjunto de todos los puntos en un plano que se encuentran a la misma distancia de un punto dado.

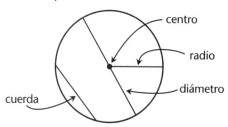

centro
radio
diámetro
cuerda

circle graph/gráfica circular (pág. 500) Una gráfica en la cual todo el círculo representa un entero o el 100%.

circumference/circunferencia (pág. 233) La distancia que hay alrededor de un círculo.

combination/combinación (pág. 556) Una selección de elementos en la cual el orden no es importante.

commutative property of addition/propiedad conmutativa de la suma (pág. 105) Cambiar el orden de los números en un problema de suma no afecta el resultado.

commutative property of multiplication/ propiedad conmutativa de la multiplicación (pág. 281) Cambiar el orden de los factores en un problema de multiplicación no afecta el producto.

compatible numbers/números compatibles (pág. 583) Los números que tienen sumas, diferencias, productos o cocientes fáciles de calcular.

complementary angles/ángulos complementarios (pág. 82) Dos ángulos cuyas medidas suman 90°.

complementary events/sucesos complementarios (pág. 386) Dos sucesos en donde uno o el otro debe ocurrir, pero no pueden ocurrir ambos al mismo tiempo.

composite number/número compuesto (pág. 150) Un número entero mayor que 1 y que tiene más de dos factores.

concave/cóncavo (pág. 382) Cuando al menos un ángulo de un polígono apunta hacia adentro, el polígono es cóncavo. *Véase también* polygon/polígono.

cone/cono (pág. 568) Un cuerpo geométrico con una base curva y un vértice.

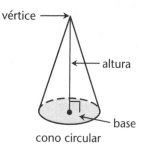

vértice
altura
base
cono circular

congruent/congruentes (pág. 217, 267) Dos figuras que tienen la misma forma y el mismo tamaño son congruentes.

construction/construcción (pág. 219) Una figura que se dibuja usando solamente regla recta y compás.

convex/convexo (pág. 382) Cuando todos los ángulos de un polígono apuntan hacia afuera, el polígono es convexo. *Véase también* polygon/polígono.

coordinate/coordenada (pág. 93) Un número de un par ordenado que da la ubicación de un punto a la izquierda o a la derecha del cero, o arriba o abajo del cero. *Véase también* coordinate plane/plano de coordenadas.

coordinate plane/plano de coordenadas (pág. 93) Una cuadrícula con un eje horizontal y un eje vertical que se cortan en un punto.

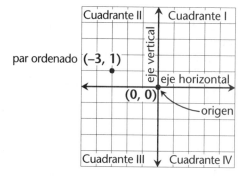

Cuadrante II | Cuadrante I
eje vertical
par ordenado (−3, 1)
eje horizontal
(0, 0)
origen
Cuadrante III | Cuadrante IV

corresponding angles/ángulos correspondientes (pág. 424) Ángulos que están en la misma posición con respecto a dos rectas y una transversal.

1
2
Los ángulos 1 y 2 son ángulos correspondientes.

corresponding parts/partes correspondientes (pág. 412) Cuando dos figuras son semejantes, para cada ángulo o lado de una de las figuras hay un ángulo o un lado semejante en la otra figura.

counting principle/principio de conteo (pág. 533) Para hallar el número de permutaciones, puedes multiplicar el número de opciones de cada punto donde hay que elegir.

cross products/productos cruzados (pág. 329)
Los productos iguales formados a partir de un par de razones equivalentes, al multiplicar el numerador de cada fracción por el denominador de la otra fracción.

cube/cubo (pág. 18) Un cuerpo geométrico cerrado con seis superficies cuadradas.

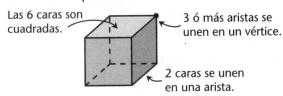

Las 6 caras son cuadradas.
3 ó más aristas se unen en un vértice.
2 caras se unen en una arista.

cylinder/cilindro (pág. 457) Un cuerpo geométrico que tiene una superficie curva y dos bases paralelas y congruentes.

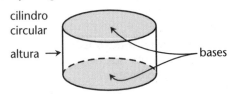

cilindro circular
altura →
bases

D ▸▸▸▸▸▸▸▸▸▸▸▸▸▸▸▸▸▸▸▸▸▸▸▸▸▸

decimal places/lugares decimales (pág. 191) La posición de los dígitos de un número, la cual determina sus valores.

degree/grado (pág. 78) Una unidad de medida de un ángulo que es $\frac{1}{360}$ de un giro completo.

denominator/denominador (pág. 584) El número de abajo de una fracción, que indica en cuántas partes iguales se divide el entero.

diameter/diámetro (pág. 218) Una cuerda que pasa por el centro de un círculo. La longitud de un diámetro se llama *el* diámetro. *Véase también* circle/círculo.

distributive property/propiedad distributiva (pág. 237) Cada sumando dentro de unos paréntesis se puede multiplicar por un factor fuera de los paréntesis. Por ejemplo: $5\left(2 + \frac{3}{5}\right) = (5 \cdot 2) + \left(5 \cdot \frac{3}{5}\right)$.

divisible/divisible (pág. 150) Cuando un número se puede dividir exactamente por otro número, es divisible por ese número.

E ▸▸▸▸▸▸▸▸▸▸▸▸▸▸▸▸▸▸▸▸▸▸▸▸▸▸

edge/arista (pág. 19, 398) Un segmento de un cuerpo geométrico en el que dos caras se encuentran. *Véase también* cube/cubo y prism/prisma.

equally likely/igualmente probable (pág. 30) Cuando la probabilidad de dos o más resultados es la misma, los resultados son igualmente probables.

equation/ecuación (pág. 16) Un enunciado matemático que indica que dos cantidades o expresiones son iguales.

equilateral triangle/triángulo equilátero (pág. 217) Un triángulo con tres lados congruentes.

equivalent fractions/fracciones equivalentes (pág. 163) Fracciones que representan la misma cantidad.

evaluate/evaluar (pág. 61, 119) Realizar operaciones matemáticas en el orden correcto o sustituir una variable por un valor y llevar a cabo la operación en el orden correcto. *Véase también* order of operations/orden de las operaciones.

event/suceso (pág. 28) Un grupo de uno o más resultados.

experiment/experimento (pág. 28) Una actividad cuyos resultados se puedan observar y escribir.

experimental probability/probabilidad experimental (pág. 28) Una probabilidad determinada por repetir un experimento un cierto número de veces y observar los resultados. Para calcular la probabilidad experimental, puedes dividir el número de veces que ocurre un resultado por el número de veces que se hace el experimento.

exponent/exponente (pág. 17, 20) Un número elevado que indica cuántas veces la base es un factor en un producto. *Véase también* exponential form/forma exponencial.

exponential form/forma exponencial (pág. 17) Una manera de escribir un número usando exponentes. Un número que se puede escribir usando un exponente y una base es una potencia de la base.

8 es una potencia de 2

forma normal $\quad 8 = 2 \cdot 2 \cdot 2 = 2^3 \quad$
exponente
forma exponencial
base

expression/expresión (pág. 60) Una frase matemática que puede contener números, variables y símbolos de operaciones.

exterior angle/ángulo externo (pág. 424) Un ángulo que está afuera de dos rectas cortadas por una transversal.

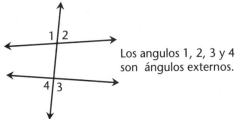

Los angulos 1, 2, 3 y 4 son ángulos externos.

F ▸▸▸▸▸▸▸▸▸▸▸▸▸▸▸▸▸▸▸▸▸▸▸▸▸▸

face/cara (pág. 19, 397) Una superficie plana de un cuerpo geométrico. *Véase también* cube/cubo y prism/prisma.

factor/factor (pág. 150) Cuando un número entero divide a otro número entero sin residuo, el primer número es un factor del segundo.

fitted line/recta de aproximación (pág. 332)
Una recta que se puede dibujar en un diagrama de dispersión de manera que aproximadamente la mitad de los puntos queden arriba de la recta y la otra mitad debajo. *Véase también* scatter plot/diagrama de dispersión.

frequency/frecuencia (pág. 5) El número de veces que un dato ocurre.

frequency table/tabla de frecuencia (pág. 5, 7) Una tabla que muestra con qué frecuencia ocurre cada dato.

function/función (pág. 119) Una relación de entrada y salida. Para cada entrada hay exactamente una salida. La salida depende de la entrada.

G ▸

geometric probability/probabilidad geométrica (pág. 387) Una probabilidad teórica basada en el área.

greatest common factor/máximo común divisor (pág. 154) El número mayor que sea factor de dos o más números.

H ▸

height of a polygon/altura de un polígono (pág. 383, 514) *Véase* parallelogram/paralelogramo y trapezoid/trapecio.

height of a space figure/altura de un cuerpo geométrico (pág. 398, 457, 547, 568) *Véase* prism/prisma, cylinder/cilindro, pyramid/pirámide y cone/cono.

histogram/histograma (pág. 318) Un tipo especial de gráfica de barras que muestra las frecuencias de datos en intervalos de igual ancho. Cada barra se toca con la siguiente.

horizontal axis/eje horizontal (pág. 3) Una recta horizontal en una gráfica, que se designa con las categorías o con la escala. *Véase también* coordinate plane/plano de coordenadas.

I ▸

image/imagen (pág. 264) La figura resultante de una transformación.

impossible event/suceso imposible (pág. 33) Un suceso que tiene una probabilidad de 0.

inequality/desigualdad (pág. 90, 380) Una enunciado matemático que indica que una cantidad o expresión es mayor o menor que otra.

integer/entero (pág. 89) Un número entero o el opuesto de un número entero, el cual es cualquier número en el conjunto de números..., –3, –2, –1, 0, 1, 2, 3,... .

interior angle/ángulo interno (pág. 424) Un ángulo que está entre dos rectas cortadas por una transversal.

Los ángulos 1, 2, 3 y 4 son ángulos internos.

intersect/cortarse (pág. 92) Cuando dos figuras geométricas comparten por lo menos un punto, se cortan.

interval/interval (pág. 4) El espacio entre los puntos de una escala.

inverse operations/operaciones inversas (pág. 135) Operaciones que se pueden "deshacer" una a otra, como suma y resta o multiplicación y división.

isosceles triangle/triángulo isósceles (pág. 217) Un triángulo que tiene por lo menos dos lados congruentes.

L ▸

least common denominator/mínimo común denominador (pág. 165) El mínimo común múltiplo de los denominadores de dos o más fracciones.

least common multiple/mínimo común múltiplo (pág. 155) El número menor de los múltiplos comunes de dos o más números.

line graph/gráfica lineal (pág. 4) Una gráfica en la cual los puntos marcados están unidos por medio de segmentos. Puede mostrar cambios que suceden con el tiempo.

line symmetry/simetría lineal (pág. 268) Si la mitad de una figura es una reflexión de la otra mitad, la figura tiene simetría lineal.

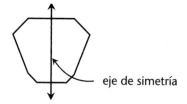

eje de simetría

lower extreme/extremo inferior (pág. 492) El dato de menor valor en un conjunto de datos. *Véase también* box-and-whisker plot/gráfica de frecuencias acumuladas.

lower quartile/cuartil inferior (pág. 492) La mediana de los valores de los datos que son menores que la mediana del conjunto total de datos. *Véase también* box-and-whisker plot/gráfica de frecuencias acumuladas.

lowest terms/mínima expresión (pág. 163) Una fracción está en su mínima expresión cuando el máximo común divisor del numerador y del denominador es 1.

M ▸

mass/masa (pág. 440) La cantidad de materia de un objeto.

mean/media (pág. 595) En un conjunto de datos numéricos, la suma de todos los datos dividida por el número de datos.

median/mediana (pág. 315) El elemento medio de un conjunto de datos ordenados de menor a mayor. Si no hay un número medio simple, es el número medio entre los dos datos que está más cerca del medio.

mixed number/número mixto (pág. 178) La suma de un número entero que no sea cero y una fracción entre 0 y 1.

mode/moda (pág. 315) El dato que ocurre con mayor frecuencia en un conjunto de datos. Puede haber más de una moda.

multiple/múltiplo (pág. 154) Un múltiplo de un número entero es el producto de ese número y otro número entero que no sea cero.

multistage experiment/experimento múltiple (pág. 365) Una situación que involucra dos o más sucesos que pasan uno después de otro.

N ▸

negative/negativo (pág. 89) Menor que cero.

net/patrón (pág. 399) Un modelo plano que se puede cortar y doblar para formar un cuerpo geométrico sin separaciones ni superposiciones.

network/red (pág. 442) Vértices unidos por arcos.

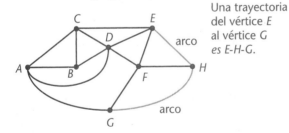

Una trayectoria del vértice *E* al vértice *G* es E-H-G.

numerator/numerador (pág. 584) El número de arriba de una fracción, que indica cuántas partes del entero hay que considerar.

O ▸

obtuse angle/ángulo obtuso (pág. 83) Un ángulo cuya medida es mayor que 90°. *Véase también* angle/ángulo.

obtuse triangle/triángulo obtusángulo (pág. 415) Un triángulo con un ángulo obtuso.

opposites/opuestos (pág. 91) Dos números que están a la misma distancia del 0 pero a lados opuestos en una recta numérica. El opuesto de 3 es –3.

order of operations/orden de las operaciones (pág. 61) El orden correcto para llevar a cabo las operaciones: operaciones dentro de los signos de agrupamiento primero, exponentes después, luego multiplicación y división de izquierda a derecha, y finalmente suma y resta de izquierda a derecha.

ordered pair/par ordenado (pág. 93) Un par de números que se usan para identificar y marcar puntos en un plano de coordenadas. *Véase también* coordinate plane/plano de coordenadas.

origin/origen (pág. 93) *Véase* coordinate plane/plano de coordenadas.

outcome/resultado (pág. 28) El resultado de un experimento.

P ▸

parallel/paralelo (pág. 92) En un plano, dos rectas que no se cortan son paralelas.

parallelogram/paralelogramo (pág. 383) Un polígono de cuatro lados con pares de lados opuestos paralelos.

La distancia perpendicular entre las bases de un paralelogramo es su altura.

bases

percent/por ciento (pág. 3) Por ciento significa "de cada 100".

percent of change/porcentaje de cambio (pág. 475) El porcentaje por el cual una cantidad aumenta o disminuye con respecto a la cantidad original.

permutation/permutación (pág. 530) Un agrupación posible de un grupo de elementos en la cual el orden es importante.

perpendicular/perpendicular (pág. 92) Dos rectas que se cortan en ángulos de 90° son perpendiculares.

plane/plano (pág. 92) Una superficie plana que se extiende infinitamente.

polygon/polígono (pág. 382) Una figura cerrada hecha con segmentos dibujados en una superficie plana y que no se cruzan.

polígonos convexos   polígonos cóncavos

positive/positivo (pág. 89) Mayor que cero.

power/potencia (pág. 17) *Véase* exponential form/forma exponencial.

prime factorization/descomposición en factores primos (pág. 151) La expresión de un número escrito como el producto de factores primos.

árbol de factorización

$12 = 2 \cdot 2 \cdot 3$

prime number/número primo (pág. 150) Un número entero mayor que 1 y que tiene exactamente dos factores, 1 y el mismo número.

principal square root/raíz cuadrada principal (pág. 396) La raíz cuadrada positiva. Su símbolo es $\sqrt{}$.

prism/prisma (pág. 398) Un cuerpo geométrico con superficies que tienen forma de polígonos. Dos de las caras, las bases, son paralelas y congruentes. Las otras caras son paralelogramos. En un prisma *rectangular,* las otras caras son rectángulos.

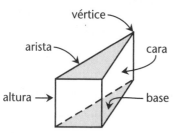

prisma triangular rectangular

probability/probabilidad (pág. 28) Un número entre 0 y 1 que te indica la posibilidad de que pase algo.

proportion/proporción (pág. 314) Una ecuación que indica que dos razones son equivalentes.

pyramid/pirámide (pág. 547) Un cuerpo geométrico que tiene una base con forma de polígono. Las otras caras son triángulos que se encuentran en un vértice simple.

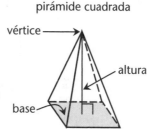

pirámide cuadrada

Q ▸▸▸▸▸▸▸▸▸▸▸▸▸▸▸▸▸▸▸▸▸▸▸▸▸▸▸▸

quadrilateral/cuadrilátero (pág. 383) Un polígono de cuatro lados.

R ▸▸▸▸▸▸▸▸▸▸▸▸▸▸▸▸▸▸▸▸▸▸▸▸▸▸▸▸

radius (plural: radii)/radio (pág. 218) Un segmento cuyos extremos son el centro y un punto cualquiera de un círculo dado. La longitud de un radio se llama *el* radio. *Véase también* circle/círculo.

range/gama (pág. 316) La diferencia entre el valor mayor y el valor menor de un grupo de datos numéricos.

rate/relación (pág. 313) Una razón que compara cantidades medidas en diferentes unidades.

ratio/razón (pág. 313) Una comparación de dos o más cantidades por medio de una división. La razón entre 6 y 8 se puede expresar como 6 a 8, 6 : 8 ó $\frac{6}{8}$.

ray/rayo (pág. 77) Una parte de una recta que empieza en un extremo y se extiende infinitamente en una dirección.

extremo

reciprocals/recíprocos (pág. 238) Dos números cuyo producto es 1.

reflection/reflexión (pág. 267) La inversión de una figura a través de una recta.

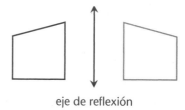

eje de reflexión

repeating decimal/decimal periódico (pág. 252) Un número decimal en el cual un dígito o una secuencia de dígitos se repite.

rhombus/rombo (pág. 514) Un paralelogramo que tiene cuatro lados congruentes.

right angle/ángulo recto (pág. 83) Un ángulo que mide 90°. *Véase también* angle/ángulo.

right triangle/triángulo rectángulo (pág. 415) Un triángulo que tiene un ángulo recto.

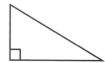

rise/distancia vertical (pág. 461) *Véase* slope/pendiente.

rotation/rotación (pág. 264) Un giro de una figura alrededor de un punto fijo, el centro de rotación, un cierto número de grados ya sea en el sentido de las agujas del reloj o en sentido contrario.

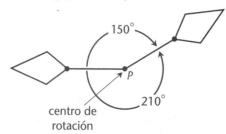

rotational symmetries/simetrías rotacionales (pág. 265) Los números de grados que una figura se puede rotar hasta quedar en la posición original.

rotational symmetry/simetría rotacional (pág. 265) Cuando una figura se puede rotar menos de 360° alrededor de su centro y quedar en su posición original, la figura tiene simetría rotacional.

run/distancia horizontal (pág. 461) *Véase* slope/pendiente.

S ▸▸▸▸▸▸▸▸▸▸▸▸▸▸▸▸▸▸▸▸▸▸▸▸▸▸▸▸▸▸▸

scale of a drawing/escala de un dibujo (pág. 413) La razón entre una medida de longitud de un dibujo y la medida de la parte correspondiente en el objeto representado.

scale on a graph/escala en una gráfica (pág. 4) Los números escritos a lo largo de un eje de la gráfica.

scalene triangle/triángulo escaleno (pág. 217) Un triángulo sin lados congruentes.

scatter plot/diagrama de dispersión (pág. 332) Una gráfica de un conjunto de puntos en un plano de coordenadas que representa la relación entre dos cantidades.

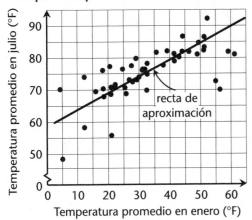

Temperatura promedio en 50 ciudades de EE.UU.

recta de aproximación

scientific notation/notación científica (pág. 197) Un número está en notación científica cuando está escrito como el producto de un decimal mayor o igual a 1 y menor que 10, y una potencia de 10. Por ejemplo:

$$\text{forma normal} \rightarrow 5261 = 5.261 \cdot 10^3 \rightarrow \text{notación científica}$$

sector/sector (pág. 500) Una región con forma de porción de torta, en un círculo marcado por dos radios y un arco.

sequence/secuencia (pág. 14) Una lista ordenada de números u objetos.

similar/semejante (pág. 295, 417) Dos figuras son semejantes si tienen la misma forma pero no necesariamente el mismo tamaño. En los polígonos semejantes, las medidas de los ángulos correspondientes son iguales, y las razones entre las longitudes de los lados correspondientes son iguales.

slope/pendiente (pág. 461) La razón entre el cambio vertical y el cambio horizontal que sufre una recta.

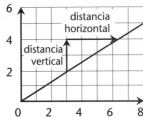

solution of an equation/solución de una ecuación (pág. 134) El valor de una variable que hace verdadera una ecuación.

solving an equation/resolver una ecuación (pág. 134) El proceso de hallar una solución.

square root/raíz cuadrada (pág. 396) Si $A = s^2$, entonces s es la raíz cuadrada de A. Por ejemplo, 5 y −5 son raíces cuadradas de 25. El símbolo para una raíz cuadrada positiva es $\sqrt{\ }$. El símbolo para una raíz cuadrada negativa es $\sqrt{\ }$.

standard form/forma normal (pág. 17) *Véase* exponential form/forma exponencial.

stem-and-leaf plot/tabla arborescente (pág. 316) Un despliegue de datos en donde cada número está representado por un *tallo* (los dígitos que están más a la izquierda) y una *hoja* (los dígitos que están más a la derecha).

straight angle/ángulo llano (pág. 83) Un ángulo cuya medida es 180°. *Véase también* angle/ángulo.

supplementary angles/ángulos suplementarios (pág. 81) Dos ángulos cuyas medidas suman 180°.

surface area of a prism/área superficial de un prisma (pág. 399) La suma de las áreas de las caras de un prisma.

T ▸▸▸▸▸▸▸▸▸▸▸▸▸▸▸▸▸▸▸▸▸▸▸▸▸▸▸▸▸▸▸

term number/número del término (pág. 14) Un número que indica la posición del término en una progresión.

term of a sequence/término de una progresión (pág. 14) Un número individual u objeto de una progresión.

terminating decimal/decimal exacto (pág. 253) Un número decimal en el cual los dígitos se detienen, o terminan.

tessellation/teselados (pág. 565) Un conjunto de mosaicos que usa polígonos congruentes y un patrón que se repite para cubrir un plano sin separaciones ni superposiciones.

theoretical probability/probabilidad teórica (pág. 30) Una probabilidad que se puede determinar sin hacer un experimento. Para calcular una probabilidad teórica, puedes dividir el número de resultados favorables por el número de resultados posibles.

transformation/transformación (pág. 291) Un cambio que se le hace a la forma, tamaño o posición de una figura.

translation/traslación (pág. 291) Una transformación que desliza cada punto de una figura a la misma distancia y en la misma dirección.

transversal/transversal (pág. 423) Una recta que corta dos rectas en puntos separados en un plano.

La recta *t* es una transversal de las rectas *m* y *n*.

trapezoid/trapecio (pág. 514) Un cuadrilátero que tiene solamente un par de lados opuestos paralelos.

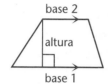

traversable/atravesable (pág. 449) Cuando una red se puede dibujar sin levantar el lápiz del papel y sin dibujar ningún arco más de una vez, la red es atravesable.

tree diagram/diagrama en árbol (pág. 168) Un despliegue de los resultados posibles de un experimento.

triangle/triángulo (pág. 58) Un polígono de tres lados.

U ▸

unit rate/relación unitaria (pág. 313) Una razón que compara una cantidad con una unidad de otra cantidad.

upper extreme/extremo superior (pág. 492) El dato de mayor valor en un conjunto de datos. *Véase también* box-and-whisker plot/gráfica de frecuencias acumuladas.

upper quartile/cuartil superior (pág. 492) La mediana de los valores de los datos que son mayores que la mediana del conjunto total de datos. *Véase también* box-and-whisker plot/gráfica de frecuencias acumuladas.

V ▸

variable/variable (pág. 16) Una cantidad, normalmente representada por una letra, que es desconocida o que cambia.

vertex of an angle/vértice de un ángulo (pág. 78) El extremo común de dos rayos que forman un ángulo. *Véase también* angle/ángulo.

vertex of a cube (plural: vertices)/vértice de un cubo (pág. 19) Un punto en donde tres o más aristas de un cubo se encuentran. Véase también cube/cubo.

vertex of a network/vértice de una red (pág. 442) Un punto en una red. *Véase también* network/red.

vertex of a prism/vértice de un prisma (pág. 398) Un punto en donde tres o más aristas de un prisma se encuentran. *Véase también* prism/prisma.

vertex of a tessellation/vértice de un teselado (pág. 565) Un punto en donde las esquinas de los polígonos de un teselado se tocan.

vertical angles/ángulos verticales (pág. 424) Dos ángulos cuyos lados forman dos pares de rayos opuestos.

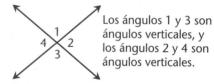

Los ángulos 1 y 3 son ángulos verticales, y los ángulos 2 y 4 son ángulos verticales.

vertical axis/eje vertical (pág. 3) Una recta vertical en una gráfica, designada con las categorías o con la escala. *Véase también* coordinate plane/plano de coordenadas.

volume/volumen (pág. 18) La cantidad de espacio dentro de un cuerpo geométrico. El volumen se mide en unidades cúbicas.

W ▸

weighted network/red con designaciones (pág. 444) Una red en la cual los arcos se designan con números que representan cosas tales como distancia y tiempo.

X ▸

***x*-axis/eje de *x* (pág. 292)** La recta numérica horizontal de un plano de coordenadas. *Véase también* coordinate plane/plano de coordenadas.

Y ▸

***y*-axis/eje de *y* (pág. 292)** La recta numérica vertical de un plano de coordenadas. *Véase también* coordinate plane/plano de coordenadas.

MIDDLE GRADES

MATH*Thematics*

MODULE
1

Making Choices

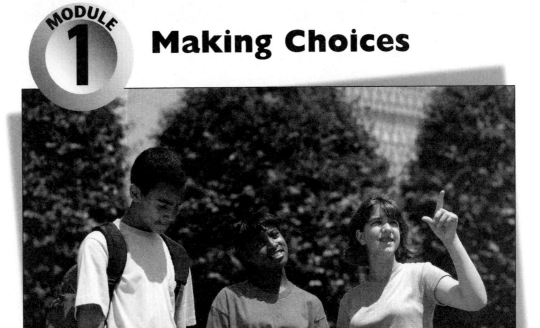

- Planning and Teaching Suggestions, p. 1-8
- Labsheets, p. 1-49
- Extended Explorations, p. 1-61
- Blackline Masters, p. 1-64

MAKING CHOICES

Module Overview

Making informed decisions about real-world situations provides the context for reviewing the problem solving process and ways for students to assess their work. Students use ideas from statistics, probability, and algebra to represent situations and construct models to solve problems.

Module Objectives

Section	Objectives	NCTM Standards
1	◆ Understand the concept of percent. ◆ Interpret bar graphs. ◆ Interpret line graphs. ◆ Complete a frequency table with ungrouped data. ◆ Use bar graphs to compare frequencies.	1, 2, 3, 4, 10
2	◆ Model a number sequence with a word sentence, a table, a graph, or an equation. ◆ Predict the nth term of a number sequence. ◆ Understand that exponents represent repeated multiplication. ◆ Identify the pattern in a sequence that involves exponents. ◆ Find the volume of a cube.	1, 2, 3, 4, 5, 8, 9, 12
3	◆ Identify outcomes of an experiment. ◆ Use a number from 0 to 1 to estimate probability. ◆ Find and use an experimental probability. ◆ Find the theoretical probability of an event. ◆ Compare the experimental and the theoretical probability of an event.	1, 2, 3, 4, 11
4	◆ Use the 4-step approach to problem solving. ◆ Choose and apply problem solving strategies.	1, 2, 3, 4
5	◆ Use the Problem Solving Scale for self-assessment. ◆ Use the Connections Scale for self-assessment.	1, 2, 3, 4
6	◆ Use the Mathematical Language Scale for self-assessment. ◆ Use the order of operations to evaluate whole-number numerical expressions with grouping symbols and exponents. ◆ Use the Representations Scale for self-assessment. ◆ Decide when to use a bar graph or a line graph to represent a set of data.	1, 2, 3, 4, 9, 10

Topic Spiraling

Section	Connections to Prior and Future Concepts
1	Bar graphs were introduced in Module 3 of Book 1, and line graphs were explored in Module 8. Section 1 of Book 2 reviews them and introduces frequency tables. The concept of percent is also reviewed. More data displays are explored in Modules 5 and 7.
2	Section 2 expands work on sequences, variables, and exponents in Modules 1 and 4 of Book 1, focusing on algebraic and graphic representations of sequences and on patterns with exponents. Negative exponents are taught in Module 3. Section 2 also covers areas of squares and volumes of cubes from Book 1, Modules 4 and 7. More on these topics is in Modules 6–8 of Book 2.
3	Section 3 explores experimental and theoretical probability, introduced in Module 4 of Book 1. Tree diagrams and geometric probability are covered in Modules 3, 5, and 6.
4	Section 4 revisits problem solving strategies and the 4-step approach to problem solving studied in Module 1 of Book 1. Equations are used to solve problems in Modules 2–4 and 7.
5	Section 5 reviews the problem solving and connections scales for self-assessment from Book 1 Module 1. These scales, the presentation scale, and scales in Section 6 are used throughout.
6	Section 6 reviews the mathematical language and representations scales for self-assessment. The order of operations is reviewed from Module 1 of Book 1, and work with grouping symbols and exponents is included. These skills are used with integers, fractions, and decimals in Module 4. Students also choose between a bar graph and a line graph, a topic explored further in Module 7.

Integration

Mathematical Connections	1	2	3	4	5	6
algebra (including patterns and functions)		**13–25**	37		52	60, 61, 66, 70
geometry	10	18–25		45, 48	56–58	66, 69
data analysis, probability, discrete math	**2–12***	**13–25**	**26–39**	46, 47	52	62–65, 67–71

Interdisciplinary Connections and Applications						
social studies and geography	7, 9	22				
reading and language arts		13			50	
science	7, 9					70
home economics		23				67
health, physical education, and sports	2–3, 8		35	40–42, 45		
communication	1, 11		38	46		69, 71
education, computers, recreation, business	4–6, 12	17, 19, 24	36			62–65

* Bold page numbers *indicate that a topic is used throughout the section.*

Guide for Assigning Homework

Regular Scheduling (45 min class period)

Section/ P&A Pages	Core Assignment	Extended Assignment	exercises to note		
			Additional Practice/Review	Open-ended Problems	Special Problems
1 pp. 8–12	**Day 1:** 1–3, 6–10 (even), 12–14, SR 28–30	1–5, 6–10 (even), 12–14, Chal 15, SR 28–30	EP, p. 12; TB, p. 588; PA 4, 5–11 (odd)	PA 4; St Sk, p. 12	
	Day 2: 16, 18, 20, *ROS 21, SR 22–27	16–20, *ROS 21, SR 22–27	TB, pp. 584, 593, 594; PA 17, 19	ROS 21; Mod Proj 1–3	Mod Proj 1–3
2 pp. 21–25	**Day 1:** 4–11, SR 33–34	2, Chal 3, 4–10 (even), 11, SR 33–34	EP, p. 25; PA 1, 2	Std Test, p. 25	
	Day 2: 14–24, 26, 28, 30, *ROS 32, SR 35–37	14–24, 26, 28, 30, Chal 31, *ROS 32, SR 35–37	TB, p. 585; PA 12, 13, 25, 27, 29, Career 38–39		
3 pp. 34–39	**Day 1:** SR 31–36	SR 31–36	EP, p. 39; TB, pp. 585, 586, 595		
	Day 2: 1–5, *6, 7–12	1–5, *6, 7–12			
	Day 3: 13, 15, 16–24 (even), 27, ROS 30	13, 15, 16–24 (even), 27, Chal 28–29, ROS 30, *Ext 37–38	PA 14, 17–25 (odd)	Mod Proj 4–5	PA 26; Mod Proj 4–5
4 pp. 45–49	**Day 1:** 2, 3, SR 8–11	2, 3, SR 8–11	EP, p. 47	E^2, p. 48	E^2, p. 48; PA 1
	Day 2: 4, 5, ROS 7	4, 5, Chal 6, ROS 7		ROS 7; Mod Proj 6–8	Mod Proj 6–8
5 pp. 56–58	**Day 1:** 1–3, SR 8–14	1–3, SR 8–14	EP, p. 58		
	Day 2: 4, 5, ROS 7, SR 15–20	4, 5, *Chal 6, ROS 7, SR 15–20	TB, pp. 582–583		
6 pp. 66–71	**Day 1:** 4–11, 16, 17	4–11, Chal 15, 16, 17	EP, p. 70; PA 1–3, 12–14		
	Day 2: 18, 22–24, *ROS 26, SR 27–34	18, 22–24, *ROS 26, SR 27–34	TB, p. 591; PA 19–21	ROS 26; Mod Proj 9–11, 12–16	PA 25; Mod Proj 9–11, 12–16
Review/ Assess	Review and Assess (PE), Quick Quizzes (TRB), Mid-Module Quiz (TRB), Module Tests— Forms A and B (TRB), Standardized Assessment (TRB)				Allow 5 days
Enrich/ Assess	E^2 (PE) and Alternate E^2 (TRB), Module Project (PE), Module Performance Assessment (TRB)				
Yearly Pacing	**Mod 1:** 18 days		**Remaining:** 122 days		**Total:** 140 days

Key: PA = Practice & Application; ROS = Reflecting on the Section; SR = Spiral Review; TB = Toolbox; EP = Extra Skill Practice; Ext = Extension; *more time

Block Scheduling (90 min class period)

	Day 1	Day 2	Day 3	Day 4	Day 5	Day 6	
Teach	Sec 1	Sec 2	Sec 3	Sec 4	Sec 5	Sec 6	Allow 3 days review/assess/projects
Apply/ Assess (P&A)	Sec 1: 1–3, 6, 8, 10, 12–14, 16, 18, 20, *ROS 21, SR 22–30	Sec 2: 4–10 (even), 11, 14, 16, 20–24, 26, 28, ROS 32, SR 33–37	Sec 3: 2, 4–6, 8, 10, 12, 13, 15, 16–24 (even), 27, ROS 30, SR 31–36	Sec 4: 2–5, ROS 7, SR 8–11	Sec 5: 1–5, *ROS 7, SR 8–20	Sec 6: 4, 6, 8–11, 16–18, 22–24, *ROS 26, SR 27–34	
Yearly Pacing	**Mod 1:** 9 days			**Remaining:** 61 days		**Total:** 70 days	

MODULE 1

Materials List

Section	Materials
1	Labsheet 1A, ruler
2	Labsheets 2A and 2B, 25 square tiles or graph paper
3	Labsheets 3A–3D, 18 chips, 2 number cubes or dice (red and blue), data from Project Question 3
4	15 index cards numbered from 1 to 15
5	Labsheet 5A, marker, solutions to Question 12 on page 43
6	Data from Module Project Question 4; for Completing the Module Project: data and tables or graphs from Module Project Questions 4 and 11; for Review and Assessment (R and A): graph paper

Support Materials in this Resource Book

Section	Practice	Study Guide	Assessment	Enrichment
1	Section 1	Section 1	Quick Quiz	
2	Section 2	Section 2	Quick Quiz	
3	Section 3	Section 3	Quick Quiz Mid-Module Quiz	Technology Activity
4	Section 4	Section 4	Quick Quiz	Alternate Extended Exploration
5	Section 5	Section 5	Quick Quiz	
6	Section 6	Section 6	Quick Quiz	
Review/ Assess	Sections 1–6		Module Tests Forms A and B Standardized Assessment Module Performance Assessment	

Classroom Ideas

Bulletin Boards:
- magazine articles and data displays about Olympic athletes or events
- examples of patterns in the real world (speed of falling objects, Calories burned and exercise, etc.)
- real-world problems and solutions using problem solving strategies

Student Work Displays:
- homework and television watching data displays
- summaries and visual displays from the E^2
- data presentations from the module project

Interest Center:
- a variety of probability games

Visitors/Field Trips:
- game designer, traffic planner, statistician

Technology:
- Module 1 Technology Activity in TRB for Section 3
- *McDougal Littell Mathpack Stats!*, CD-ROM/disks Mac/Win

The Math Gazette
Making Choices

Sneak Preview!

Over the next four weeks in our mathematics class, we will be applying problem solving and reasoning skills and developing statistics, probability, geometry, and pre-algebra concepts while completing a thematic unit on Making Choices. Some of the topics we will be discussing are:

✗ using data to make decisions

✗ determining how likely the options are to happen

✗ using reasoning

✗ evaluating decisions

✗ communicating decisions

We will look at how mathematics can be used to help make wise decisions in everyday situations.

Ask Your Student

How could you find the volume of a cereal box? (Sec. 2)

What does a probability of $\frac{1}{6}$ mean? (Sec. 3)

What are the steps in the problem solving model? (Sec. 4)

Connections

Literature:
Students will read the poem *Smart*, by Shel Silverstein and an excerpt from *Alesia*, by Eloise Greenfield and Alesia Revis. You may enjoy reading other Shel Silverstein poems with your student.

Study Skills:
Students analyze data on how academic performance is affected by the amount of time spent on homework and watching television.

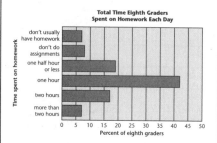

Health:
Claims about the effect of an active life style on average life expectancy are investigated.

Consumer Topic:
Students investigate how advertisers use commercials on television to influence consumers.

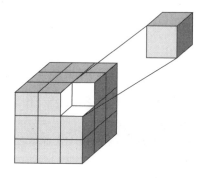

E² Project

Following Section 4, students will have approximately one week to complete the E^2 project, *The Painted Cube*. This project requires students to use spatial skills to determine the number of painted faces on small cubes cut from a larger cube that has been painted.

Students may use some of the following materials for the project:

✗ grid paper, scissors, and tape for constructing cubes

✗ wooden blocks or sugar cubes

Making Choices

Section Title	Mathematics Your Student Will Be Learning	Activities
1: Going for the Gold	◆ interpreting bar graphs and line graphs ◆ reviewing the concept of percent ◆ completing frequency tables	◆ conduct a survey on the amount of time students spend on homework ◆ present and analyze the survey results using a bar graph
2: Patterns and Predictions	◆ modeling sequences with tables, graphs, and equations ◆ generalizing patterns involving exponents	◆ use squares, cubes, and graphs to analyze patterns
3: Likely or Unlikely?	◆ determining the outcomes of an experiment ◆ determining experimental and theoretical probabilities	◆ use probability to develop a strategy for playing a game
4: What Can You Expect?	◆ using the 4-step model for approaching problems ◆ using problem solving strategies	◆ analyze claims about exercise and average life expectancy ◆ analyze a card game
5: Creative Solutions	◆ solving problems ◆ using Assessment Scales to evaluate problem solving and making connections	◆ assess student solutions to problems from Section 4
6: The Clear Choice	◆ using the order of operations ◆ using Assessment Scales to evaluate use of mathematical language and representations in problem solving	◆ analyze how the amount of time spent watching television affects academic performance

MODULE 1

Activities to do at Home

◆ How do I spend my time? Help your student keep a log of the amount of time spent on homework and watching television each day. Use the information presented in Sections 1 and 6 to discuss the results. You may also want to include other activities such as time spent sleeping, eating, reading for pleasure, playing sports, and helping at home, and have your student construct a graph of the results. (Begin after Sec. 1 and discuss results after Sec. 6.)

◆ Where are statistics and probability used? Ask your student to look for examples of bar, line, and other graphs in newspapers, magazines, and on television and explain whether the graphs are appropriate and contain all the necessary information. Or, have your student look for examples of uses of probability and explain what the probabilities mean and how they might have been determined. (After Sec. 3)

Related Topics

You may want to discuss these related topics with your student:

 Statistics

 Games of chance

 Television advertising

 Health and fitness

 Methods of assessing performance

Section ① Data Displays

Section Planner

DAYS FOR MODULE 1

1 2 **3 4 5 6 7 8 9 10 11 12 13**

SECTION 1

First Day
Setting the Stage, *p. 2*
Exploration 1, *pp. 3–4*

Second Day
Exploration 2, *pp. 5–6*
Key Concepts, *p. 7*

Block Schedule

Day 1
Setting the Stage, Exploration 1, Exploration 2, Key Concepts

RESOURCE ORGANIZER

Teaching Resources
• Practice and Applications, Sec. 1
• Study Guide, Sec. 1
• Warm-Up, Sec. 1
• Quick Quiz, Sec. 1

Section Overview

In Section 1 students will begin their study with an exploration of bar graphs and line graphs. They will learn how to use these graphs to read, display, and analyze information that may help them to make good choices in daily life. Key terms used are *bar graph, vertical* and *horizontal axes, percent, line graph, interval,* and *frequency table.* Students will study the components of bar and line graphs that make it easier to compare data on two graphs, for example, the title, numerical scale, and the intervals of the axes. They will examine the use of a double line graph to compare data that change over time. A review of percent can be found in the Toolbox on page 588. Some students may need to review this topic since these skills will be needed in this section when they study bar graphs whose data are given in percent form.

As students practice drawing their own bar graphs and line plots, they will learn how to use a frequency table to record data that will be displayed on a graph. They will examine the data on the graphs and draw inferences from them.

SECTION OBJECTIVES

Exploration 1
• understand the concept of percent
• interpret bar graphs
• interpret line graphs

Exploration 2
• complete a frequency table with ungrouped data
• use bar graphs to compare frequencies

ASSESSMENT OPTIONS

Checkpoint Questions
• Question 7 on p. 3
• Question 12 on p. 4
• Question 14 on p. 6

Embedded Assessment
• For a list of embedded assessment exercises see p. 1-12.

Performance Task/Portfolio
• Exercise 4 on p. 8 (open-ended)
• Exercise 16 on p. 9
• Exercise 21 on p. 10 (research)
• Module Project on p. 11

SECTION 1 MATERIALS

Exploration 2
◆ Labsheet 1A
◆ ruler

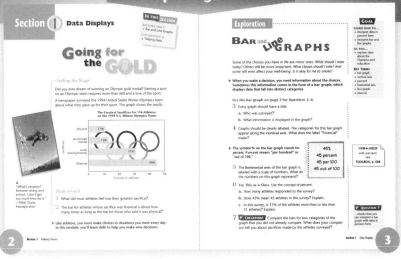

Setting the Stage

MOTIVATE

Have the whole class read the information about the bar graph. By show of hands, have students answer the question, "Did you ever dream of winning an Olympic gold medal?" Allow students to share their experiences in competition involving sports, music, drama, chess, or other extracurricular activities. This opportunity for students to discuss their talents and interests is a great way for the teacher and classmates to get to know each other.

Exploration 1

PLAN

Classroom Management

Exploration 1 is best completed individually or in small groups. *Question 6* is highlighted for the whole class. This offers a chance to check students' ability to interpret a bar graph with data in percent form. As students work through *Questions 8–11* on page 4, make certain they are interpreting the line graph correctly. If a majority of students have questions, take time for a whole-class discussion. Otherwise, allow students to work without interruption. You may want to have each student record all answers in a notebook or binder set up for this year's mathematics class.

GUIDE

Developing Math Concepts

For *Question 6*, students should be able to use mental math. Since 45% represents 45 out of 100, then 45 out of 114 athletes would be less than 45% of the athletes. Use other examples such as 45 out of 92 athletes and 45 out of 200 athletes. With enough examples, students should be able to give the required answers without actually computing.

Writing Have students keep a journal of mathematical terms. Providing a classroom list of terms for all students to use as a reference will assist students in communicating their understanding using correct mathematical language.

Common Error Many students will not see why bar graphs are useful in some cases, while line graphs are more useful in other situations. Point out the line graph shows change over time for one quantity, while a bar graph shows a comparison of several different quantities. In some cases, either type of graph is appropriate, but not always.

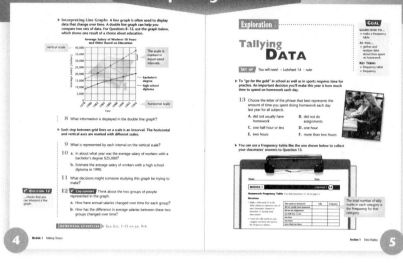

Teacher Support for Pupil Pages 4–5

Exploration 1 continued

Classroom Examples
Below is a line graph that shows the voter turnout in federal elections in the United States for the years 1980–1996. State the scale along the vertical axis and along the horizontal axis.

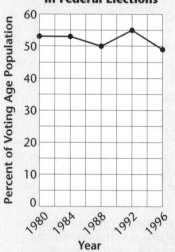

National Voter Turnout in Federal Elections

Answer: The scale along the vertical axis goes from 0% to 60%. The scale along the horizontal axis goes from 1980 to 1996 and is divided into 4-year intervals.

Checkpoint For *Question 12*, having students raise their hand as they complete the checkpoint will allow you to give immediate feedback. Taking the time to ensure students are proceeding correctly will save time later and eliminate continual checks and reteaching.

HOMEWORK EXERCISES

See the Suggested Assignment for Day 1 on page 1-12. For Exercise Notes, see page 1-12.

Exploration 2

PLAN

Classroom Management
Exploration 2 is best performed individually. Each student will need a copy of the Labsheet 1A and a ruler. *Question 20* on page 6 is highlighted for discussion. This provides the opportunity to check students' understanding before assigning homework.

GUIDE

Developing Math Concepts
Some students may need to be reminded of the convenience of grouping tally marks by five. Point out the difference between *tally mark* and *frequency*. The term *frequency* will be used regularly in this program. Stress the importance of a clear, concise title to explain what the graph represents.

Common Error Some students will forget to label each axis. Point out that someone else reading the graph would not know how to interpret the graph if there are no labels.

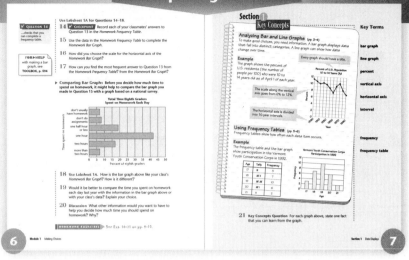

Exploration 2 continued

Checkpoint In order for students to complete the exploration correctly, check *Question 14* for accuracy as each student completes the frequency table.

Classroom Examples
The table and the graph show the number of threatened species in six categories. Use the graph and the table to describe the data.

Category	Tally	Frequency
Mammals	JHT III	8
Birds	JHT JHT II	12
Amphibians	JHT	5
Snails	JHT I	6
Clams	II	2
Insects	JHT IIII	9

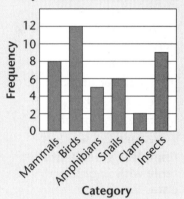

**Number of Threatened
Species in the United States**

Answer: Sample Response: The most threatened category is birds, and the least threatened category is clams.

■ HOMEWORK EXERCISES ▶

See the Suggested Assignment for Day 2 on page 1-12. For Exercise Notes, see page 1-12.

CLOSE

Closure Question Describe what line graphs, bar graphs, and frequency tables show.

Answer: Line graphs show how data change over time, bar graphs show data that fall into distinct categories, and a frequency table shows how often data items occur.

Customizing Instruction

Home Involvement Those helping students at home will find the Key Concepts on page 7 a handy reference to the key ideas, terms, and skills of Section 1.

Absent Students For students who were absent for all or part of this section, the blackline Study Guide for Section 1 may be used to present the ideas, concepts, and skills of Section 1.

Extra Help For students who need additional practice, the blackline Practice and Applications for Section 1 provides additional exercises that may be used to confirm the skills of Section 1. The Extra Skill Practice on page 12 also provides additional exercises.

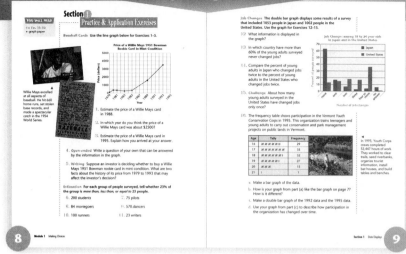

SUGGESTED ASSIGNMENT

Core Course
Day 1: Exs. 1–3, 6–10 even,
   12–14, 28–30
Day 2: Exs. 16, 18, 20–27

Extended Course
Day 1: Exs. 1–5, 6–10 even,
   12–15, 28–30
Day 2: Exs. 16–27

Block Schedule
Day 1: Exs. 1–3, 6, 8, 10,
   12–14, 16, 18, 20–30

EMBEDDED ASSESSMENT

These section objectives are
tested by the exercises
listed.

**Understand the concept of
percent.**
   Exercises 6, 8, 10

Interpret bar graphs.
   Exercises 12–14

Interpret line graphs.
   Exercises 1–3

**Complete a frequency
table with ungrouped
data.**
   Exercises 18, 20

**Use bar graphs to com-
pare frequencies.**
   Exercise 16

Practice & Application

EXERCISE NOTES

Writing For *Ex. 5*, discuss your
expectations of students for
exercises that involve writing.
For example, you might require
them to use complete sentences
and correct grammar and to use
mathematical terms correctly.

Developing Math Concepts
For *Exs. 6–11* be sure students
understand the difference
between exact and estimated
answers. Point out that these
exercises require estimated
answers.

Background Information For
Exs. 12–15, point out that until
recent years, workers in the
United States were more likely
to keep the same job for many
years, in some cases working for
the same company all their
lives. Because of global eco-
nomic changes, this is now less
common.

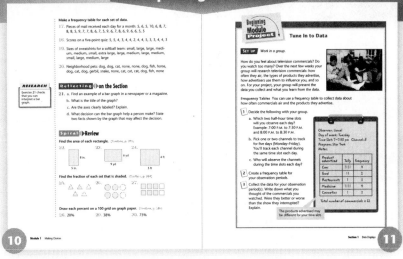

Practice & Application

Developing Math Concepts

For *Exs. 19–20*, point out that the data used to create a frequency table may not always be numerical, even though frequencies themselves are always numerical.

Closing the Section

Remind students the purpose of this section was to learn skills to help them make wise decisions. Therefore, their answer to *Reflecting on the Section Exercise 21* on page 10 should represent their skills using graphs, constructing graphs, and making decisions based on graphs. *USA Today* is a source of many graphs if students are having difficulty in locating graphs.

Beginning the Module Project

Students will be working with the same group on this project throughout the module. Decide on a system for students to use in storing their project work. This will help eliminate lost materials and will help provide access to materials throughout the completion of this module. Depending on your students' level of group skills, you may need to review or teach skills and expectations required for successful group work. To assist students with the collection of data, take time each day to check on their progress. Provide a time line for each task.

QUICK QUIZ ON THIS SECTION

1. What is the difference between data that can be displayed in a bar graph and data that can be displayed in a line graph?

2. Use the data in the following frequency table to make a bar graph showing the favorite subjects of 70 students.

Favorite subject	Frequency
Mathematics	28
Science	11
English	17
Social studies	14

3. Make a frequency table for this set of data about the number of CD's bought in the past month: 2, 0, 6, 1, 2, 5, 0, 1, 1, 0, 4, 3, 2, 0, 12, 2, 4, 3.

For answers, see Quick Quiz blackline on p. 1-64.

Section ② Sequences and Exponents

Section Planner

DAYS FOR MODULE 1

| 1 | 2 | 3 | 4 | 5 | 6 | 7 | 8 | 9 | 10 | 11 | 12 | 13 |

SECTION 2

First Day
Setting the Stage, p. 13
Exploration 1, pp. 14–16

Second Day
Exploration 2, pp. 17–19
Key Concepts, p. 20

Block Schedule

Day 2
Setting the Stage, Exploration 1,
Exploration 2, Key Concepts

RESOURCE ORGANIZER

Teaching Resources
- Practice and Applications, Sec. 2
- Study Guide, Sec. 2
- Warm-Up, Sec. 2
- Quick Quiz, Sec. 2

Section Overview

In Section 2, students will find and use patterns to make the kinds of predictions that can help them make good choices in a variety of decision-making situations. Students will learn how to identify patterns involving sequences of numbers or shapes, and how to continue a pattern. Geometric models will help them to visualize the rule for a sequence. They will write equations that describe the rule of a sequence by relating the term number to the term. Students will use their equations to predict terms in a sequence. Students will also explore sequences by graphing the sequences on a coordinate plane. Section 3 will expose students to geometric sequences, though that term will not be introduced. *Power, exponent, base, exponential form* of a sequence, and *standard form* of a sequence are some of the new vocabulary words that are introduced in this section. Students will use exponents to predict a term in a sequence. They will work with sequences in exponential form to model areas of squares and volumes of cubes. They will then use these sequences to find the areas of other squares and the volumes of other cubes.

SECTION OBJECTIVES

Exploration 1
- model a number sequence with a word sentence, a table, a graph, or an equation
- predict the nth term of a number sequence

Exploration 2
- understand that exponents represent repeated multiplication
- identify the pattern in a sequence that involves exponents
- find the volume of a cube

ASSESSMENT OPTIONS

Checkpoint Questions
- Question 10 on p. 15
- Question 12 on p. 16
- Question 16 on p. 18
- Question 20 on p. 19

Embedded Assessment
- For a list of embedded assessment exercises see p. 1-19.

Performance Task/Portfolio
- Exercise 3 on p. 21 (challenge)
- Exercise 4 on p. 22
- Exercise 30 on p. 23
- Exercise 32 on p. 24 (visual thinking)
- ★ Exercises 38–39 on p. 24 (career)
- Standardized Testing on p. 25

★= a problem solving task that can be assessed using the Assessment Scales (reviewed in Sections 4–6)

SECTION 2 MATERIALS

Exploration 1
- ◆ Labsheets 2A and 2B
- ◆ 25 square tiles or graph paper

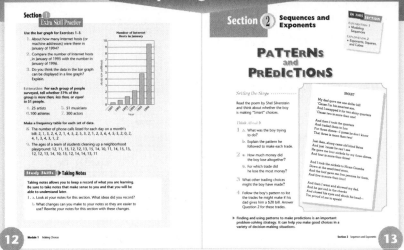

Setting the Stage

MOTIVATE

The poem on page 13 may be read orally, or you may choose four students to act out the poem for the class. To get more students involved, have each group of four students act out the poem. They can answer *Questions 1–4* as a class or in each group. If you have each group act out the poem and answer the questions, each student records the answers following the procedure you've developed for the year.

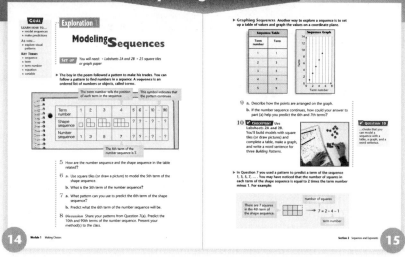

Exploration 1

PLAN

Classroom Management
Prepare Labsheets 2A and 2B for each student. Provide graph paper and enough tiles for each student to have 25 tiles. If you do not have enough tiles, pairs of students can work together. Make certain each student records the information and each student is involved in creating the pattern. Continue to have the tiles available for those students who need them throughout the module. For **Question 8**, provide enough time for students to present their method to the class.

GUIDE

Developing Math Concepts
Graphing sequences using a table of values will eventually lead students to see that *term number* and *term* correspond to *x* and *y* when ordered pairs of the form (*x*, *y*) are graphed in the coordinate plane. The material between **Questions 10** and **11** is very important in helping students learn how to write an equation for a sequence and then make predictions. For **Question 11**, you may need to include more examples to review the procedure for writing an equation.

Common Error Students confuse the *term number* with the *term*. Point out the term number is the position for each term. It indicates *where* you will find the term in the sequence. For example, the term number 5 indicates you will find the term in the fifth position when the terms are listed sequentially. The fifth term is the actual shape or number appearing in the fifth position.

Checkpoint Prior to **Question 10**, write word sentences for the pattern in **Question 9**, not an equation. Students will use a word sentence to write an equation on the following pages. For **Question 12** on page 16, students will be using word sentences from their labsheets to write an equation.

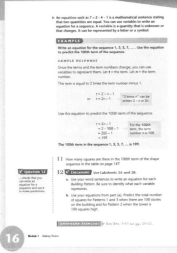

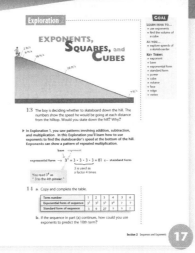

Exploration 1 continued

Classroom Examples

Write an equation for the sequence 1, 4, 7, 10, ... Use the equation to predict the 100th term of the sequence.

Sample Answer: Let t = the term. Let n = the term number.

The term is equal to 3 times the term number minus 2.

$$t = 3n - 2$$

Use this equation to predict the 100th term of the sequence.

$$\begin{aligned} t &= 3n - 2 \\ &= 3 \cdot 100 - 2 \\ &= 300 - 2 \\ &= 298 \end{aligned}$$

The 100th term is 298.

▶ HOMEWORK EXERCISES

See the Suggested Assignment for Day 1 on page 1-19. For Exercise Notes, see page 1-19.

Exploration 2

PLAN

Classroom Management
Provide a set of cubes for students to work with volume patterns. This exploration may be completed individually or in small groups. Each student should have a cube as you discuss *Question 18*. If you do not have enough cubes, you can have pairs or groups of students share. Give each student an opportunity to point out each term and show what volume means.

Customizing Instruction

Alternative Approach For *Question 8* on page 14, have students present methods in their group and have the group present one of the methods to the class.

Technology After students have completed Labsheets 2A and 2B, have them use a graphing calculator to set up and graph a table of values. You may want to use a computer program to demonstrate how to set up and graph a table of values. Have individual students, pairs of students, or the class set up and graph the patterns from Labsheets 2A and 2B to check their work. Have students use the graphing calculator or computer program to complete other patterns.

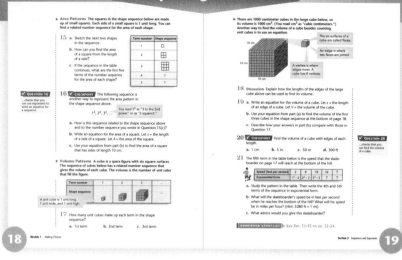

Exploration 2 continued

GUIDE

Developing Math Concepts
Students who have memorized equations for area and volume will develop a better sense of these concepts if they can use manipulatives to determine area and volume.

Checkpoint For *Question 16*, remind students that this is similar to previous patterns, but now exponents are involved. Students should demonstrate understanding before continuing the exploration. For *Question 20*, have students record how they found the volume rather than just writing the final answer. By having students show their work, you can diagnose areas of weakness and strength.

Common Error Students who lack understanding of exponents will multiply the base number times the exponent. You may need to provide extra examples to emphasize the correct procedure.

Classroom Examples
Find the volume of a cube when the length of an edge is 7.1 in.

Answer: $V = s^3$
$$= (7.1)^3$$
$$= 7.1 \cdot 7.1 \cdot 7.1$$
$$= 357.911$$

The volume is 357.911 in.^{3}

HOMEWORK EXERCISES ▶

See the Suggested Assignment for Day 2 on page 1-19. For Exercise Notes, see page 1-19.

CLOSE

Closure Question Write the formulas for the area of a square and the volume of a cube in two ways, one of which uses exponents. State what each variable represents in the formulas.

Sample Response: Let s = the length of a side of the square or the cube, A = the area of the square, and V = the volume of a cube. Then $A = s \cdot s$ or $A = s^2$, and $V = s \cdot s \cdot s$ or $V = s^3$.

Customizing Instruction

Visual Learners Providing square tiles will help students visualize the patterns. A two-dimensional drawing is very abstract for many students. Provide the opportunity to use the manipulatives as often as possible.

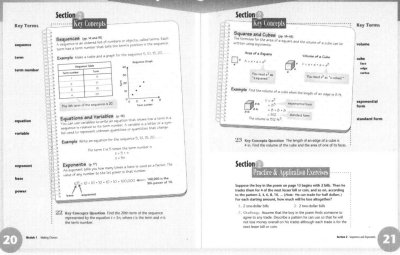

SUGGESTED ASSIGNMENT

Core Course

Day 1: Exs. 4–11, 33, 34
Day 2: Exs. 14–24, 26, 28, 30, 32, 35–37

Extended Course

Day 1: Exs. 2–4, 6, 8, 10, 11, 33, 34
Day 2: Exs. 14–24, 26, 28, 30–32, 35–37

Block Schedule

Day 2: Exs. 4–10 even, 11, 14, 16, 20–24, 26, 32–37

EMBEDDED ASSESSMENT

These section objectives are tested by the exercises listed.

Model a number sequence with a word sentence, a table, a graph, or an equation.

Exercises 4a–d, 6, 8, 10

Predict the *n*th term of a number sequence.

Exercises 4e, 10, 11b

Understand that exponents represent repeated multiplication.

Exercises 14, 16, 20–22

Identify the pattern in a sequence that involves exponents.

Exercises 23, 28

Find the volume of a cube.

Exercises 24–26

Practice & Application

EXERCISE NOTES

Challenge *Ex. 3* may be solved in a group. Have groups act out their solutions to prove the pattern is correct.

The following is a reduced image of pupil pages 22–23.

Page 22

4. Use the shape sequence in the table.

   a. Draw pictures of the 5th and 6th terms of the sequence.

   b. Write the number sequence that matches the first six terms of the shape sequence.

   c. Write a word sentence to describe a pattern you could use to predict the 7th term of the number sequence.

   d. Make a table of values for the first 10 terms of the number sequence. Use it to make a graph of the sequence.

   e. Use your graph to predict the 15th term of the number sequence.

Term number	Shape sequence
1	
2	
3	
4	
⋮	⋮

Write an equation for each word sentence. Use t for the term and n for the term number.

5. The term is six times the term number.

6. The term is one less than the term number.

7. The term is five more than the term number.

8. The term is half the term number.

For each sequence, make a table, draw a graph, and write an equation. Then predict the 100th term.

9. 7, 14, 21, 28, …   10. 199, 198, 197, 196, …

11. **Social Studies** Arizona and Oregon became states on the same day, February 14, but in different years. Arizona's first year as a state was Oregon's 54th year.

Arizona's years of statehood	1	2	3	4	…
Oregon's years of statehood	54	55	56	57	…

   a. Arizona became a state in 1912. When did Oregon become a state?

   b. When Arizona celebrates 100 years of statehood, how many years will Oregon have been a state?

22 Module 1 Making Choices

Page 23

Write each product in exponential form.

12. 2 · 2 · 2   13. 3 · 3   14. 7 · 7 · 7 · 7 · 7

Write each power in standard form.

15. 5^2 16. 4^3 17. 11^4 18. 6^5

19. 10^6 20. 0^{15} 21. 1^{30} 22. 1592^1

23. Predict the 100th term of the sequence 2^3, 4^3, 6^3, 8^3, …

Find the volume of a cube with edges of each length.

24. 7 mm   25. 11 ft   26. 80 cm   27. 25 in.

Chinese Noodles To make dragon's beard noodles, a chef takes noodle dough, stretches it, and then folds it in half. The chef repeats this process, making more noodles with each fold. An experienced noodle maker can stretch and fold the dough 8 times.

28. Suppose a chef folds the dough 8 times. How many noodles will there be?

29. How many folds are required to make about 500 noodles?

30. a. Copy and complete the table.

Side length (cm)	10	20	30	40
Area of a square (cm²)	?	?	?	?

   b. How does the area of a square change when you multiply the length of each side by 2? by 3? by 4?

   c. Copy and complete the table.

Edge length (cm)	10	20	30	40
Volume of a cube (cm³)	?	?	?	?

   d. How does the volume of a cube change when you multiply the length of each edge by 2? by 3? by 4?

   e. **Writing** Compare your answers to parts (b) and (d). Is the effect on area of doubling a side length the same as the effect on volume of doubling an edge length? Explain.

31. **Challenge** The volume of a cube is 700 cm³. Estimate the length of an edge. Explain your method.

Section 2 Sequences and Exponents **23**

Practice & Application

Manipulatives For *Ex. 4* it may be helpful for some students to use tiles to discover the pattern.

Background Information In *Ex. 11* you might point out that Arizona was the last of the 48 states (before Alaska and Hawaii) to be admitted to the Union. The state was very sparsely settled until the advent of air conditioning.

Developing Math Concepts If students are unsure about exponential form and standard form for *Exs. 12–22*, have them refer to page 17.

Multicultural Note Some students in your class may be of Asian descent. For *Exs. 28–29*, you could allow these students to share their knowledge of dragon's beard noodles or other similar noodles that are common to their native cuisine.

Customizing Instruction

Home Involvement Those helping students at home will find the Key Concepts on pages 20 and 21 a handy reference to the key ideas, terms, and skills of Section 2.

Absent Students For students who were absent for all or part of this section, the blackline Study Guide for Section 2 may be used to present the ideas, concepts, and skills of Section 2.

Extra Help For students who need additional practice, the blackline Practice and Applications for Section 2 provides additional exercises that may be used to confirm the skills of Section 2. The Extra Skill Practice on page 25 also provides additional answers.

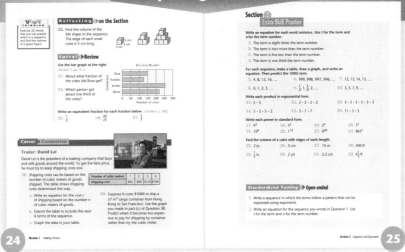

Closing the Section

Remind students that the purpose of this section was to find and use patterns to make predictions. *Reflecting on the Section Exercise 32* asks students to demonstrate their ability to find a pattern and predict. Explain your expectation for students to clearly communicate their understanding using all the skills presented in this section. It may be helpful to use the Key Concepts on pages 20–21 as a model for parts of their answer.

QUICK QUIZ ON THIS SECTION

1. Write an equation for the following word sentence, using *t* for the term and *n* for the term number: *The term is two more than five times the term number.*

2. Make a table, draw a graph, and write an equation for this sequence. Then predict the 200th term.

   5, 11, 17, 23, ...

3. Write 11 • 11 • 11 • 11 in exponential form.

4. Find the volume of a cube with edges of length 14 mm.

5. Predict the 50th term of the sequence 3^3 , 6^3 , 9^3 , ...

For answers, see Quick Quiz blackline on p. 1-65.

Section ③ Probability

Section Planner

DAYS FOR MODULE 1

1 2 3 4 **5 6 7** 8 9 10 11 12 13

SECTION 3

First Day
Setting the Stage, *pp. 26–27*

Second Day
Exploration 1, *pp. 27–29*

Third Day
Exploration 2, *pp. 30–32*
Key Concepts, *p. 33*

Block Schedule

Day 3
Setting the Stage, Exploration 1, Exploration 2, Key Concepts

RESOURCE ORGANIZER

Teaching Resources
• Practice and Applications, Sec. 3
• Study Guide, Sec. 3
• Technology Activity, Sec. 3
• Mid-Module Quiz
• Warm-Up, Sec. 3
• Quick Quiz, Sec. 3

Section Overview

Students will perform die-rolling experiments in Section 3 so they can learn about experimental and theoretical probabilities. They will learn how probabilities can help them make good choices in a game. The key terms *experiment, outcome, probability, experimental probability, equally likely outcomes, event,* and *theoretical probability* are all presented. The explorations will suggest that over the long run, an experimental probability will approach the theoretical probability of an experiment. The technology page shows students how they can use probability software to quickly and easily simulate an experiment with a large number of trials. When impossible and certain events are defined, the students learn how to use a number line to display probabilities.

Students will express their experimental probabilities as reduced fractions. They will also use fractions to compare probabilities. It is expected that students will be proficient in these skills. Refer students who need to review the skill to Toolbox page 585 for reducing fractions or to Toolbox page 586 for comparing fractions.

SECTION OBJECTIVES

Exploration 1
• identify outcomes of an experiment
• use a number from 0 to 1 to estimate probability
• find and use an experimental probability

Exploration 2
• find the theoretical probability of an event
• compare the experimental and the theoretical probability of an event

ASSESSMENT OPTIONS

Checkpoint Questions
• Question 6 on p. 28
• Question 13 on p. 30

Embedded Assessment
• For a list of embedded assessment exercises see p. 1-27.

Performance Task/Portfolio
• Exercise 5 on p. 34
• Exercise 26 on p. 36 (home involvement)
• Exercise 27 on p. 37 (writing)
• Exercises 28–29 on p. 37 (challenge)
• Exercise 30 on p. 37 (discussion)
• Module Project on p. 38
★ Standardized Testing on p. 39

★ = a problem solving task that can be assessed using the Assessment Scales (reviewed in Sections 4–6)

SECTION 3 MATERIALS

Setting the Stage
◆ Labsheet 3A
◆ 18 chips for each student
◆ 2 number cubes or dice

Exploration 1
◆ Labsheets 3A and 3B
◆ 18 chips
◆ 2 number cubes or dice

Exploration 2
◆ Labsheets 3C and 3D
◆ 2 number cubes or dice (red and blue)

Module Project on page 38
◆ Data from Project Question 3

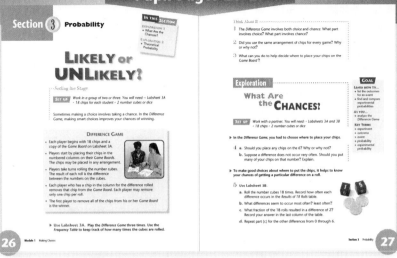

Setting the Stage

MOTIVATE

Students will work in groups of two or three to play the *Difference Game*. Each student will need Labsheet 3A, 18 chips or markers to place on the *Game Board* (Labsheet 3A), and 2 number cubes or two spinners with numbers 1 through 6. Have the students read the game directions. Go through the procedure asking questions such as the following: *What do you do before rolling the dice?* (place chips on game board) *Does each player have the chips in the same place?* (No) *How do you know what chip to take off?* (the difference between the two numbers rolled) *Who takes off a chip?* (all players) *How many chips do you remove?* (one) *Who is the winner?* (first player with all chips gone) *Do you get to move chips around once the game begins?* (No) *What else do you have to do besides play the game?* (record how many times the cube was rolled on the frequency table) *How many games do you play?* (three) Monitor students as they play the game. For those students who have finished the three games, have them write responses to *Questions 1–3* while waiting for everyone to finish their games. Then discuss *Questions 1–3*.

Exploration 1

PLAN

Classroom Management This exploration is best performed in groups of two. As students work through *Questions 4* and *5* they will need the materials for the game, Labsheets 3A and 3B. Make certain students are recording the correct fraction for *Question 5(c)*.

GUIDE

Developing Math Concepts The concept of probability can be intimidating for some students until they have dealt with lots of real-world examples. You may want to give several examples similar to those in *Exs. 1–4* on page 34. These exercises show events that a 7th grader would encounter where the probability is *zero, one, greater than one half,* or *less than one half.*

Common Error Students who have difficulty with fractions may have more success if they look at the part/whole relationship. The *part* of the rolls out of the *total* number of rolls represents the fraction.

Managing Labsheets For Labsheet 3B, have only one person from each group collect and report data from the other groups. Another method is to have one person from each group add the data to the 72 Rolls Table on a overhead, board, or computer display.

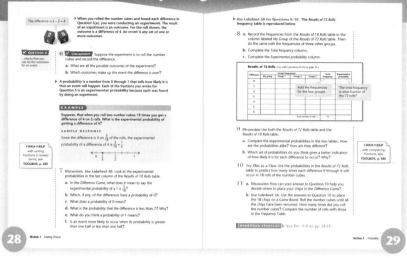

Exploration 1 continued

Checkpoint Prior to *Question 6*, make certain students understand the terms *experiment*, *outcome*, and *event*. Have students give several examples for each term. Explain that *Question 6* refers to the difference game they have just played. Some students will need *Question 6(b)* to be clarified. Have the students think back to the game. "Remember when you played the game and your difference was even? What outcomes made that happen?"

Classroom Examples

Suppose that when you throw two darts at a dart board 30 times you get an odd sum on 12 of the throws. What is the experimental probability of an odd sum? Graph your answer on a number line.

Sample Answer: Since the sum is odd on $\frac{12}{30}$ of the throws, the experimental probability of an odd sum is $\frac{12}{30} = \frac{2}{5}$.

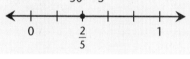

Question 7 is highlighted for discussion. Give enough time to discuss each part of the question using the *Example* above it for clarification. Have several different students explain the answers. *Questions 9* and *11* are also highlighted for discussion, and *Question 10* is highlighted for whole-class discussion. This allows the results of the whole class to be combined. After completing *Question 11(b)*, have the groups and the class draw conclusions.

HOMEWORK EXERCISES

See the Suggested Assignment for Day 1 on page 1-27. For Exercise Notes, see page 1-27.

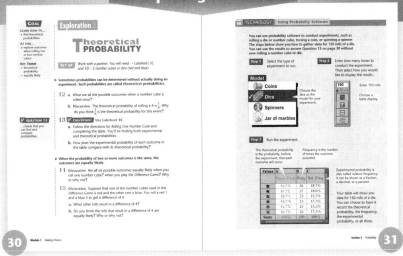

Exploration 2

PLAN

Classroom Management
Exploration 2 is best performed in groups of two. Each student needs Labsheets 3C and 3D, a red number cube, and a blue number cube. Discuss the following terminology: *theoretical probability* and *equally likely*.

Managing Time
This exploration will require more explanation and discussion, as well as time for the experiments. If enough time is available, have the students use a spinner similar to the one in Key Concepts on page 33. Have them predict what the probability of their outcomes will be and then have them spin 60 times to verify their prediction. Some students will only be able to make a connection to the information on Key Concepts page after completing the spins. Discuss the results to review the concepts of experimental and theoretical probability.

GUIDE

Developing Math Concepts
Experimental probability may make more sense to some students than theoretical probability because they can actually perform experiments to derive their answers for experimental probability. Help students make the connection to theoretical probability by using several examples from their experiences. For *Question 12*, make certain students can explain why the probability for each number is $\frac{1}{6}$.

Questions 14 and *15* are highlighted for discussion. You may want to provide other examples for students to help clarify what *equally likely* means. Have all students verbalize examples of equally likely results. Monitor students for correct use of Labsheet 3D for *Questions 16–18* on page 32.

Checkpoint
Prior to *Question 13*, students should verbalize the difference between experimental and theoretical probability. For Labsheet 3C, check students' completion of *Question 13(a)* before they complete *Question 13(b)*.

Ongoing Assessment
Have students explain what they are doing as they conduct their experiments. Check their terminology and ask questions using the terminology.

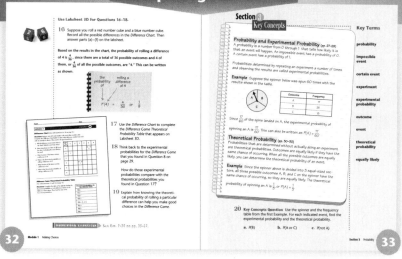

Exploration 2 continued

Classroom Examples
Give the theoretical probability of selecting a vowel from the 26 letters of the alphabet.

Answer: Since each letter has the same chance of being selected as any other letter, the theoretical probability of selecting a vowel is $\frac{5}{26}$.

▌ HOMEWORK EXERCISES ▶

See the Suggested Assignment for Day 2 on page 1-27. For Exercise Notes, see page 1-27.

CLOSE

Closure Question Explain the difference between experimental probability and theoretical probability.

Answer: Experimental probability is probability found by performing experiments. Theoretical probability is calculated probability, or probability that is determined without doing an experiment.

Customizing Instruction

Home Involvement Those helping students at home will find the Key Concepts on page 33 a handy reference to the key ideas, terms, and skills of Section 3.

Absent Students For students who were absent for all or part of this section, the blackline Study Guide for Section 3 may be used to present the ideas, concepts, and skills of Section 3.

Extra Help For students who need additional practice, the blackline Practice and Applications for Section 3 provides additional exercises that may be used to confirm the skills of Section 3. The Extra Skill Practice on page 33 also provides additional exercises.

Technology Providing the opportunity for students to use probability software allows students to observe the outcomes of several experiments in a short period of time. Most students benefit from performing the experiment themselves and using the software to validate their experience.

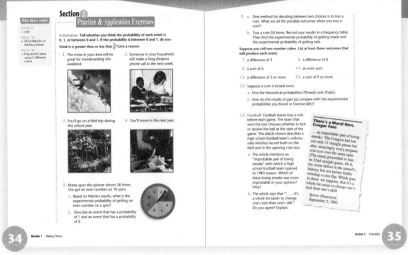

34 Module 1 Making Choices

Section 3 Probability **35**

SUGGESTED ASSIGNMENT

Core Course
Day 1: Exs. 31–36
Day 2: Exs. 1–12
Day 3: Exs. 13, 15, 16–24 even, 27, 30

Extended Course
Day 1: Exs. 31–36
Day 2: Exs. 1–12
Day 3: Exs. 13, 15, 16–24 even, 27–30, 37, 38

Block Schedule
Day 3: Exs. 2, 4–6, 8, 10, 12, 13, 15, 16–24 even, 27, 30–36

EMBEDDED ASSESSMENT

These section objectives are tested by the exercises listed.

Identify outcomes of an experiment.
Exercises 6a, 8, 10, 12

Use a number from 0 to 1 to estimate probability.
Exercises 2, 4

Find and use an experimental probability.
Exercises 5a, 6b

Find the theoretical probability of an event.
Exercises 16, 18, 20, 22, 24

Compare the experimental and the theoretical probability of an event.
Exercises 13, 27

Practice & Application

EXERCISE NOTES

Estimation For *Exs. 1–4*, stress that the answers involve estimation, not an exact answer.

Reading For *Ex. 14*, have students read the article orally and discuss the events in the article before they try to answer the questions.

Developing Math Concepts
When answering *Question 14(b)*, students should make reference to what they did during this section to support their explanation. For *Exs. 25* and *26*, you may need to explain the game procedure.

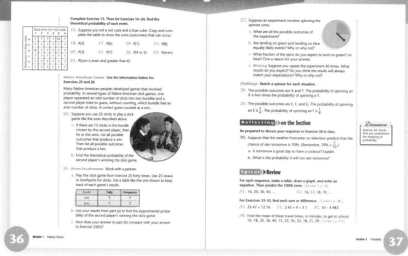

Practice & Application

Manipulatives Students will need toothpicks, straws, or something similar to complete *Ex. 26*.

Home Involvement *Ex. 26* provides an opportunity for students to play the game. Have students bring back a signature and comment from home about the game. An additional activity is *Ex. 38*. Have students write about their experience; how long the activity lasted, who participated, their experimental probability, their prediction, and the actual number of cubes for each color.

Writing Remind students to answer all the questions posed in *Ex. 27(d)*. For those students with difficulties in writing, have someone record their responses or accept oral responses.

MODULE 1 ◆ SECTION 3

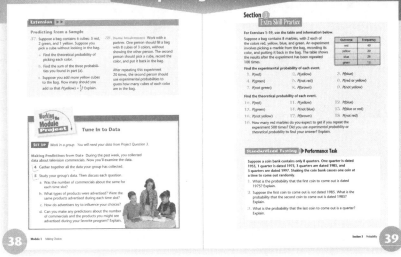

Have students work in their
original groups and retrieve the
data about commercials from
storage. Each student should
record the groups responses for
Questions 4 and *5*. Monitor
each group by asking questions
to assess students' involvement,
understanding, as well as accuracy and completeness of their
responses. Have students store
their findings and answers to
Question 5 for future use.

Closing the Section

Students have had several experiences with probability which
should lead them to understand
the probability in everyday situations such as weather forecasting. *Reflecting on the Section
Exercise 30* allows students to
apply the skills they have
learned in this section. Stress
that students should communicate their understanding of
probability by correctly using
terminology and by connecting
examples from the section to
weather forecasting. Students
should be prepared to discuss
their response in small groups or
in whole-class discussion.

QUICK QUIZ ON THIS SECTION

1. Evelyn spins the spinner shown
   60 times and gets white on 28
   spins. What is the experimental
   probability of getting white?

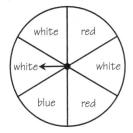

2. What is the theoretical probability of getting white in the
   situation of *Question 1*?

3. Suppose you roll three number
   cubes. List three outcomes
   that will produce an odd sum
   greater than 11.

For answers, see Quick Quiz
blackline on p. 1-66.

MODULE 1 ◆ SECTION 3

Section ④ Problem Solving

Section Planner

DAYS FOR MODULE 1

1 2 3 4 5 6 7 8 9 10 11 12 13

SECTION 4

First Day
Setting the Stage, p. 40
Exploration 1, pp. 41–42

Second Day
Exploration 2, p. 43
Key Concepts, p. 44

Block Schedule

Day 4
Setting the Stage, Exploration 1,
Exploration 2, Key Concepts

RESOURCE ORGANIZER

Teaching Resources
• Practice and Applications, Sec. 4
• Study Guide, Sec. 4
• Warm-Up, Sec. 4
• Quick Quiz, Sec. 4

Section Overview

In Section 4, students investigate a problem that involves interpreting and analyzing information in order to make choices about a real life situation. In exploring the problem, they will study a 4-step approach to problem solving. The four steps involved in the problem-solving approach are outlined in the *Key Concepts* summary and include understanding the problem, making a plan, carrying out the plan, and looking back. Students examine and practice these concepts as they develop a strategy for predicting the outcomes of a game. As they investigate different kinds of problems in the Practice and Application exercises, they will discover that different strategies are required for different kinds of problems. Strategies used include looking for a pattern; making a diagram, a list, or a table; solving an equation; guessing and checking; and looking for a pattern. On the Student Self Assessment page, students will use five scales to assess how well they approached and solved the problems in the exercises.

The focus in this section is on a problem-solving strategy rather than on vocabulary, so no new vocabulary is introduced.

SECTION OBJECTIVES

Exploration 1
• use the 4-step approach to problem solving

Exploration 2
• choose and apply problem solving strategies

ASSESSMENT OPTIONS

Embedded Assessment
• For a list of embedded assessment exercises see p. 1-33.

Performance Task/Portfolio
⋆ Exercise 1 on p. 45 (writing)
⋆ Exercises 4–5 on p. 45
⋆ Exercises 6 on p. 45 (challenge)
⋆ Exercises 7 on p. 46 (oral report)
⋆ Module Project on p. 46
⋆ Extended Exploration on p. 48

⋆ = a problem solving task that can be assessed using the Assessment Scales (reviewed in Sections 4–6)

SECTION 4 MATERIALS

Exploration 2
◆ 15 index cards numbered from 1 to 15

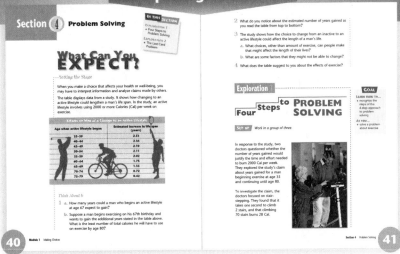

Setting the Stage

MOTIVATE

Discuss what is meant by an "active" lifestyle. Point out the information in the table is based on calories used per week on exercise. In a small group or as a whole class, have students read and answer *Questions 1–4*. Make sure that students interpret the table correctly.

Exploration I

PLAN

Classroom Management
Exploration 1 is best performed in groups of three. Have each group read out loud and discuss the information preceding the questions. For *Question 5*, remind students to use their own words even though they are working as a group. *Question 7* requires each student to solve the problem individually. *Question 8* allows the group members to check with each other but requires students to respond using their own words. *Question 9* is highlighted for whole-class discussion. The discussion should result in a class description for each problem-solving step.

GUIDE

Writing Using the 4-step problem solving method as an outline for writing about solutions will result in clear, concise, and comprehensive communication.

Common Error Although students follow the problem-solving steps, they tend to skip the last step. Getting students to check if their solution is reasonable will eliminate many errors.

Classroom Examples
For the following problem, explain how you could use the 4-step approach to problem solving to find a solution:
Rowena wants to exercise by jogging a mile each day around her neighborhood. She wants to find a route where she begins and ends at her house. How can Rowena solve this problem?

Sample Answer: Step 1: The problem is that Rowena needs to find a 1-mile jogging route around her neighborhood that begins and ends at her house. She needs to know the distances of the streets around her house and where the streets are in relation to each other.

Step 2: Rowena can use several problem-solving strategies, such as make a picture or draw a diagram (a map of the streets in her neighborhood, in this case), make an organized list, guess and check, or act it out. Step 3: Rowena can measure the distances of the streets in her neighborhood by making a map of her neighborhood where she would like to run and then using a bicycle that has an odometer or riding in a car and using its odometer to find the distances of each street on the map. Then she can make several routes and see if they are close to 1 mile long by adding up the distances of the streets she will jog on. Step 4: Rowena can check her measurements and the addition of the lengths of the streets. She can also extend the problem by finding more than one route to jog on so that she can see different people in her neighborhood when she jogs.

HOMEWORK EXERCISES

See the Suggested Assignment for Day 1 on page 1-33. For Exercise Notes, see page 1-33.

MODULE 1 ◆ SECTION 4

Exploration 2

PLAN

Classroom Management
Exploration 2 is best performed in groups with a set of cards for each group. If you have a class list of problem-solving strategies, have students take a moment to review the list. If there is not a list, this would be a good time to create a class list of problem-solving strategies for all students to use as a reference. Make certain students are placing the card correctly as indicated in the pictures. Students will be using their solutions for the *Last Card Problem* for 16 and 20 cards in Section 5. Therefore, you may want to collect the solutions and place them in storage for future use with Section 5 on page 51.

Managing Time
Prior to the exploration prepare sets of cards numbered from 1 through 15.

GUIDE

Developing Math Concepts
Post the *Key Concepts 4-Step Approach to Problem Solving* next to the class-generated 4-Step Approach. Point out the similarities in each problem-solving step. Encourage students to remember and apply the steps as they solve problems.

Classroom Examples
Using seven cards for the *Last Card Problem*, use words to describe how the experiment is worked out. Describe what is common in all of the cards that are placed under.

Answer: 1 is placed face up, 2 is placed under, 3 is placed up, 4 is placed under, 5 is placed face up, 6 is placed under, 7 is placed face up, 2 is placed under, 4 is placed face up, 6 is placed under, 2 is placed face up, 6 is placed under, 6 is placed face up.

The last card is 6. All of the cards that are placed under are even.

HOMEWORK EXERCISES

See the Suggested Assignment for Day 2 on page 1-33. For Exercise Notes, see page 1-33.

CLOSE

Closure Question List each step in the 4-step Approach to Problem Solving in this section and briefly explain each step.

Answer: Understand the problem, make a plan, carry out the plan, look back. In the first step, you identify the question and gather the necessary information. In the second step, you decide on a problem solving strategy. In the third step, you solve the problem. In the fourth step, you check to make sure that your solution is accurate and makes sense.

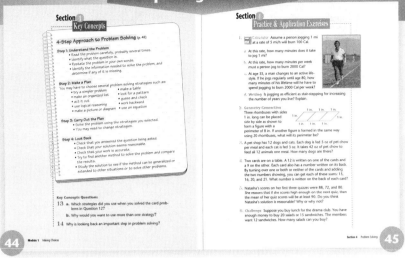

SUGGESTED ASSIGNMENT

Core Course
Day 1: Exs. 2, 3, 8–11
Day 2: Exs. 4, 5, 7

Extended Course
Day 1: Exs. 2, 3, 8–11
Day 2: Exs. 4–7

Block Schedule
Day 4: Exs. 2–5, 7–11

EMBEDDED ASSESSMENT

These section objectives are tested by the exercises listed.

Use the 4-step approach to problem solving.
Exercise 2

Choose and apply problem solving strategies.
Exercise 4

Practice & Application

EXERCISE NOTES

Managing Time For *Exs. 1–6*, using the 4-step approach in a complete and comprehensive manner will take more time. Allow the needed time for students to solve the problems as well as discuss the process. Having students use the 4-Step Approach as an outline for communicating their solutions will allow you to assess students' strengths and weaknesses.

Geometry Connection For *Ex. 2*, some students may need to be reminded of the definition of a rhombus. Drawing a picture, making a table, or using rhombuses are strategies for solving *Ex. 2*. Encourage students to make connections to previous problems as they solve this exercise.

Developing Math Concepts *Ex. 3* and *Ex. 4* may need clarification by reading aloud, acting out, or drawing a picture. Working in a group for *Ex. 6* may cause less frustration. Using a ratio or making a table may help students obtain the solution. Students will use different strategies to solve *Ex. 6*.

Customizing Instruction

Home Involvement Those helping students at home will find the Key Concepts on page 44 a handy reference to the key ideas, terms, and skills of Section 4.

Absent Students For students who were absent for all or part of this section, the blackline Study Guide for Section 4 may be used to present the ideas, concepts, and skills of Section 4.

Extra Help For students who need additional practice, the blackline Practice and Applications for Section 4 provides additional exercises that may be used to confirm the skills of Section 4. The Extra Skill Practice on page 47 also provides additional exercises.

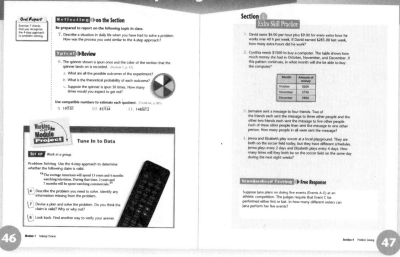

Working on the Module Project

Have students work in their original groups and retrieve the data about commercials from storage. Using the data collected, students follow the 4-step approach to determine if the claim is valid. Make certain students are following the directions in *Questions 6–8* and are applying the skills from this section. A complete, concise, and comprehensive solution should be written by all members of the group.

Closing the Section

Using the 4-step approach to problem solving extends beyond the mathematics classroom. Students should be able to recognize the connection between problem solving in mathematics and everyday problem solving. The application of the 4-step approach is of value in each student's life as he or she encounters problems inside and outside school. *Reflecting on the Section Exercise 7* provides an opportunity for students to share these connections and applications. Have each student write a description for *Exercise 7*. Then have students or groups of students present the process for approaching and solving as many different situations in daily life as possible. These presentations should be enjoyable, interesting, and informative.

QUICK QUIZ ON THIS SECTION

1. You have $1000 to spend stocking the school store with T-shirts, sweat shirts, and hats. How could you use a 4-step approach in deciding how to place your order?

2. A farmer has 200 ft of fencing. What is the largest rectangular area that can be enclosed?

3. Joey swims every third day and lifts weights every fifth day. Today he both swims and lifts weights. On how many days will he both swim and lift weights in the next 6 weeks?

4. The rectangles in this sequence are twice as wide as they are high. What will be the perimeter of the 100th rectangle?

For answers, see Quick Quiz blackline on p. 1-67.

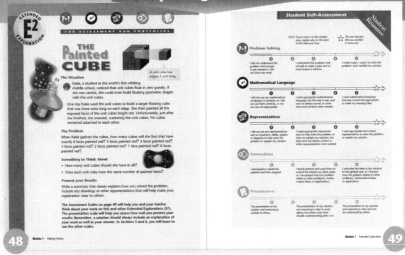

Extended Exploration

The extended exploration will take several days to solve and present results. First have students read *The Situation*. Using a model to act out the situation will give students a visual of the situation. Have students make their own model as a problem-solving strategy. If students use your model, it will eliminate the opportunity to apply their own skills. Make reference to the classroom or personal list of problem-solving strategies and 4-step approach as skills to be used to solve this problem. Next have students read *The Problem* and then state the problem in their own words. Just as they solved problems in the previous

section, students will be solving the extended exploration. They have started by discussing the first step, understanding the problem. Now they will record explanations as they work through each step of the 4-step approach. Next have them read *Something to Think About* and *Present your Results*. Discuss the Presentation Assessment Scale. It is helpful if students see and discuss examples for a score of one, three, and five. Modeling what a score of five looks like will allow students to know what they are striving to achieve. *Problem Solving* and *Connections* are presented in Section 5. *Mathematical Language* and *Representations* are presented in Section 6. For students who have studied this program, the

Assessment Scale will be familiar. Therefore, a review and examples of your expectations will be sufficient. For students who have not used the Assessment Scale, in-depth discussion and examples will be necessary. It will take longer for these students to reach a score of five on all the Assessment Scales, but there will be improvement. Because the extended exploration takes three to five days, provide students with a time line for completion. Check with the students each day for questions and progress.

Section Planner

SECTION 5

First Day
Setting the Stage, *p. 50*
Exploration 1, *pp. 51–52*

Second Day
Exploration 2, *pp. 53–55*
Key Concepts, *p. 55*

Block Schedule

Day 5
Setting the Stage, Exploration 1,
Exploration 2, Key Concepts

RESOURCE ORGANIZER

Teaching Resources
• Practice and Applications, Sec. 5
• Study Guide, Sec. 5
• Warm-Up, Sec. 5
• Quick Quiz, Sec. 5

Section Overview

Section 5 will ask students to evaluate their solutions to the problems in Section 4 by evaluating the strategies they used. Thus, students should be very familiar with all the strategies for making a plan that were outlined in that section. In this section, students will work with two of the problem solving scales on page 49 as they assess the strategies they used. Students can score at one of five levels on each scale. Each level on a scale includes one or more of the four steps in the 4-step approach to problem solving. In this section, students will focus on the *Problem Solving Scale* and the *Connections Scale*. Students will use the Problem Solving Scale to assess how well they apply the 4-step approach. The Connections Scale will help students assess the connections they make to other problems, mathematical concepts, or applications.

SECTION OBJECTIVES

Exploration 1
• use the *Problem Solving Scale* for self-assessment

Exploration 2
• use the *Connections Scale* for self-assessment

ASSESSMENT OPTIONS

Checkpoint Questions
• Question 8 on p. 52
• Question 11 on p. 54

Embedded Assessment
• For a list of embedded assessment exercises see p. 1-40.

Performance Task/Portfolio
★Exercise 1 on p. 56 (visual thinking)
★Exercise 4 on p. 56
• Exercise 7 on p. 57 (journal)
★Standardized Testing on p. 58

★= a problem solving task that can be assessed using the Assessment Scales (reviewed in Sections 4–6)

SECTION 5 MATERIALS

Exploration 2
◆ Labsheet 5A
◆ marker for highlighting
◆ solutions to Question 12 on page 43

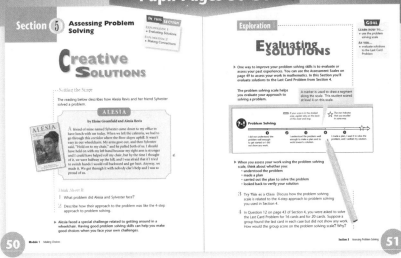

Setting the Stage

MOTIVATE

Have students read the description of how Alesia and her friend solved a problem. Students can read silently, in groups, or as a whole class. Discuss *Questions 1* and *2*. Students may want to share similar situations. Discuss the approach used to solve the problem and how it leads to making good choices. Point out that solving problems in daily life is similar in approach to solving mathematical problems. Most of the time people use the 4-step approach so naturally that they are unaware that they have good problem-solving skills.

Exploration I

PLAN

Classroom Management Have students note that the purpose for this exploration is to improve problem-solving skills through the use of assessment. An effective way to improve is to look at what you did and find the strengths and weaknesses. This exploration is best performed as a whole class if students have not used the Assessment Scales. Otherwise the exploration may be done individually with whole-class discussion for *Questions 3* and *5*. Have student retrieve their solutions for the *Last Card Problem* from Section 4.

Managing Time Section 5 will take less time if students are familiar with the Assessment Scale. If students are not familiar with the scale, it is important to take the time for a comprehensive discussion and to model the Assessment Scale for improvement and success in reaching the score of 5 for each scale.

GUIDE

Developing Math Concepts Students should be looking for patterns. Mathematics is the language of patterns. Remind students the importance of recording in order to find patterns.

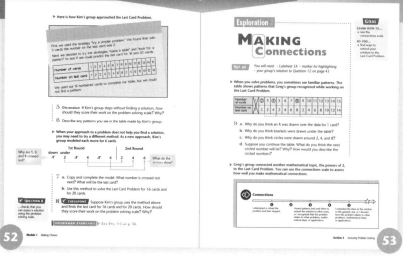

Exploration 1 continued

Classroom Examples
Using the Classroom Example from Exploration 1 of Section 4, how can you score at level 5 on the problem solving scale?

Sample Answer: You can make a plan, use it to find a route that is 1 mile long and begins and ends at Rowena's house, and then verify the length of the route.

Checkpoint *Question 8* checks students' understanding of the problem-solving assessment scale. Make certain each student can explain why they chose the score.

▶ HOMEWORK EXERCISES

See the Suggested Assignment for Day 1 on page 1-40. For Exercise Notes, see page 1-40.

Exploration 2

PLAN

Classroom Management
Provide Labsheet 5A and a high-lighter for each student. *Question 9* is best performed in small groups for students to ver-balize their thinking. *Question 10* is highlighted for discussion. Make certain students explain what a connection is and why the group earned the score. Connections can be difficult for students. Therefore, several examples as well as discussion of *Questions 10–17* will be helpful. After *Question 16*, have students take note of their strengths and weaknesses. A set of cards for students to use in groups and individually will be needed for the exploration and homework exercises.

Customizing Instruction

Alternative Approach If students do not have solu-tions from Section 4, model the problem and provide cards for students to review the problem.

Visual Learners Have sets of cards for students who still need to act out the problem, draw pictures, or dia-grams to visualize what is occurring with the cards.

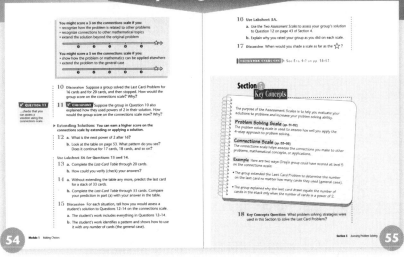

Exploration 2 continued

GUIDE

Developing Math Concepts
Review powers of 2 and have
students quickly list powers of 2
(2, 4, 8, 16, 32, ...). Students
who list 2, 4, 8, 10 are listing
multiples of 2.

Checkpoint *Question 11*
checks students' understanding
of the connections scale. Make
certain students can explain
why they chose the score.

Classroom Examples

**Using the Classroom Example
from Exploration 1 of Section
4, how can you score at level 5
on the connections scale?**

Sample Answer: You could find
the lengths of the streets that
Rowena has to run on and make
generalizations for possible
1-mile jogging routes. For example, Rowena has to run on the
street that her house is on
because her route begins and
ends at her house.

HOMEWORK EXERCISES

See the Suggested Assignment
for Day 2 on page 1-40. For
Exercise Notes, see page 1-40.

CLOSE

Closure Question When assessing your work, how could you
score a 5 on the Problem Solving
Scale? on the Connections
Scale?

Answer: If I made a plan, used it to
solve the problem, and verified
my work; If I extended the ideas
in the solution to a general case,
or I showed how the problem
relates to other problems, mathematical ideas, or applications.

Customizing Instruction

Home Involvement Those helping students at home
will find the Key Concepts on page 55 a handy reference to the key ideas, terms, and skills of Section 5.
Having students share their problems and Assessment
Scale with parents can open home-school communication. The card problem is enjoyable for students to
share with their family.

Absent Students For students who were absent for
all or part of this section, the blackline Study Guide for
Section 5 may be used to present the ideas, concepts,
and skills of Section 5.

Extra Help For students who need additional practice, the blackline Practice and Applications for Section
5 provides additional exercises that may be used to
confirm the skills of Section 5. Having students work
with a partner helps them to build confidence in solving problems. Giving students extra time and assis-
tance for the first few problems may give them the
skills to continue working on their own rather than
skipping problems. The Extra Skill Practice on page 58
provides additional exercises.

MODULE 1 ◆ SECTION 5

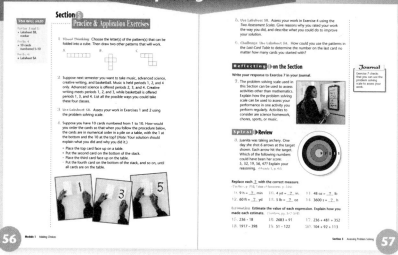

SUGGESTED ASSIGNMENT

Core Course
Day 1: Exs. 1–3, 8–14
Day 2: Exs. 4, 5, 7, 15–20

Extended Course
Day 1: Exs. 1–3, 8–14
Day 2: Exs. 4–7, 15–20

Block Schedule
Day 5: Exs. 1–5, 7–20

EMBEDDED ASSESSMENT

These section objectives are tested by the exercises listed.

Use the *Problem Solving Scale* for self-assessment.
Exercises 1–3

Use the *Connections Scale* for self-assessment.
Exercises 4, 5

Practice & Application

EXERCISE NOTES

Visual Learners Graph paper will be useful for *Ex. 1* because some students will want to cut out shapes to check their solution.

Problem Solving For *Exs. 1, 2,* and *4*, students will be applying the 4-step problem-solving approach along with appropriate problem-solving strategies. Encourage them to look back and use the skills they have developed in solving other problems. Point out that students will be using Labsheets 5A and 5B which contain Assessment Scales. Knowing what is expected (assessed) will help students achieve a higher score.

Writing *Ex. 4* requires perseverance and students should be recording their process as they solve the problem.

Closing the Section

The purpose of this section was to improve problem-solving skills through assessment, as well as to make connections to everyday situations. *Reflecting on the Section Exercise 7* checks students' ability to use the Assessment Scale in an everyday situation.

QUICK QUIZ ON THIS SECTION

1. Give an example of how a student could get 5 on the problem-solving scale and 1 on the connections scale.

2. Sammie has 3 shirts, 2 pairs of pants, 2 pairs of shoes, and 3 pairs of socks. How many different outfits does she have?

3. For question 2 write down the number of choices for each category and the number of different combinations. How are the numbers related? What do you think the answer would be for a person with 10 shirts, 15 pairs of pants, 8 pairs of shoes, and 20 pairs of socks?

For answers, see Quick Quiz blackline on p. 1-68.

Section ⑥ Expressions and Representations

Section Planner

DAYS FOR MODULE 1
| 1 | 2 | 3 | 4 | 5 | 6 | 7 | 8 | 9 | 10 | 11 | 12 | 13 |

SECTION 6

First Day
Setting the Stage, *p. 59*
Exploration 1, *pp. 60–61*

Second Day
Exploration 2, *pp. 62–65*
Key Concepts, *p. 65*

Block Schedule

Day 6
Setting the Stage, Exploration 1,
Exploration 2, Key Concepts

RESOURCE ORGANIZER

Teaching Resources
• Practice and Applications, Sec. 6
• Study Guide, Sec. 6
• Module Tests Forms A and B
• Standardized Assessment
• Module Performance Assessment
• Warm-Up, Sec. 6
• Quick Quiz, Sec. 6

Section Overview

In Section 6 students will examine ways to assess and improve their mathematical communication skills. They will study the mathematical meanings of *expression*, *order of operations*, and *evaluating an expression*. Then they will use the *Mathematical Language Scale* to evaluate how well they use mathematical vocabulary and symbols. Students will study grouping symbols and the order of operations, discussing how each is related to the language of mathematics.

In Exploration 2, students will explore how models, or representations, such as equations, tables, graphs, and diagrams will help them communicate mathematical ideas and solutions to problems. They will use the *Representations Scale* to assess how well they use representations. For example, they will decide when a line graph can appropriately display information. The technology page shows students how to use spreadsheets to create a bar graph.

Where necessary for review of bar graphs and line graphs, which are discussed in this section, students should refer to the Key Concepts summary on page 7 in Section 1.

SECTION OBJECTIVES

Exploration 1
• use the *Mathematical Language Scale* for self-assessment
• use the order of operations to evaluate whole-number numerical expressions with grouping symbols and exponents

Exploration 2
• use the *Representations Scale* for self-assessment
• decide when to use a bar graph or a line graph to represent a set of data

ASSESSMENT OPTIONS

Checkpoint Questions
• Question 11 on p. 61
• Question 15 on p. 63

Embedded Assessment
• For a list of embedded assessment exercises see p. 1-46.

Performance Task/Portfolio
★ Exercise 16 on p.66
★ Exercise 26 on p. 68 (discussion)
★ Module Project on pp. 69, 71

★ = a problem solving task that can be assessed using the Assessment Scales (reviewed in Sections 4–6)

SECTION 6 MATERIALS

Module Project on page 69
◆ data from Module Project Question 4

Module Project on page 71
◆ data and tables or graphs from Module Project Questions 4 and 11

Review and Assessment on page 72
◆ graph paper

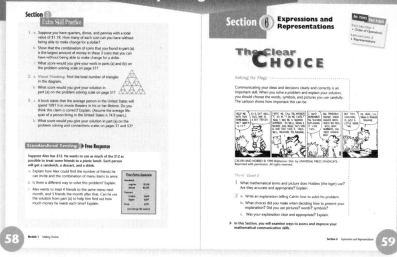

Setting the Stage

MOTIVATE

Read the introduction and comic strip to the whole class, or after students have read the comic strip, choose one student to read the part of Calvin and another student read the part of Hobbes. After students have written a response, discuss **Questions 1** and **2**. Emphasize the importance of communicating ideas clearly and correctly. Have students share situations when problems arose due to miscommunication. Point out the purpose of this section is to examine ways to assess and improve mathematical communication skills which will be used throughout the year.

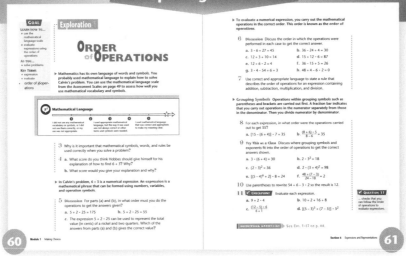

Exploration 1

PLAN

Classroom Management
Depending on the level and experience of the students, this exploration can be performed individually, in a small group, or as a whole class. As indicated earlier, it is important to use mathematical terms correctly. Therefore, make certain students understand the terms *expression, evaluate,* and other terms used in the module. *Questions 5* and *6* are highlighted for discussion which can be done in small group or as a whole class. Make certain students are reading all of the material. *Question 9* is highlighted for whole class discussion. This allows for all students to hear the thinking of classmates and gives students an opportunity to verbalize order of operations. As students discuss grouping symbols, model the step-by-step format shown on page 65 in the Key Concepts.

GUIDE

Developing Math Concepts
When reading *Question 9(a)*, point out that 3 · (6 + 4) can be read as *3 times the quantity six plus four*. Point out that some problems have symbols within symbols that affect the solution, for example, as in *Question 9(e)*. Stress that operations within the innermost pair of grouping symbols should be performed first. *Question 9(f)* shows the importance of performing all operations in the numerator and then performing all the operations in the denominator before dividing the numerator by the denominator.

Classroom Examples
Follow the order of operations to evaluate the expression $7 - 4 + [(18 - 3) \div 5]^3 \cdot 2$.

Answer:

$7 - 4 + [(18 - 3) \div 5]^3 \cdot 2$
$7 - 4 + [15 \div 5]^3 \cdot 2$
$7 - 4 + 3^3 \cdot 2$
$7 - 4 + 27 \cdot 2$
$7 - 4 + 54$
57

Common Error Students who skip steps or lack understanding of grouping symbols will have difficulty. Students should complete one calculation at a time. Have students record and verbalize what to do as you model solutions.

Checkpoint *Question 11* should be completed using the step-by-step format shown in the Key Concepts on page 65. Make certain students complete *Question 11* correctly before doing *Exs. 1–15* in Practice and Application on page 66.

Ongoing Assessment Ask students questions about their work as they complete the exploration. This will allow you to assess, clear up misconceptions, and allow other students to hear classmates' thinking.

HOMEWORK EXERCISES

See the Suggested Assignment for Day 1 on page 1-46. For Exercise Notes, see page 1-46.

MODULE 1 ◆ SECTION 6

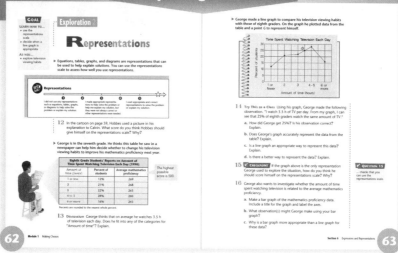

Exploration 2

PLAN	**GUIDE**

Classroom Management

Depending on the level and experience of the students, this exploration can be performed individually, in a small group, or as a whole class. *Question 13* is highlighted for discussion which can be done in a small group or as a whole class. *Question 14* is highlighted for whole class discussion. Have students reflect back to Section 1, Exploration 1, when line graphs were used to represent change over time. Comparing the line graph from Section 1 and George's line graph should help students to see when a line graph is appropriate.

Classroom Examples

Using the Classroom Example from Exploration 1 of Section 4, how can you score at level 5 on the representations scale?

Sample Answer: You could draw an accurate map of Rowena's neighborhood and draw a diagram of one or more possible jogging routes that she could take.

Checkpoint *Question 15* will check students' understanding of the representation scale. Therefore, writing a complete explanation will lead to a more valuable assessment.

Common Error Students who make a bar graph incorrectly for *Question 16(a)* would benefit by following a model such as the one on page 7 of Section 1 in the Key Concepts.

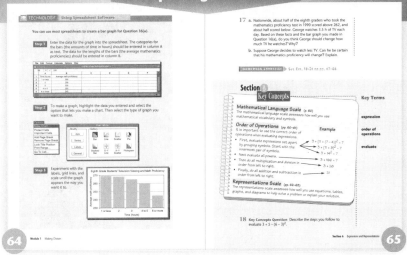

HOMEWORK EXERCISES ▶

See the Suggested Assignment for Day 2 on page 1-46. For Exercise Notes, see page 1-46.

CLOSE

Closure Question State the Order of Operations.

Answer: Complete operations inside parentheses, evaluate powers, do multiplication and division from left to right, do addition and subtraction from left to right.

Customizing Instruction

Technology If you do not have access to a lab for students to use a spreadsheet, one computer in the classroom can be used to demonstrate page 64. Pairs of students can take turns at the computer for practice. Once students see the use of spreadsheet, they can incorporate spreadsheets into any lesson that includes collecting class data.

Home Involvement Those helping students at home will find the Key Concepts on page 65 a handy reference to the key ideas, terms, and skills of Section 6.

Absent Students For students who were absent for all or part of this section, the blackline Study Guide for Section 6 may be used to present the ideas, concepts, and skills of Section 6.

Extra Help For students who need additional practice, the blackline Practice and Applications for Section 6 provides additional exercises that may be used to confirm the skills of Section 6. The Extra Skill Practice on page 70 also provides additional exercises.

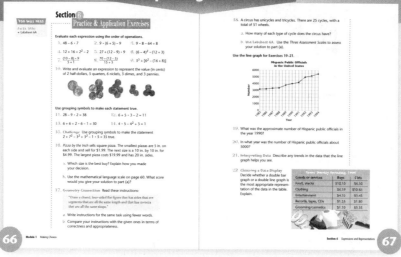

SUGGESTED ASSIGNMENT

Core Course
Day 1: Exs. 4–11, 16, 17
Day 2: Exs. 18, 22–24, 26–34

Extended Course
Day 1: Exs. 4–11, 15–17
Day 2: Exs. 18, 22–24, 26–34

Block Schedule
Day 6: Exs. 4, 6, 8–11, 16–18,
22–24, 26–34

EMBEDDED ASSESSMENT

These section objectives are
tested by the exercises listed.

**Use the *Mathematical
Language Scale* for
self-assessment.**

Exercises 16, 17

**Use the order of opera-
tions to evaluate whole-
number numerical
expressions with grouping
symbols and exponents.**

Exercises 4, 6, 8–10

**Use the *Representations
Scale* for self-assessment.**

Exercises 18, 23, 24

**Decide when to use a bar
graph or a line graph to
represent a set of data.**

Exercise 22

Practice & Application

EXERCISE NOTES

Challenge For *Ex. 15*, have
students reflect on *Ex. 9* and the
multiple use of grouping
symbols.

Assessment Students will need
Labsheet 6A to assess their solution for *Ex. 18*. Point out the
importance of reading the
assessment wording before solving the problem. When students
follow the Assessment Scale,
their solution includes more
than the final answer. If students know what is expected,
they are more likely to score five
or above on all assessment
scales.

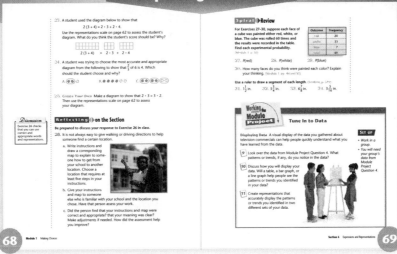

Closing the Section

The purpose of this section was to examine ways to assess and improve mathematical communication skills which will be used throughout the year. *Reflecting on the Section Exercise 26* provides assessment of students' ability to communicate using appropriate words and representations, in this case, a map. Have students work on *Ex. 26(a)* independently. For *Ex. 26(b)*, have students actually follow the instructions if possible. This will help them to assess the instructions. Remind students to follow only the instructions given and not add any. Students should give feedback to the original writer so they may evaluate their strengths and weaknesses. Have each student write a comprehensive response to *Ex. 26(c)*.

Have students work in their original groups and retrieve the data about commercials from storage. Using the data collected, students follow directions for *Questions 9–11* to complete a visual display of their data. Point out to students that this display should represent the skills they have learned during the module. Use the Assessment Scales listed on page 49 in order to understand what is expected. Monitor the students as they work in their group to make certain each member is involved. Each person should have a record for all parts of the project.

QUICK QUIZ ON THIS SECTION

1. Evaluate
   $14 + 10 \cdot 2 - 16 \div 8$.

2. Use parentheses to rewrite
   $104 \div 2 + 6 - 2 + 1$ so the
   result is 10.

3. Write instructions for drawing
   an isosceles right triangle for
   someone who doesn't understand the meaning of any of
   the three words *isosceles*, *right*,
   or *triangle*.

4. Make a diagram to show that
   $(2 + 5)^2 = 2^2 + 2 \cdot 2 \cdot 5 + 5^2$.

5. Use the representations scale
   to assess your diagram in
   question 4.

For answers, see Quick Quiz
blackline on p. 1-69.

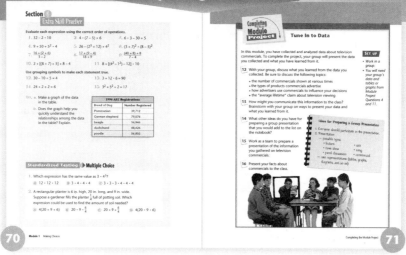

Completing the Module Project

Take class time to discuss **Questions 12–16** on page 71. Monitor groups for completion of **Questions 12–13**. Record their final decision on presentation format in **Question 15**. This will give you an idea of the variety and length of the presentations. Encourage the students to be creative, correct, and comprehensive. Assign students areas of the classroom or school for their displays to be shared. Set a time line for presentations and make a video tape if possible. The presentations or displays provide an opportunity to invite parents to see what is happening in the classroom.

MODULE 1   LABSHEET **1A**

Homework Frequency Table (Use with Questions 14–18 on page 6.)

Directions

- Make a tally mark (I) in the *Tally* column to represent each of your classmates' answers to Question 13. Include your own answer.

- Count the tally marks in each category and write the total in the *Frequency* column.

Time spent on homework	Tally	Frequency
did not usually have homework		
did not do assignments		
one half hour or less		
one hour		
two hours		
more than two hours		

Homework Bar Graph (Use with Questions 15–18 on page 6.)

Directions Use the data from the frequency table above to complete the bar graph. The bars have been started for you along the vertical axis. Remember to include labels or a scale along each axis.

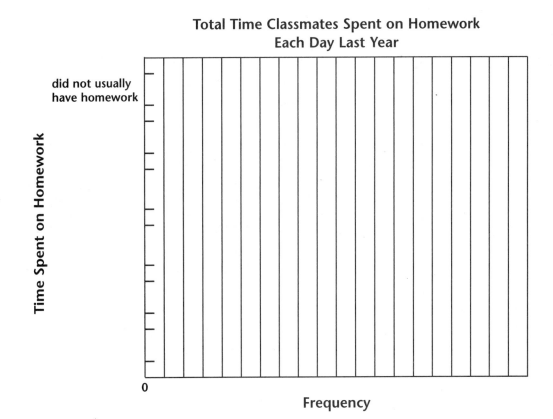

Total Time Classmates Spent on Homework Each Day Last Year

did not usually have homework

Time Spent on Homework

0

Frequency

Name _____   Date _____

Building Patterns (Use with Questions 10 and 12 on pages 15–16.)

Directions For each pattern:

• Model the shape sequence for the first 5 terms with square tiles (or draw pictures).

• Use your models and any patterns you notice to complete the table. Make a graph of the first 5 terms of the sequence.

• Write a word sentence that explains how to find the total number of squares if you know the number of stories in the building or the number of squares in the tower.

Pattern 1   1-story building   2-story building   3-story building

Number of stories in the building	Total number of squares
1	3
2	
3	
4	
5	
10	
90	

Word Sentence:

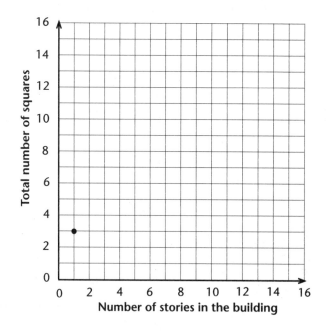

Patterns 2 and 3 are on Labsheet 2B.

Name _____   Date _____

Building Patterns continued (Use with Questions 10 and 12 on pages 15–16.)

Pattern 2   1 square in tower   2 squares in tower   3 squares in tower

 The tower is shaded.

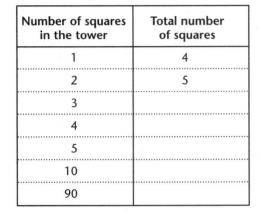

Number of squares in the tower	Total number of squares
1	4
2	5
3	
4	
5	
10	
90	

Word Sentence: _____

Pattern 3   1-story building with tower   2-story building with tower   3-story building with tower

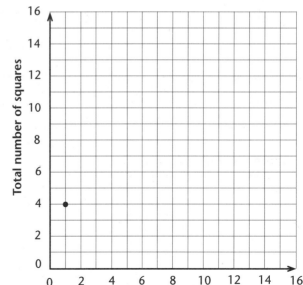

Number of stories in the building	Total number of squares
1	4
2	
3	
4	
5	
10	
90	

Word Sentence: _____

Game Board (Use with *Setting the Stage* on page 26 and with Question 11(b) on page 29.)

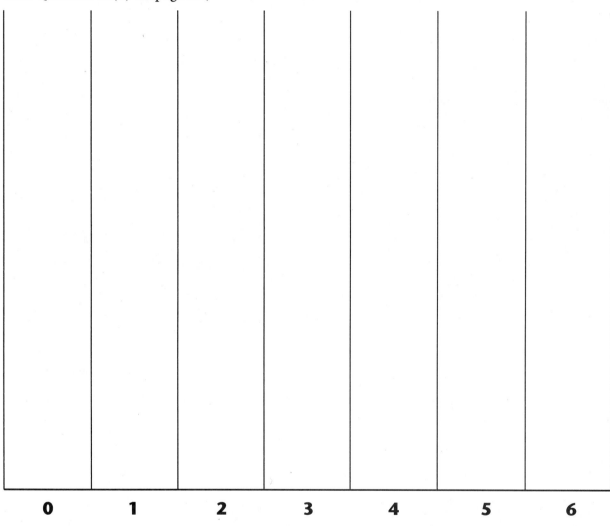

0	**1**	**2**	**3**	**4**	**5**	**6**

Frequency Table (Use with *Setting the Stage* on page 26 and with Question 11(b) on page 29.)

Game	Tally of rolls	Total number of rolls
1		
2		
3		

MODULE 1   **LABSHEET** **3B**

Results of 18 Rolls (Use with Questions 5, 7(a) and (b), 8, and 9 on pages 27–29.)

Difference	Tally	Frequency	Fraction of rolls
0			
1			
2			
3			
4			
5			
6			
Total number of rolls →		18	

Results of 72 Rolls (Use with Questions 8–10 on page 29.)

Difference	Group frequencies				Total frequency	Experimental probability
	My group	Group 1	Group 2	Group 3		
0						
1						
2						
3						
4						
5						
6						
			Total number of rolls →		72	

MODULE 1   **LABSHEET** **3C**

Rolling One Number Cube (Use with Question 13 on page 30.)

Directions Follow the steps below to complete the table showing the *Results of Rolling One Number Cube*.

- Find the theoretical probability of each outcome and record it in the last column of the table.

- Find the sum of the theoretical probabilities of the six outcomes and record it in the table.

- Take turns rolling a number cube 30 times. Keep a tally of your results. Record the frequency of each outcome for your group.

- Record the results from four other groups in the table. Then add the frequencies to get a total frequency of each outcome for 150 rolls.

- Find the experimental probability of each outcome based on the frequencies for 150 rolls.

Results of Rolling One Number Cube

Outcome	Tally	— Frequencies for 30 rolls					Frequency for 150 rolls	Probabilities — Experimental	Theoretical
		My group	Group 1	Group 2	Group 3	Group 4			
1									
2									
3									
4									
5									$\frac{1}{6}$
6									
Sum of theoretical probabilities →									

| MODULE 1 | LABSHEET (3D) |

Difference Chart (Use with Questions 16–18 on page 32.)

Directions Suppose you roll a red number cube and a blue number cube. Complete the *Difference Chart* below to show what difference results from each roll. An example is shown. Then answer the questions below.

a. Which difference occurs most often in the chart? Which occurs least often?

b. How many boxes are there to fill in on the chart (including the ones filled in for you)?

c. What fraction of the boxes contain a difference of 4?

d. What is the theoretical probability of rolling a difference of 4?

e. What fraction of the boxes contain a difference of 6?

f. What is the theoretical probability of rolling a difference of 6?

Blue / Red	1	2	3	4	5	6
1					(5 – 1) / 4	
2	1					
3						
4			(4 – 3) / 1			
5						
6						

Difference Game Theoretical Probability Table

(Use with Questions 17 and 18 on page 32.)

Directions Complete the table at the right by finding the theoretical probability of each difference shown in the *Difference Chart* above. Then find the sum of the theoretical probabilities.

Theoretical Probabilities for the *Difference Game*
$P(0) =$
$P(1) =$
$P(2) =$
$P(3) =$
$P(4) = \frac{4}{36}$, or $\frac{1}{9}$
$P(5) =$
$P(6) =$
Sum =

MODULE 1   **LABSHEET** (5A)

Last-Card Table (Use with Questions 13 and 14 on page 54 and Exercise 6 on page 57.)

Directions Use the table below and follow the directions in Questions 13 and 14 on page 54 to extend your solution to the Last Card Problem.

Number of cards	1	2	3	4	5	6	7	8	9	10	11	12	13	14	15	16	17	18	19	20
Number on last card	1	2	2	4	2	4	6	8	2	4	6	8	10	12	14					

Number of cards	21	22	23	24	25	26	27	28	29	30	31	32	33
Number on last card													

Two Assessment Scales (Use with Question 16 on page 55.)

Directions Use a marker to draw a segment along each scale to the point that describes your group's work for Question 12 on page 43 of Section 4.

▬▬ *If your score is in the shaded area, explain why on the back of this sheet and stop.*

☆ *The star indicates that you excelled in some way.*

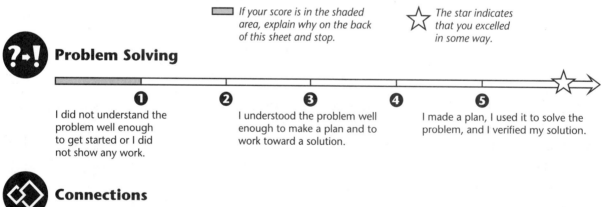

Problem Solving

❶ I did not understand the problem well enough to get started or I did not show any work.

❷

❸ I understood the problem well enough to make a plan and to work toward a solution.

❹

❺ I made a plan, I used it to solve the problem, and I verified my solution.

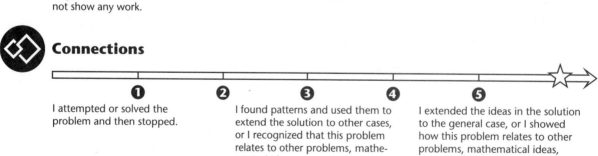

Connections

❶ I attempted or solved the problem and then stopped.

❷

❸ I found patterns and used them to extend the solution to other cases, or I recognized that this problem relates to other problems, mathematical ideas, or applications.

❹

❺ I extended the ideas in the solution to the general case, or I showed how this problem relates to other problems, mathematical ideas, or applications.

MODULE 1   LABSHEET **5B**

Problem Solving Scales for Exercises 1 and 2 (Use with

Exercise 3 on page 56.)

▭ *If your score is in the shaded area, explain why on the back of this sheet and stop.*

☆ *The star indicates that you excelled in some way.*

 Problem Solving

❶ **❷** **❸** **❹** **❺** ☆→

I did not understand the problem well enough to get started or I did not show any work.

I understood the problem well enough to make a plan and to work toward a solution.

I made a plan, I used it to solve the problem, and I verified my solution.

 Problem Solving

❶ **❷** **❸** **❹** **❺** ☆→

I did not understand the problem well enough to get started or I did not show any work.

I understood the problem well enough to make a plan and to work toward a solution.

I made a plan, I used it to solve the problem, and I verified my solution.

Two Assessment Scales for Exercise 4 (Use with Exercise 5 on

page 57.)

▭ *If your score is in the shaded area, explain why on the back of this sheet and stop.*

☆ *The star indicates that you excelled in some way.*

 Problem Solving

❶ **❷** **❸** **❹** **❺** ☆→

I did not understand the problem well enough to get started or I did not show any work.

I understood the problem well enough to make a plan and to work toward a solution.

I made a plan, I used it to solve the problem, and I verified my solution.

◈ **Connections**

❶ **❷** **❸** **❹** **❺** ☆→

I attempted or solved the problem and then stopped.

I found patterns and used them to extend the solution to other cases, or I recognized that this problem relates to other problems, mathematical ideas, or applications.

I extended the ideas in the solution to the general case, or I showed how this problem relates to other problems, mathematical ideas, or applications.

MODULE 1   **LABSHEET** 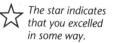 6A

Three Assessment Scales (Use with Exercise 18 on page 67.)

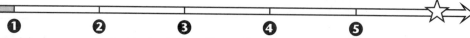 If your score is in the shaded area, explain why on the back of this sheet and stop.   ☆ The star indicates that you excelled in some way.

 Problem Solving

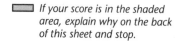

❶ I did not understand the problem well enough to get started or I did not show any work.

❷ ❸ I understood the problem well enough to make a plan and to work toward a solution.

❹ ❺ I made a plan, I used it to solve the problem, and I verified my solution.

 Representations

❶ I did not use any representations such as equations, tables, graphs, or diagrams to help solve the problem or explain my solution.

❷ ❸ I made appropriate representations to help solve the problem or help me explain my solution, but they were not always correct or other representations were needed.

❹ ❺ I used appropriate and correct representations to solve the problem or explain my solution.

 Connections

❶ I attempted or solved the problem and then stopped.

❷ ❸ I found patterns and used them to extend the solution to other cases, or I recognized that this problem relates to other problems, mathematical ideas, or applications.

❹ ❺ I extended the ideas in the solution to the general case, or I showed how this problem relates to other problems, mathematical ideas, or applications.

Name _____   Problem _____

☆ *The star indicates
that you excelled
in some way.*

Problem Solving

①   **②**   **③**   **④**   **⑤**

You did not understand
the problem well enough
to get started or you did
not show any work.

You understood the problem
well enough to make a plan
and to work toward a solution.

You made a plan, you used it to
solve the problem, and you verified
your solution.

Mathematical Language

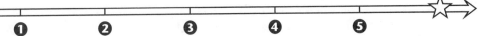

①   **②**   **③**   **④**   **⑤**

You did not use any mathematical
vocabulary or symbols, or you did
not use them correctly, or your
use was not appropriate.

You used appropriate mathematical
language, but the way it was used
was not always correct or other
terms and symbols were needed.

You used mathematical language
that was correct and appropriate
to make your meaning clear.

Representations

①   **②**   **③**   **④**   **⑤**

You did not use any representations
such as equations, tables, graphs,
or diagrams to help solve the
problem or explain your solution.

You made appropriate representations to help solve the problem or
help you explain your solution, but
they were not always correct or
other representations were needed.

You used appropriate and correct
representations to solve the problem
or explain your solution.

Connections

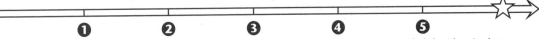

①   **②**   **③**   **④**   **⑤**

You attempted or solved the
problem and then stopped.

You found patterns and used them to
extend the solution to other cases,
or you recognized that this problem
relates to other problems, mathematical ideas, or applications.

You extended the ideas in the
solutionto the general case, or you
showed how this problem relates
to other problems, mathematical
ideas, or applications.

Presentation

①   **②**   **③**   **④**   **⑤**

The presentation of your
solution and reasoning is
unclear to others.

The presentation of your solution
and reasoning is clear in most
places, but others may have
trouble understanding parts of it.

The presentation of your solution
and reasoning is clear and can
be understood by others.

Content Used: _____   **Computational Errors:** Yes ☐ No ☐

Notes on Errors: _____
_____

Name _____   Problem _____

STUDENT SELF-ASSESSMENT SCALES

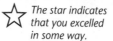 *If your score is in the shaded area, explain why on the back of this sheet and stop.*

☆ *The star indicates that you excelled in some way.*

 ### Problem Solving

❶ ❷ ❸ ❹ ❺ ☆→

I did not understand the problem well enough to get started or I did not show any work.

I understood the problem well enough to make a plan and to work toward a solution.

I made a plan, I used it to solve the problem, and I verified my solution.

 ### Mathematical Language

❶ ❷ ❸ ❹ ❺ ☆→

I did not use any mathematical vocabulary or symbols, or I did not use them correctly, or my use was not appropriate.

I used appropriate mathematical language, but the way it was used was not always correct or other terms and symbols were needed.

I used mathematical language that was correct and appropriate to make my meaning clear.

 ### Representations

❶ ❷ ❸ ❹ ❺ ☆→

I did not use any representations such as equations, tables, graphs, or diagrams to help solve the problem or explain my solution.

I made appropriate representations to help solve the problem or help me explain my solution, but they were not always correct or other representations were needed.

I used appropriate and correct representations to solve the problem or explain my solution.

 ### Connections

❶ ❷ ❸ ❹ ❺ ☆→

I attempted or solved the problem and then stopped.

I found patterns and used them to extend the solution to other cases, or I recognized that this problem relates to other problems, mathematical ideas, or applications.

I extended the ideas in the solution to the general case, or I showed how this problem relates to other problems, mathematical ideas, or applications.

 ### Presentation

❶ ❷ ❸ ❹ ❺ ☆→

The presentation of my solution and reasoning is unclear to others.

The presentation of my solution and reasoning is clear in most places, but others may have trouble understanding parts of it.

The presentation of my solution and reasoning is clear and can be understood by others.

The Painted Cube (E² on textbook page 48)

There is only one answer to this problem, but expect the representations to vary. Students may build the cube, draw a picture, use base plans, or in some other way represent the colored cube. All of the *Math Thematics* Assessment Scales should be used to assess student work.

The sample response below shows part of a student's solution.

Partial Solution

I drew a picture of the large cube to get a better idea about which faces were painted. I needed to see inside the large cube so I also drew the three layers of the cube.

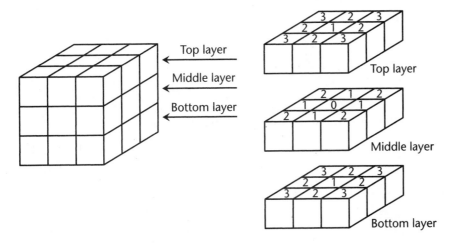

The numbers in the drawings tell how many faces on each small cube are painted. I organized my results in a table.

Number of painted faces	6	5	4	3	2	1	0
Number of small cubes	0	0	0	8	12	6	1

I wondered if it was possible to get 4, 5, or 6 painted faces. I looked at other cubes. My results are below.

Dimensions of large cube	Total number of small cubes	Number of painted faces on small cubes						
		6	5	4	3	2	1	0
$1 \times 1 \times 1$	1	1	0	0	0	0	0	0
$2 \times 2 \times 2$	8	0	0	0	8	0	0	0
$3 \times 3 \times 3$	27	0	0	0	8	12	6	1
$4 \times 4 \times 4$	64	0	0	0	8	24	24	8
$5 \times 5 \times 5$	125	0	0	0	8	36	54	27
$n \times n \times n, n \geq 2$	$n \cdot n \cdot n$	0	0	0	8	$12 \cdot (n-2)$	$6 \cdot (n-2) \cdot (n-2)$	$(n-2) \cdot (n-2) \cdot (n-2)$

I found a general rule for find the number of painted faces if the dimensions of the cube are greater than or equal to 2. I also realized that you could never paint 4 or 5 faces no matter what the size of your large cube.

MODULE 1   **ALTERNATE E²**

Making Soup

The Situation

A backpacker has two pots, one holds exactly $5\frac{1}{2}$ cups and one holds

exactly $3\frac{1}{2}$ cups. The backpacker needs exactly 4 cups of water to make

some soup. The backpacker also has a large plastic bottle of water, but the
container has no measurements marked on it.

The Problem

Using only the two pots, explain how the backpacker can measure exactly
4 cups of water without wasting any water.

Something to Think About

• What problem solving strategies could you use?
• How could the backpacker get 2 cups of water?

Present Your Results

Explain the procedure the backpacker should follow to get exactly 4 cups
of water. Include any drawings that will help make your solution easier to
understand.

Making Soup

The Problem Solving, Representations, and Presentation Scales of the *Math Thematics* Assessment Scales should be used to assess student work. Students should show a step-by-step approach to measuring exactly 4 cups of water.

The sample response below shows part of a student's solution.

Partial Solution

Step 1: Fill the $5\frac{1}{2}$-cup pot with water.

Step 2: Pour water from the $5\frac{1}{2}$-cup pot into the $3\frac{1}{2}$-cup pot until it's full. There are now 2 cups of water in the large pot.

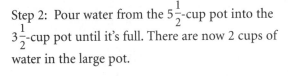

Step 3: Pour out the water in the $3\frac{1}{2}$-cup pot, but keep the 2 cups of water in the large pot.

Step 4: Pour the 2 cups of water from the large pot into the small pot.

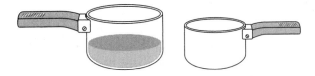

Step 5: Fill the $5\frac{1}{2}$-cup pot with water.

Step 6: Pour the water from the large pot into the small pot until the small one is full. Since only $1\frac{1}{2}$ cups of water can be poured in the small pot, the large pot has $5\frac{1}{2} - 1\frac{1}{2} = 4$ cups of water!

Extention: If there was another container available, the backpacker could place the 2 cups of water from Step 2 into the extra container. Then the backpacker would repeat Steps 1 and 2 to get another 2 cups of water.

Write each fraction as a percent.

1. $\dfrac{61}{100}$

2. $\dfrac{13}{25}$

3. $\dfrac{165}{200}$

Write each percent as a fraction in lowest terms.

4. 87%

5. 5%

6. 72%

1. What is the difference between the data that can be displayed in a bar graph and the data that can be displayed in a line graph?

2. Use the data in the frequency table to make a bar graph showing the favorite subjects of 70 students.

3. Make a frequency table for this set of data about the number of CD's bought in the past month: 2, 0, 6, 1, 2, 5, 0, 1, 1, 0, 4, 3, 2, 0, 12, 2, 4, 3.

Favorite subject	Frequency
Mathematics	28
Science	11
English	17
Social studies	14

ANSWERS

Warm-Ups: 1. 61% 2. 52% 3. 82.5% 4. $\dfrac{87}{100}$ 5. $\dfrac{1}{20}$ 6. $\dfrac{18}{25}$

Quick Quiz: 1. In a bar graph, data are distinct categories, such as favorite colors. In a line graph, data are usually some measurement (number) taken over time, such as one's height. 2.

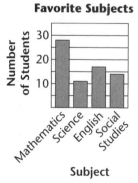

Favorite Subjects

3.

Number of CDs	Tally	Frequency
0	IIII	4
1	III	3
2	IIII	4
3	II	2
4	II	2
5	I	1
6	I	1
12	I	1

Write the next three numbers.

1. 5, 15, 25, 35, …

2. 300, 298, 296, 294, …

3. 2, 22, 222, 2222, …

4. 1, 3, 2, 4, 3, 5, 4, 6, …

| MODULE 1 SECTION 2 | QUICK QUIZ |

1. Write an equation for the following word sentence, using *t* for the term and *n* for the term number: *The term is two more than five times the term number.*

2. Make a table, draw a graph, and write an equation for this sequence. Then predict the 200th term.

   5, 11, 17, 23, …

3. Write $11 \cdot 11 \cdot 11 \cdot 11$ in exponential form.

4. Find the volume of a cube with edges of length 14 mm.

5. Predict the 50th term of the sequence 3^3, 6^3, 9^3, … .

ANSWERS

Warm-Ups: 1. 45, 55, 65 **2.** 292, 290, 288 **3.** 22222, 222222, 2222222 **4.** 5, 7, 6

Quick Quiz: 1. $t = 5n + 2$ **2.** Sequence Table   Sequence Graph $t = 6n - 1$; 1199
3. 11^4 **4.** 2744 mm^3
5. 3,375,000

Term number	Term
1	5
2	11
3	17
4	23

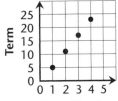

Write the fraction in simplest form.

1. $\dfrac{12}{52}$ **2.** $\dfrac{16}{16}$

3. $\dfrac{0}{8}$ **4.** $\dfrac{7}{29}$

5. Order the fractions from least to greatest.

$\dfrac{1}{2}, \dfrac{3}{8}, \dfrac{3}{4}, \dfrac{5}{6}, \dfrac{6}{5}, \dfrac{1}{3}$

MODULE 1   SECTION 3   **QUICK QUIZ**

1. Evelyn spins the spinner shown 60 times and gets white on 28 spins. What is the theoretical probability of getting white?

2. What is the experimental probability of getting white in the situation of Question 1?

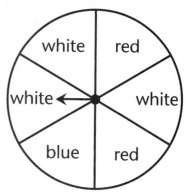

3. Suppose you roll three number cubes. List three outcomes that will produce an odd sum greater than 11.

ANSWERS

Warm-Ups: 1. $\dfrac{3}{13}$ **2.** 1 **3.** 0 **4.** $\dfrac{7}{29}$ **5.** $\dfrac{1}{3}, \dfrac{3}{8}, \dfrac{1}{2}, \dfrac{3}{4}, \dfrac{5}{6}, \dfrac{6}{5}$

Quick Quiz: 1. 50% **2.** $\dfrac{7}{15}$ **3.** Sample Response: 3, 5, 5; 3, 4, 6; 4, 4, 5

Tell which problem solving strategy or strategies you would use to solve each problem.

1. finding a path through a maze

2. deciding in what order you should deliver packages that are to be delivered to different locations

3. trying to find your lost keys

4. how you can rearrange the furniture in your room

MODULE 1 SECTION 4   **QUICK QUIZ**

1. You have $1000 to spend stocking the school store with T-shirts, sweatshirts, and hats. How could you use a 4-step approach in deciding how to place your order?

2. A farmer has 200 ft of fencing. What is the largest rectangular area that can be enclosed?

3. Joey swims every third day and lifts weights every fifth day. Today he both swims and lifts weights. On how many days will he both swim and lift weights in the next 6 weeks?

4. The rectangles in this sequence are twice as wide as they are high. What will be the perimeter of the 100th rectangle?

ANSWERS

Warm-Ups: 1. work backward   **2.** make an organized list and make a diagram   **3.** act it out (retrace your steps) and use logical reasoning   **4.** draw a diagram

Quick Quiz: 1. Sample Response: First decide what kinds of clothing students want to buy. Get prices from the manufacturer. Conduct a student poll. Determine the fraction of students who wish to purchase each item. Use guess and check to find the numbers of each type of clothing you can buy that are in the same proportions as student poll numbers with price below $1000. (For example, if $\frac{1}{4}$ of students want hats, $\frac{1}{2}$ sweatshirts, and $\frac{1}{4}$ T-shirts, estimate how much it would cost to buy 25 hats, 50 sweatshirts, and 25 T-shirts. Revise estimate and check again.)   **2.** a square area 50 ft on each side   **3.** 2 times   **4.** 600 ft

MODULE 1 SECTION 5 — WARM-UPS

Match each action with the appropriate step in the 4-Step Solving Approach.

A. Make a Plan

B. Look Back

C. Understand the Problem

D. Carry Out the Plan

1. You want to earn money during the summer.
2. You decide to start a lawn mowing business.
3. You advertise and find clients for your business and mow lawns throughout the summer.
4. You ask your clients if they were pleased with your service and if there is anything that they would like done differently.

MODULE 1 SECTION 5 — QUICK QUIZ

1. Give an example of how a student could get 5 on the problem-solving scale and 1 on the connections scale.
2. Sammie has 3 shirts, 2 pairs of pants, 2 pairs of shoes, and 3 pairs of socks. How many different outfits does she have?
3. For question 2 write down the number of choices for each category and the number of different combinations. How are the numbers related? What do you think the answer would be for a person with 10 shirts, 15 pairs of pants, 8 pairs of shoes, and 20 pairs of socks?

ANSWERS

Warm-Ups: 1. C **2.** A **3.** D **4.** B

Quick Quiz: 1. It is possible to solve a problem correctly but not to make any connections with other types of problems. **2.** 36 **3.** 3, 2, 2, 3; if you multiply the numbers of choices per category together, you get the number of combinations; 24,000.

1. $87 + 258 + 390$

2. $12 \cdot 42 \cdot 71$

Tell whether to use a table, line graph, or bar graph.

3. to show changes over time

4. to find an exact value

5. to compare data

1. Evaluate $14 + 10 \cdot 2 - 16 \div 8$.

2. Use parentheses to rewrite $104 \div 2 + 6 - 2 + 1$ so the result is 10.

3. Write instructions for drawing an isosceles right triangle for someone who doesn't understand the meaning of any of the three words *isosceles*, *right*, or *triangle*.

4. Make a diagram to show that $(2 + 5)^2 = 2^2 + 2 \cdot 2 \cdot 5 + 5^2$.

5. Use the representations scale to assess your diagram in question 4.

ANSWERS

Warm-Ups: 1. 735 **2.** 35,784 **3.** line graph **4.** table **5.** bar graph

Quick Quiz: 1. 32 **2.** $104 \div (2 + 6) - (2 + 1)$ **3.** Sample Response: Draw a corner (like the corner of your paper), with the two sides that make up the corner of equal length. Draw a slanted segment that connects the two ends of the sides that make up the corner.

4. 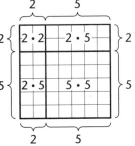   **5.** Answers will vary.

MODULE 1 SECTION 1   **PRACTICE AND APPLICATIONS**

For use with Exploration 1

Use the bar graph for Exercises 1–10.

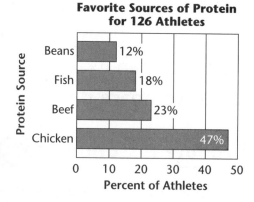

Favorite Sources of Protein for 126 Athletes

1. **a.** Who was surveyed?

   b. What information is displayed in the graph?

2. **a.** What source of protein did most athletes choose as their favorite?

   b. What source of protein did the fewest athletes choose as their favorite?

3. What do the numbers on the horizontal axis mean?

4. The bar for athletes who chose beans as their favorite source of protein is about how many times as long as the bar for athletes who chose beef? chicken?

5. How many athletes responded to the survey?

6. In this survey, is 18% of the athletes *more than* or *less than* 18 athletes?

7. Compare the bars for beans and fish. What does your comparison tell you about the percent of athletes who prefer fish to beans?

8. Compare the bars for beans and chicken. What does your comparison tell you about the percent of athletes who prefer chicken to beans?

9. Compare the bars for beans and beef. What does your comparison tell you about the percent of athletes who prefer beans to beef?

10. Almost half of the athletes surveyed chose chicken as their favorite source of protein. About how many athletes chose chicken?

(continued)

MODULE 1 SECTION 1   **PRACTICE AND APPLICATIONS**

For use with Exploration 2

11. What is the letter of the phrase that best represents the average amount of time you spent each day last year exercising?

    a. did not usually exercise   **b.** 20 minutes

    c. 30 minutes   **d.** 45 minutes

    e. one hour   **f.** more than one hour

12. Use a frequency table like the one shown below to collect data about classmates, friends, or relatives for the question in Exercise 11.

Exercise Frequency Table

Time spent exercising	Tally	Frequency
usually did not exercise		
20 minutes		
30 minutes		
45 minutes		
one hour		
more than one hour		

13. Use the data in the *Exercise Frequency Table* to make an *Exercise Bar Graph* that has horizontal bars.

14. How did you choose the scale for the horizontal axis of the *Exercise Bar Graph*?

15. How did you find the most frequent answer to Exercise 11 from the *Exercise Frequency Table*? from the *Exercise Bar Graph*?

16. How is your *Exercise Bar Graph* like the bar graph shown below?

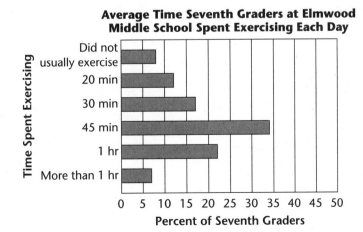

MODULE 1 SECTION 2   PRACTICE AND APPLICATIONS

For use with Exploration 1

Use the table for Exercises 1–3.

Term number	1	2	3	4	5	6	...	10	...	90
Shape sequence					?	?	?	...	?	...
Number sequence	2	4	6	8	?	?	...	?	...	?

1. How are the number sequence and the shape sequence related?

2. a. Draw a picture to model the 5th term of the shape sequence.

   b. What is the 5th term of the number sequence?

3. a. What pattern can you use to predict the 6th term of the shape sequence?

   b. Predict what the 6th term of the number sequence will be.

   c. Predict the 10th and 90th terms of the number sequence.

4. Write an equation for each word sentence. Use t for the term and n for the term number.

   a. The term is seven times the term number.

   b. The term is two less than the term number.

   c. The term is six more than the term number.

   d. The term is one fourth the term number.

5. For each sequence, make a table, draw a graph, and write an equation. Then predict the 10th term.

   a. 6, 12, 18, 24, ...   **b.** 28, 26, 24, 22, ...

6. The formula for the volume of a cube is $V = s^3$, where $V =$ the volume of the cube and $s =$ the length of an edge of the cube. Cynthia makes a jewelry box in the shape of a cube to give to her mother. The length of one side of the cube is 3 in.

   a. What is the volume of the jewelry box?

   b. What is the area of the top surface of the jewelry box?

(continued)

MODULE 1 SECTION 2   PRACTICE AND APPLICATIONS

For use with Exploration 2

7. Write each product in exponential form.

    a. $2 \cdot 2 \cdot 2 \cdot 2 \cdot 2$ **b.** $3 \cdot 3 \cdot 3$ **c.** $8 \cdot 8$

    d. $5 \cdot 5 \cdot 5 \cdot 5$ **e.** $9 \cdot 9$ **f.** $4 \cdot 4 \cdot 4$

    g. $6 \cdot 6 \cdot 6 \cdot 2$ **h.** $8 \cdot 3 \cdot 3$ **i.** $7 \cdot 2 \cdot 2 \cdot 2 \cdot 2$

8. Write each power in standard form.

    a. 7^2 **b.** 5^3 **c.** 2^5

    d. 12^2 **e.** 0^{12} **f.** 10^8

    g. 1436^1 **h.** 4^4 **i.** 1^{30}

9. Predict the 100th term of each sequence.

    a. $3^2, 6^2, 9^2, 12^2, \dots$ **b.** $2^5, 4^5, 6^5, 8^5, \dots$

10. Find the volume of a cube with edges of each length.

    a. 1 ft   **b.** 3 in.   **c.** 8 m

    d. 15 ft   **e.** 40 cm   **f.** 200 m

    g. 60 cm   **h.** 8 ft   **i.** 14 mm

    j. $\frac{1}{4}$ ft   **k.** 3.1 cm   **l.** $2\frac{1}{2}$ m

11. Copy and complete each table.

    a.

Side length (cm)	5	10	15	20
Area of a square (cm^2)	?	?	?	?

    b.

Edge length (cm)	5	10	15	20
Volume of a cube (cm^3)	?	?	?	?

12. The length of a side of a square room is 18 feet. How many square feet of carpet would be needed to cover the floor of the room?

MODULE 1 SECTION 3   **PRACTICE AND APPLICATIONS**

For use with Exploration 1

1. Tell whether you think the probability of each event is 0, 1, or somewhere in between. If the probability is in between, do you think it is greater than or less than $\frac{1}{2}$? Give a reason for your answer.

   a. You will visit the zoo this year.   **b.** You will go swimming this weekend.

   c. Someone in your household will go to the grocery store this week.   **d.** You will hike to the top of a mountain today.

2. Jackie spun the spinner shown at the right 38 times. She got an odd number on 16 spins.

   a. Based on Jackie's results, what is the experimental probability of getting an odd number on a spin?

   b. Describe an event that has a probability of 1 and an event that has a probability of 0.

3. What are all the possible outcomes when you toss a number cube?

4. Toss a coin 30 times. Record your results in a frequency table. Then find the experimental probability of getting heads and the experimental probability of getting tails.

5. Suppose you spin the two spinners shown at the right. List at least 3 outcomes that will produce each event.

   a. a difference of 2   **b.** a difference of 0

   c. a sum of 8   **d.** an even sum

   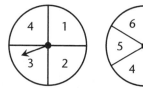

6. Suppose a bag contains 12 marbles, with 3 each of the colors red, yellow, blue, and green. An experiment involves picking a marble from the bag and putting it back in the bag. The table shows the results after the experiment has been repeated 100 times. Find each experimental probability.

Outcome	Frequency
red	24
yellow	30
blue	26
green	20

   a. $P(\text{red})$ **b.** $P(\text{yellow})$ **c.** $P(\text{blue})$

   d. $P(\text{green})$ **e.** $P(\text{not green})$ **f.** $P(\text{green or yellow})$

   g. $P(\text{not red})$ **h.** $P(\text{purple})$ **i.** $P(\text{not yellow})$

   (continued)

For use with Exploration 2

7. Suppose a number cube is rolled once. Find the theoretical probabilities $P(1)$, $P(2)$, and $P(5)$.

8. Suppose you spin the two spinners shown below. Copy and complete the table to show the sums (outcomes) that can occur.

Spinner 1   Spinner 2

Spinner 2	Spinner 1			
	1	2	3	4
1				
2				
3				
4				
5				
6				

Find the theoretical probability of each event.

a. $P(2)$ **b.** $P(6)$ **c.** $P(1)$

d. $P(8)$ **e.** $P(3)$ **f.** $P(7)$

g. $P(4 \text{ or } 5)$ **h.** $P(\text{even})$ **i.** $P(12)$

9. Suppose an experiment involves spinning the spinner once.

a. What are all the possible outcomes of the experiment?

b. Are spinning an A and spinning a B equally likely events? Why or why not?

c. What fraction of the spins do you expect to land on A? on B? Give a reason for your answer.

d. Suppose you repeat the experiment 30 times. What results do you expect? Do you think the results will always match your expectations? Why or why not?

10. Sketch a spinner for each situation.

a. The possible outcomes are J and K. The probability of spinning a J is three times the probability of spinning a K.

b. The possible outcomes are A, B, and C. The probability of spinning an A is $\frac{1}{2}$. The probability of spinning B is $\frac{1}{4}$.

MODULE 1 SECTION 4   **PRACTICE AND APPLICATIONS**

For use with Exploration 1

1. Assume a person bicycling 1 mi at a rate of 10 mi/h will burn 80 Cal.

   a. At this rate, how many minutes does it take to cycle 1 mi?

   b. At this rate, how many minutes per week must a person bicycle to burn 2000 Cal?

2. Denise earns $7.00 per hour plus $2.00 for every sale she makes. If Denise earned $239 for 25 hours of work last week, how many sales did she make?

For use with Exploration 2

3. Four equilateral triangles can be placed side by side as shown to form a parallelogram with a perimeter of 6 in. If another parallelogram is formed the same way using 30 triangles, what will its perimeter be?

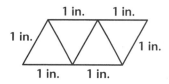

4. A farmer has 8 cows and horses. Each cow is fed 6 lb of hay per meal and each horse is fed 8 lb. It takes 52 lb of hay to feed all 8 animals one meal. How many horses are there?

5. Derrick's scores on his first three science tests are 88, 86, and 87. What score must he get on his fourth test to raise his average to 90?

6. Renzo needs $600 to buy some speakers. The table shows how much money he had in March, April, and May. If this pattern continues, in what month will he be able to buy the speakers?

Month	Amount of money
March	$90
April	$165
May	$240

7. Peter Pan Preschool has a phone relay to inform parents if the preschool is closed during bad weather. The director calls three parents who each call four other parents. These four parents then each call three other parents who each call two more parents. How many parents are called in all?

8. The chess club has enough money to buy 8 boards or 64 chess pieces. The members decide to buy 32 chess pieces. How many boards can they buy?

Name _____ Date _____

For use with Exploration 1

1. Jared wanted to find the total number of squares in the diagram shown at the right.

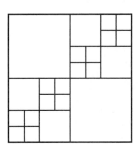

a. Jared decided to solve the problem above by first counting the number of small squares. Then he planned on counting the larger squares. He counted 27 total squares and recorded 27 as his answer. How would you score Jared's work on the problem solving scale? Why?

b. Solve the problem. Is your solution the same as Jared's?

c. What score would you give your solution in part (b) on the problem solving scale?

2. a. Suppose you have quarters, dimes, and pennies with a total value of $1.08. How many of each coin can you have without being able to make change for a dollar?

b. What score would you give your work in part (a) on the problem solving scale?

For use with Exploration 2

3. a. Suppose Julia has $15. She wants to buy at least one of each type of book at the book sale and she wants to use as much of $15 as possible to buy some gifts. How many of each type of book should Julia buy?

b. What score would you give your solution in part (a) on the problem solving and connections scale?

Book Sale

Mysteries	$1.95
Novel	$2.35
Science	$2.65
Fantasy	$1.45
Nature	$2.95

Name _____   Date _____

For use with Exploration 1

1. Evaluate each expression using the order of operations.

  a. $36 - 4 \cdot 5$

  b. $8 \cdot (3 + 7) - 5$

  c. $7 \cdot 6 - 40 \div 5$

  d. $15 + 18 \div 3^2 - 6$

  e. $36 \div (15 - 6) \cdot 4$

  f. $(8 - 3)^2 \cdot (14 - 8)$

  g. $\dfrac{(12 - 5) \cdot 6}{7 - 4}$

  h. $\dfrac{80 \div (6 - 2)}{35 \div 7}$

  i. $2^4 \div [5^2 - (13 + 7)]$

  j. $40 - 2 \cdot 15$

  k. $6 \cdot (8 - 4) + 5$

  l. $9 \cdot 4 - 24 \div 4$

2. Write and evaluate an expression to represent the value (in cents) of 3 half dollars, 3 quarters, 8 nickels, 4 dimes, and 2 pennies.

3. Use grouping symbols to make each statement true.

  a. $25 - 8 \cdot 3 = 51$

  b. $9 + 4 \cdot 5 - 3 = 17$

  c. $9 + 9 \div 3 \cdot 5 - 3 = 12$

  d. $6 \cdot 5 - 5^2 + 2 = 3$

For use with Exploration 2

Use the line graph for Exercises 4–6.

4. What was the approximate number of students playing baseball in 1992?

5. In what year was the number of students playing baseball about 2000?

6. Describe any trends in the data that the line graph helps you see.

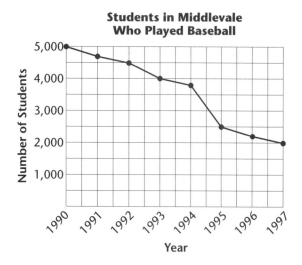

Students in Middlevale Who Played Baseball

7. A student was trying to choose the most accurate and appropriate diagram from the following to show that $\frac{3}{4}$ of 8 is 6. Which should the student choose and why?

  a. (○ ○ ○) ○

  b. (○ ○ ○)(○ ○ ○)(○ ○ ○) ○

  c. ○ ○ ○ ○ ○ ○ ○ ○

MODULE 1   SECTIONS 1–6   **PRACTICE AND APPLICATIONS**

For use with Section 1

Use the line graph for Exercises 1 and 2.

1. What is represented by each interval on the vertical scale?

2. **a.** In what year were the sales about $5000?

   b. Estimate the sales in 1997.

3. For each group of people surveyed, tell whether 36% of the group *is more than*, *less than*, or *equal to* 36 people.

   a. 300 runners

   c. 95 students

   b. 79 musicians

   d. 450 skiers

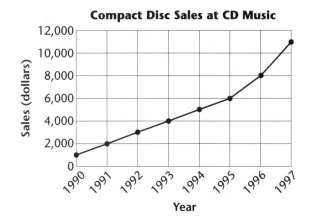

4. Make a frequency table for the data.

   Scores on a ten-point quiz: 8, 6, 9, 9, 8, 8, 7, 10, 6, 8, 8, 6, 10, 7, 9

For use with Section 2

5. **a.** Sketch the next two shapes in the shape sequence.

   b. How can you find the perimeter of a square from the length of a side?

   c. If the sequence in the table continues, what are the next two terms of the number sequence for the perimeter of each shape?

   d. Write an equation for the perimeter of a square. Let s = the length of a side of a square. Let P = the perimeter of the square. Use your equation to find the perimeter of a square that has sides of length 20 cm.

   e. Make a table of values for the first 10 terms of the number sequence. Use it to make a graph of the sequence. Use your graph to predict the 15th term of the sequence.

Term number	Shape sequence	Number sequence
1	□	4
2	⊞	8
3	▦	12

(continued)

MODULE 1 SECTIONS 1–6   **PRACTICE AND APPLICATIONS**

For use with Section 3

6. Suppose a bag contains 12 marbles, with 3 each of the colors red, yellow, blue, and green. An experiment involves picking a marble from the bag and putting it back in the bag. Find the theoretical probability of each event.

   a. $P(\text{red})$ **b.** $P(\text{yellow})$ **c.** $P(\text{not green})$

   d. $P(\text{green or yellow})$ **e.** $P(\text{not red})$ **f.** $P(\text{purple})$

   g. $P(\text{blue})$ **h.** $P(\text{blue or green})$ **i.** $P(\text{not yellow})$

For use with Section 4

7. Katie earns $8.00 per hour plus $12.00 for every extra hour she works over 40 h per week. If Katie earned $392.00 last week, how many extra hours did she work?

For use with Section 5

8. a. A book states that an average teenager in the United States should spend at least 130 h a year exercising. Do you think this is a reasonable estimate? Explain.

   b. What score would you give your solution in part (a) on the problem solving and connections scale?

For use with Section 6

9. Evaluate each expression using the order of operations.

   a. $12 + 32 \div 4^2 \cdot 7$ **b.** $39 - (3^3 + 6) + 5^2$ **c.** $(3 + 4)^2 \cdot (25 - 15)^2$

   d. $\dfrac{18 \div (4 + 2)}{9 - 8}$ **e.** $\dfrac{14 + (8 - 6)}{20 \div 5}$ **f.** $\dfrac{(45 + 5) \div 5}{8 - 6}$

   g. $4 + [(6 + 9) \div 3] + 7 - 2$ **h.** $7 + [(3^2 - 2^2) - 3] \cdot 6$

10. Use grouping symbols to make each statement true.

   a. $28 - 10 \div 6 = 3$ **b.** $8 + 2 \cdot 7 = 70$

   c. $18 \div 2 + 4 = 3$ **d.** $4^2 + 2^2 \div 4 = 5$

Name _____   Date _____

Going for the Gold   Data Displays

GOAL   **LEARN HOW TO:** • interpret data in percent form
• interpret bar and line graphs
• make a frequency table

AS YOU: • explore data about the Olympics and education
• gather and analyze data about time spent on homework

Exploration 1: Bar and Line Graphs

Analyzing Bar and Line Graphs

A **bar graph** displays data that fall into distinct categories. A bar graph should always have a title and should be clearly labeled. The categories for the bar graph at the right appear along the **vertical axis**. The **horizontal axis** is labeled with a scale of numbers.

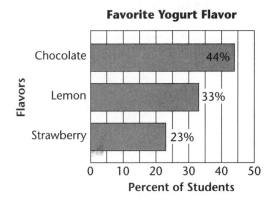

Percent

The symbol % on the bar graph above stands for *percent*. **Percent** means "per hundred" or "out of 100." Four different ways to express a percent are shown at the right.

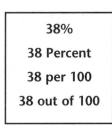

38%

38 Percent

38 per 100

38 out of 100

Interpreting Line Graphs

A **line graph** is often used to display data that change over time. The double line graph at the right compares two sets of data.

Each step between grid lines on a scale of a graph is an *interval*. The interval used for the vertical scale on the double line graph at the right is 75.

MODULE 1 SECTION 1   STUDY GUIDE

Exploration 2: Tallying Data

Using Frequency Tables

Frequency tables show how often each data item occurs. The frequency table at the right shows the number of students in two middle school classes who bought lunch in the cafeteria. The total number of tally marks in each category is the **frequency** for that category.

Students Buying Lunch

Class	Tally	Frequency
Mrs. Hall's	卌 卌 卌	15
Mr. Akee's	卌 卌 ‖	12

Example

Make a bar graph of the data given in the frequency table.

Number of Students Taking Work Home

Day	Tally	Frequency
Monday	卌 卌 卌 卌 卌	25
Tuesday	卌 卌 卌	15
Wednesday	卌 卌 卌 ‖‖	19
Thursday	卌 卌 卌 卌 卌 ‖‖	28
Friday	‖‖‖	4

Sample Response

First Give the bar graph a title.

Number of Students Taking Work Home

Next Label the axes, one to show the categories and the other to show a scale for the numerical values.

vertical axis: 0, 5, 10, 15, 20, 25, 30, 35

horizontal axis: Monday, Tuesday, Wednesday, Thursday, Friday

Then Draw the bars to model the data values in the table.

The completed graph is shown at the right.

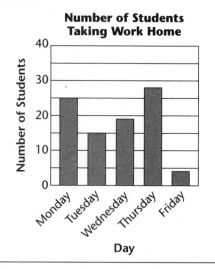

Number of Students Taking Work Home

Name _____ Date _____

Exploration 1

Use the line graph at the right for Exercises 1–4.

1. What information is displayed in the graph?

2. What are the intervals of the horizontal and vertical axes?

3. What could you predict about the enrollment in the year 2000?

4. Did the enrollment between 1996 and 1997 increase by 20%? Explain.

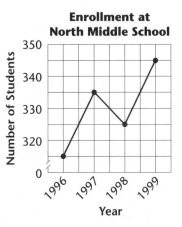

Enrollment at North Middle School

Exploration 2

Make a frequency table for each set of data.

5. Scores on an English grammar test: 88, 88, 76, 98, 100, 95, 76, 100, 85, 98, 88, 85, 76, 79, 75, 88, 91, 93, 71, 65, 88, 93, 65, 85

6. Favorite color of cross country team members: blue, red, yellow, yellow, red, green, green, orange, blue, blue, green, yellow, red

Spiral Review

Find the area of each rectangle. (Toolbox, p. 593)

7. length: 5 ft, width: 5 ft

8. length: 30 in., width: 18 in.

For Exercises 9–12, use mental math to find each value.
(Toolbox, p. 584)

9. $\frac{2}{3}$ of 18

10. $\frac{1}{2}$ of 24

11. $\frac{5}{8}$ of 16

12. $\frac{4}{5}$ of 55

13. How many squares of a 100-square grid would be shaded to show 45%?
   (Toolbox, p. 588)

Name _____ Date _____

Patterns and Prediction   Sequences and Exponents

GOAL   **LEARN HOW TO:** • model sequences
                    • make predictions
                    • use exponents
                    • find the volume of a cube

       AS YOU: • explore visual patterns
                • explore speeds of a skateboarder

Exploration 1: Modeling Sequences

Sequences

A **sequence** is an ordered list of numbers or objects called **terms**.

2, 4, 6, 8, 10, … is a sequence.

The **term number** tells the position of each term in the sequence.

The *1st term* of the sequence above is 2.
The *5th term* of the sequence above is 10.

You can use the pattern of a sequence to predict a specific term of the sequence.

Each term in the sequence is twice its term number. So, the 6th term is 12.

Equations and Variables

An **equation** is a mathematical sentence stating that two quantities are equal.

$5 = 2 + 3$ is an equation.

A **variable** is a letter used to represent a quantity that is unknown or that changes. You can use variables to write an equation that shows how each term in a sequence is related to its term number.

Let n = the term number and let t = the term. Then,

$$t = 2 \cdot n \text{ or } t = 2n$$

models the sequence shown above.

Exploration 2: Exponents, Squares, and Cubes

Exponents

An **exponent** tells you how many times a **base** is used as a factor. **Exponential form** is a way of writing repeated multiplication of a number using exponents. **Standard form** is a way of writing numbers using digits.

base   exponent
$$4^3 = 4 \cdot 4 \cdot 4 = 64$$
exponential form   standard form

The **power** of a number in exponential form is its exponent.

4^3 is read as "4 to the 3rd power" or "4 cubed."

MODULE 1 SECTION 2   **STUDY GUIDE**

Squares and Cubes

A **cube** is a space figure with six square surfaces, called **faces**. An **edge** is where two faces are joined. A **vertex** is where edges meet.

A cube has 6 faces, 12 edges, and 8 vertices.

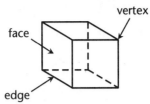

Area is the number of *unit squares* that fill a figure. A unit square is 1 unit long and 1 unit wide. The area formula for a square can be written using exponents.

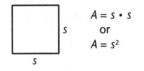

$A = s \cdot s$
or
$A = s^2$

Volume is the number of *unit cubes* that fill a figure. A unit cube is 1 unit long, 1 unit wide, and 1 unit high. The volume formula for a cube can be written using exponents.

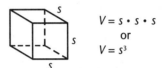

$V = s \cdot s \cdot s$
or
$V = s^3$

Example

Find the volume of a cube when the length of an edge is 6 cm.

▪ Sample Response ▪

$V = s^3$ ← volume formula for a cube
$\;\;\; = 6^3$ ← exponential form
$\;\;\; = 6 \cdot 6 \cdot 6$
$\;\;\; = 216$ ← standard form

The volume of the cube is 216 cm^3.

Name _____   Date _____

Exploration 1

**For Exercises 1–3, write an equation for each word sentence.
Use *t* for the term and *n* for the term number.**

1. The term is four times the term number.

2. The term is two less than the term number.

3. The term is six more than twice the term number.

4. Make a table, draw a graph, and write an equation for the sequence
6, 12, 18, 24, ... Then predict the 100th term.

5. Visual Thinking Sketch the 6th shape in the sequence below.

Exploration 2

Write each product in exponential form.

6. $7 \cdot 7 \cdot 7 \cdot 7 \cdot 7 \cdot 7$ **7.** $12 \cdot 12 \cdot 12 \cdot 12 \cdot 12 \cdot 12 \cdot 12 \cdot 12$

Write each power in standard form.

8. 8^3 **9.** 9^2 **10.** 50^1 **11.** 0^4

**For Exercises 12–15, find the volume of a cube with edges of
each length.**

12. 4 mm   **13.** 8 in.   **14.** 10 km   **15.** 30 ft

16. Writing Is the volume of a cube related to the area of one face of the
cube? Explain.

Spiral Review

Use the bar graph at the right. (Module 1, pp. 2–3)

17. What percent of the blooms were yellow?

18. If there were 500 blooms in all, how many of
them were white?

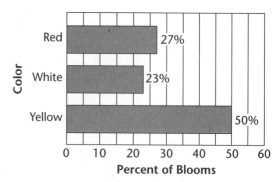

Write an equivalent fraction for each. (Toolbox, p. 585)

19. $\frac{4}{5}$ **20.** $\frac{15}{25}$ **21.** $\frac{1}{3}$ **22.** $\frac{3}{45}$

MODULE 1 SECTION 3   **STUDY GUIDE**

Likely or Unlikely   Probability

GOAL   **LEARN HOW TO:** • list the outcomes for an event
                               • find and compare experimental probabilities
                               • find theoretical probabilities

   AS YOU: • analyze a game
              • explore outcomes when rolling one or more number cubes

Exploration 1: What Are the Chances?

Probability and Experimental Probability

A **probability** is a number from 0 through 1 that tells how likely it is
that an event will happen. An **event** is any set of one or more outcomes.
An **impossible event** has a probability of 0. A **certain event** has a
probability of 1.

When you roll a number cube or spin a
spinner and record the outcome, you are
conducting an **experiment**. An **outcome**
is the result of an experiment.

When a probability is found by repeating
an experiment and recording the results,
the probability is called an **experimental
probability**. The experimental probability
is the ratio of the number of times an
event occurred to the number of times
the experiment was conducted.

Spinning the spinner below is an *experiment*.
There are two possible *outcomes*: A or B.

Suppose the spinner was spun 8 times and
"B" resulted 3 times. The experimental
probability would be $= \dfrac{3}{8}$.

Example

A pair of number cubes was rolled 32 times and
the sum was recorded. The results of this experiment are shown in the frequency table at the
right. Use the frequency table to determine the
experimental probability of rolling a sum of 5.

Sum	Frequency
2	1
3	3
4	3
5	**6**
6	4
7	5
8	4
9	4
10	2
11	1
12	0

MODULE 1 SECTION 3   **STUDY GUIDE**

Since a sum of 5 occurred in 6 of the 32 rolls, the experimental probability of a sum of 5 is $\frac{6}{32}$, or $\frac{3}{16}$. This can also be written as $P(\text{sum of } 5) = \frac{3}{16}$.

Exploration 2: Theoretical Probability

A **theoretical probability** is a probability that is determined without actually doing an experiment.

When two or more outcomes have the same chance of occurring, the outcomes are **equally likely**.

Example

Tell whether the outcomes W, X, Y, and Z on each spinner below are equally likely to occur. Then find the theoretical probability of spinning an X.

a.

b.

Sample Response

a. Since the spinner is divided into four equal-sized sectors, the four outcomes (W, X, Y, and Z) are equally likely to occur.

Since the four sectors of the spinner are the same size, the theoretical probability is

$$P(X) = \frac{1}{4}.$$

b. Since the spinner is not divided into four equal-sized sectors, the four outcomes (W, X, Y, and Z) are not equally likely to occur.

The sector labeled "X" appears to be approximately one-eighth of the whole spinner, so the theoretical probability of spinning X is

$$P(X) = \frac{1}{8}.$$

Name _____ Date _____

Exploration 1

Trisha spun the spinner shown 25 times. She got an odd number 15 times. Use this information for Exercises 1 and 2.

1. Based on Trisha's results, what is the experimental probability of getting an odd number on a spin?

2. Describe an event that has a probability of 1 and an event that has a probability of 0.

3. What are the possible outcomes when you roll a number cube?

4. Toss a coin 30 times. Record your results in a frequency table. Then find the experimental probability of getting heads and the experimental probability of getting tails.

Exploration 2

Suppose you toss two coins. Find the theoretical probability of each event.

5. P(two heads)   6. P(two tails)   7. P(one heads)   8. P(one tails)

For Exercises 9–12, suppose an experiment involves spinning this spinner once.

9. What are all the possible outcomes of the experiment?

10. Are spinning an A, B, and C equally likely events? Why or why not?

11. What fractions of the spins do you expect to land on A? on B? on C?

12. **Writing** Suppose you repeat the experiment 20 times. What results do you expect? Do you think the results will always match your expectations? Why or why not?

13. **Challenge** Sketch a spinner for this situation: The possible outcomes are Red and Green. The probability of spinning Red is three times the probability of spinning Green.

Spiral Review

For each sequence, make a table, draw a graph, and write an equation. Then predict the 100th term. (Module 1, pp. 20–21)

14. 3, 4, 5, 6, …   15. 4, 7, 10, 13, …

For Exercises 16–18, find each sum or difference. (Toolbox, p. 581)

16. 9 – 6.23   17. 37.18 + 47.25   18. 6 + 7.3 + 1.52

19. Find the mean of these running times, in seconds, at a track meet:
25.1, 23.2, 27.7, 26.0, 27.0, 25.0, 20.1, 22.5, 28.1, 23.7 (Toolbox, p. 595)

MODULE 1 SECTION 4

What Can You Expect?   Problem Solving

GOAL **LEARN HOW TO:** • recognize the steps of the 4-step approach to problem solving
• apply the 4-step approach to problem solving
AS YOU: • solve a problem
• predict outcomes

Exploration 1: Four Steps to Problem Solving

Step 1: Understand the Problem

• **Read** the **problem** carefully, probably several times.

• **Identify** what the **question** is.

• **Restate** the **problem** in your own words.

• **Identify** the **information needed** to solve the problem, and determine if any of it is missing.

Step 2: Make a Plan

You may have to choose several problem solving strategies such as:

• try a simpler problem

• make an organized list

• act it out

• use logical reasoning

• make a picture or diagram

• make a table

• look for a pattern

• guess and check

• work backward

• use an equation

Step 3: Carry Out the Plan

• Solve the problem using the strategies you selected.

• You may need to change strategies.

Step 4: Look Back

• Check that you answered the question being asked.

• Check that your solution seems reasonable.

• Check that your work is accurate.

• Try to find another method to solve the problem and compare the results.

• Study the solution to see if the method can be generalized or extended to other situations or to solve other problems.

| MODULE 1 SECTION 4 | STUDY GUIDE |

Example

A phone call costs $.35 for the first minute and $.12 for each minute thereafter. If Jordan's bill for calling her brother was $1.31. How many minutes did she talk?

■ Sample Response ■

Step 1:
- Read the problem carefully.
- Identify the question.
- Restate the problem in your own words.
- Identify the necessary information.

How many minutes did she talk?
first minute = $.35;
each additional minute = $.12;
Her bill was $1.31.

Step 2:
- Choose a strategy.

Step 3:
- Solve the problem.

Since I know how much the bill was, I will *work backward* to solve.

Subtract the charge for the first minute from the total. Divide by 12 to find the number of additional minutes.

$$\begin{array}{ccc} \$1.31 & 8 & 8 \\ -0.35 & 12\overline{)96} & +1 \\ \hline \$.96 & \underline{96} & 9 \\ & 0 & \end{array}$$

The phone call lasted 9 min.

Step 4:
- Check that you answered the question.
- Check that your answer seems reasonable.
- Check that your work is accurate.

Check:
$.35 + 8 • $.12 = $.35 + $.96
            = $1.31 ✔

Exploration 2: The Last Card Problem

Once you have solved a problem, you can use the pattern or model that you used to solve it to make predictions. For instance, in the Example above, you could predict the cost of a 30 min call by using the model $.35 + 29 • $.12 = $3.83.

Name _____   Date _____

Exploration 1

Assume a person typing 360 words at the rate of 90 words per minute earns $2.

  1. At this rate, how many minutes would it take to type 360 words?

  2. At this rate, how many words would a person need to type to earn $30?

  3. How many hours would a person need to type to earn $1000?

  4. Writing Is getting paid $10 per 1800 words better pay? Explain.

Exploration 2

  5. A restaurant has square tables that seat 2 people on each side. If two tables are placed end-to-end, then 12 people may be seated. If 10 tables are placed end-to-end, how many people may be seated?

  6. Elizabeth's scores on her first three math tests were 89, 78, and 91. She reasons that if she scores high enough on her next test, then the mean of her scores will be an A. An A at her school is 93–100. Is her reasoning correct? Explain.

  7. Inga and Dante work at a movie theater taking tickets. They are both working today, but they have different schedules. Inga works every third day and Dante works every other day. How many times will they both be working together on the same day during the next 27 days?

Spiral Review

The spinner shown is spun once and the number that the spinner lands on is recorded. (Module 1, p. 33)

  8. What are all the possible outcomes of the experiment?

  9. What is the theoretical probability of each outcome?

  10. Suppose the spinner is spun 64 times. How many times would you expect to get an 8?

Use compatible numbers to estimate each quotient.
(Toolbox, p. 582)

  11. $21 \overline{)599}$ **12.** $63 \overline{)127}$ **13.** $309 \overline{)883}$

Creative Solutions   Assessing Problem Solving

GOAL **LEARN HOW TO:** • use the problem solving scale
• use the connections scale

AS YOU: • evaluate solutions
• find ways to extend a solution

Exploration 1: Evaluating Solutions

Problem Solving Scale

This problem solving scale is used to assess how well you apply the 4-step approach to problem solving.

 Problem Solving

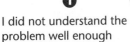

| ❶ | ❷ | ❸ | ❹ | ❺ |

I did not understand the problem well enough to get started or I did not show any work.

I understood the problem well enough to make a plan and to work toward a solution.

I made a plan, I used it to solve the problem, and I verified my solution.

When you assess your work using the problem solving scale, think about whether you:

• understood the problem

• made a plan

• carried out the plan to solve the problem

• looked back to verify your solution

Example

Suppose you were asked to find the next number in the pattern 1, 4, 7, 10, … .

To solve the problem, you used a dot pattern to represent the numbers. You determined the answer was 13. What score would you rate on the problem solving scale?

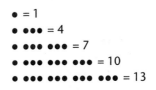

Sample Response

You would probably rate this solution a **4** on the problem solving scale because you made a plan, used it to solve the problem, but did not verify your solution.

MODULE 1 SECTION 5	STUDY GUIDE

Exploration 2: Making Connections

Connections Scale

You can use the connections scale to assess how well you make connections to other problems, mathematical concepts, or applications.

 Connections

❶ I attempted or solved the problem and then stopped.

❸ I found patterns and used them to extend the solution to other cases, or I recognized that this problem relates to other problems, mathematical ideas, or applications.

❺ I extended the ideas in the solution to the general case, or I showed how this problem relates to other problems, mathematical ideas, or applications.

You might score a **3** on the connections scale if you:

- recognize how the problem is related to other problems
- recognize connections to other mathematical topics
- extend the solution

You might score a **5** on the connections scale if you:

- show how the problem or mathematics can be applied elsewhere
- extend the problem to the general case

Example

Refer back to the problem in the previous Example.

Suppose you used a dot pattern to represent the numbers as shown below, indicating the position of each number in the pattern. You then wrote a formula for finding any number in the pattern, and used it to determine that the next number is 13. What score would you rate on the connections scale?

1st ● = 1
2nd ● ●●● = 4
3rd ● ●●● ●●● = 7
4th ● ●●● ●●● ●●● = 10
5th ● ●●● ●●● ●●● ●●● = 13

Let t = the term number.

Then $1 + 3(t - 1)$ = the number in the tth position.

Find the number in the 5th position.

$1 + 3(t - 1) = 1 + 3(5 - 1) \leftarrow t = 5$
$= 1 + 3(4) = 1 + 12 = 13$

The next number in the pattern is 13.

Sample Response

You would probably rate this solution a **5** on the connections scale because you extended the solution to the general case.

MODULE 1 SECTION 5 | PRACTICE & APPLICATION EXERCISES | STUDY GUIDE

Exploration 1

1. Choose the letter of the pattern(s) that can be folded into a square pyramid. Then draw another pattern that will work.

A. 　　**B.** 　　**C.**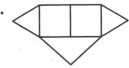

2. Suppose you did not answer Exercise 1. How would you rate your work on the problem solving scale? Why?

3. If you chose the correct letters in Exercise 1 but did not draw another pattern, how would you rate yourself on the problem solving scale? Why?

Exploration 2

4. Find the next number in the number pattern 3, 5, 7, 9, … . Extend your work to find the 200th number in the pattern. Assess your work using the connections scale.

Spiral Review

5. Matt threw three darts at the target shown at the right. All three darts hit the target, landing in two different scoring regions. Which of the following numbers could have been his score: 15, 25, 30, 45, or 70? Explain your reasoning.
(Module 1, p. 44)

Replace each ___?___ with the correct measure. (Toolbox, p. 592)

6. 5 h = ___?___ min　　**7.** 6 yd = ___?___ in.　　**8.** 4 lb = ___?___ oz

9. 45 ft = ___?___ yd　　**10.** 60 in. = ___?___ ft　　**11.** 8 h = ___?___ s

Estimation **Estimate the value of each expression. Explain how you made each estimate.** (Toolbox, p. 582)

12. 327 · 38　　　　**13.** 3572 ÷ 63　　　　**14.** 145 + 796 + 62

15. 9017 − 893　　　**16.** 99 · 143　　　　　**17.** 201 + 75 + 123

Name _____   Date _____

The Clear Choice   Expressions and Representations

GOAL   **LEARN HOW TO:** • use the mathematical language scale
              • evaluate expressions using the order of operations
              • use the representations scale
              • decide when a line graph is appropriate

AS YOU: • solve problems
           • explore television viewing habits

Exploration 1: Order of Operations

Mathematical Language Scale

This mathematical language scale is used to assess how well you use
mathematical vocabulary and symbols.

   Mathematical Language

| ❶ | ❷ | ❸ | ❹ | ❺ |

| I did not use any mathematical vocabulary or symbols, or I did not use them correctly, or my use was not appropriate. | I used appropriate mathematical language, but the way it was used was not always correct or other terms and symbols were needed. | I used mathematical language that was correct and appropriate to make my meaning clear. |

An **expression** is a mathematical phrase that can be formed using
numbers, variables, and operation symbols.

The expression $3 \cdot 4 + y$ contains the numbers 3 and 4, the variable y, and
the operation symbols $\cdot$ and $+$.

Order of Operations

To **evaluate** an expression, you carry out the mathematical operations in
the correct order. This order is known as the **order of operations**. It is
important to use the correct order of operations when evaluating
expressions.

Step 1: Carry out the operations within
grouping symbols. Start with the
innermost grouping symbols first.

Step 2: Next evaluate all powers.

Step 3: Then do all multiplication and
division in order from left to right.

Step 4: Do all addition and subtraction in
order from left to right.

$2 + [2 \cdot (8-3)^2 \div 5] \div 2$ *(Step 1)*
$= 2 + [2 \cdot 5^2 \div 5] \div 2$ *(Steps 1, 2)*
$= 2 + [2 \cdot 25 \div 5] \div 2$ *(Steps 1, 3)*
$= 2 + [50 \div 5] \div 2$ *(Step 1)*
$= 2 + 10 \div 2$ *(Step 3)*
$= 2 + 5$ *(Step 4)*
$= 7$

Name _____ Date _____

When an expression contains a fraction bar, you carry out the operations in the numerator separately from those in the denominator. Then you divide the numerator by the denominator as the final step.

Exploration 2: Representations

Representations Scale

You can use the representations scale to assess how well you use equations, tables, graphs, and diagrams to help solve a problem or explain a solution.

 Representations

 1   **2**   **3**   **4**   **5**

I did not use any representations such as equations, tables,
graphs, or diagrams to help
solve the problem or explain
my solution.

I made appropriate representations to help solve the problem
or help me explain my solution,
but they were not always correct or other representations
were needed.

I used appropriate and
correct representations
to solve the problem
or explain my solution.

Example

Zack is buying paper towels. The brand he prefers comes in two different size rolls. One size has 75 sheets and sells for $0.79. The other sells for $1.29 and has 125 sheets. Which is the better buy? Explain how you made your decision. Use the representations scale to score your solution.

■ Sample Response ■

Think: $\dfrac{\$.79}{75}$ (>, <, or =) $\dfrac{\$1.29}{125}$

To find the unit cost of each roll, do the two divisions. Then compare the unit costs.

Since $0.01032 < 0.01053\ldots$, this means

$$\dfrac{\$.79}{75} > \dfrac{\$1.29}{125}.$$

Therefore, the $1.29 package is the better buy.

$$\begin{array}{r} 0.01053 \\ 75\overline{)0.79000} \\ \underline{75} \\ 40 \\ \underline{0} \\ 400 \\ \underline{375} \\ 250 \\ \underline{225} \\ 25 \end{array}$$

$$\begin{array}{r} 0.01032 \\ 125\overline{)1.29000} \\ \underline{1\,25} \\ 40 \\ \underline{0} \\ 400 \\ \underline{375} \\ 250 \\ \underline{250} \\ 0 \end{array}$$

Since I wrote an equation, found the correct solution, and explained my solution I think I rate a **5** on the representations scale.

| MODULE 1 SECTION 6 | PRACTICE & APPLICATION EXERCISES | STUDY GUIDE |

Exploration 1

For Exercises 1–9, evaluate each expression using the order of operations.

1. $36 - 5 \cdot 6$

2. $8 \cdot (5 + 7) - 4$

3. $4 \cdot 3 - 8 \div 2$

4. $10 + 25 \div 5 + 3^2$

5. $48 \div (13 - 7) \cdot 4$

6. $(12 - 9)^2 - (12 - 9)$

7. $\dfrac{(15 + 1) \cdot 2}{6 + 2}$

8. $\dfrac{90 \div (10 \div 5)}{9 - 4}$

9. $2^3 \div [3^2 - (5 + 3)]$

10. Write and evaluate an expression to represent the value (in cents) of 3 dollars, 2 half-dollars, 7 dimes, 4 nickels, and 8 pennies.

11. Challenge Use grouping symbols to make the statement $2^3 + 6^2 - 4^2 \div 4 - 2 \cdot 3 = 7$ true.

Exploration 2

12. Jeremy's insect and spider collection consists of 5 bugs whose total number of legs are 34.

    a. If insects have 6 legs and spiders have 8 legs, how many insects and how many spiders does Jeremy have?

    b. Use the *Three Assessment Scales* shown on Labsheet 6A to assess your solution to part (a).

Spiral Review

For Exercises 13–16, suppose a spinner has equal sectors lettered A, B, C, or D. The spinner was spun 50 times and the results were recorded in the table. Find each experimental probability. (Module 1, p. 33)

Outcome	Frequency
A	10
B	15
C	20
D	5

13. $P(A)$

14. $P(B)$

15. $P(C)$

16. $P(D)$

17. How many sectors do you think were labeled with each letter? Explain your thinking. (Module 1, p. 44 and 55)

Use a ruler to draw a segment of each length. (Toolbox, p. 591)

18. $1\frac{1}{4}$ in.

19. $4\frac{3}{8}$ in.

20. $6\frac{3}{4}$ in.

21. $2\frac{11}{16}$ in.

Name _____   Date _____

For Use with Section 3

In this activity, you will see how a spreadsheet program can be used to simulate spinning a spinner with eight equal-sized sections numbered 1 through 8. Assume there is an equal chance of the spinner landing on each of the eight numbers.

To have the spreadsheet software generate a random number between 1 and 8, enter the formula =INT(RAND()*8+1) in cell A2. Use the FILL command to generate 80 random spins of the spinner as shown in the chart below.

	A	B	C	D	E	F	G	H
1				SPINNING A SPINNER: 1 TO 8				
2	3	8	6	6	1	5	2	7
3	5	1	2	3	7	1	5	8
4	2	7	2	6	7	5	6	1
5	7	4	4	8	4	5	8	8
6	2	7	3	7	7	5	8	7
7	3	4	3	7	2	7	5	1
8	6	5	1	7	7	6	4	5
9	2	2	7	3	3	2	6	2
10	7	1	3	4	6	2	7	6
11	6	4	5	3	6	2	7	2
12	VALUES	THEO. PROB	FREQ.	EXP. PROB				
13	1	0.125	7	0.0875				
14	2	0.125	13	0.1625				
15	3	0.125	9	0.1125				
16	4	0.125	7	0.0875				
17	5	0.125	10	0.125				
18	6	0.125	11	0.1375				
19	7	0.125	17	0.2125				
20	8	0.125	6	0.075				
21								
22	1 OR 2		20	0.25				
23	5, 6, 7		38	0.475				
24	EVEN NO.		37	0.4625				

1. The theoretical probability of spinning a 1 is shown in cell B13.

   a. Written as a percent, what is the theoretical probability that the spinner will land on 1? _____

   b. Explain why the theoretical probability of spinning 1 is 0.125.

      _____

In cell C13, the software counts how many times a 1 was spun. To instruct the computer to count the 1s, use the formula =COUNTIF(A2:H11,1). The computer searches from cell A2 in the upper left to H11 in the lower right to see how many times the number 1 occurs.

2. What formula can be entered in cell D13 to calculate the experimental probability of spinning a 1? _____

3. The number in cell C22 shows how many times a 1 or 2 was spun. What formula can you enter in cell C22 to get the computer to display this number? _____

4. In cell D22, the experimental probability of spinning a 1 or 2 is calculated. What is the formula for this cell? _____

5. What is the theoretical probability of spinning a 5, 6, or 7?

_____

6. What formula can you use for cell D24 to have the computer display the result shown in the chart? _____

Name _____   Date _____

MODULE 1 QUIZ   **MID-MODULE**

Use the line graph for Exercises 1–4.

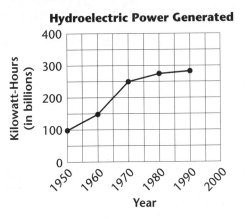

Hydroelectric Power Generated

1. How many kilowatt-hours of hydroelectric power were generated in 1980?

2. In what decade did the United States start generating more than 100 billion kilowatt-hours per year?

3. In what decade did hydroelectric power increase the most?

4. Predict how much hydroelectric power will be generated in the year 2000.

5. The table at the right shows data gathered in a survey about people's favorite kind of fruit. Make a bar graph of the data.

Favorite Fruit of 50 People Surveyed

Fruit	Frequency
apple	11
banana	8
orange	9
pear	4
strawberry	5
watermelon	3
other	10

6. Make a frequency table for the following data about the number of television sets per household:
3, 1, 2, 2, 2, 0, 1, 5, 1, 2, 3, 4, 5, 1, 1, 2, 3, 0, 1, 2.

7. Make a table, draw a graph, and write an equation for the sequence 1, 3, 9, 27, 81, … . Use your equation to predict the 50th term. Write your prediction using exponential notation.

Write each product in exponential form.

8. $12 \cdot 12 \cdot 12 \cdot 12$ 9. $7 \cdot 7 \cdot 7$ 10. $5 \cdot 5 \cdot 5 \cdot 5 \cdot 5$

Find the volume of a cube with edges of each length.

11. 16 cm   12. 30 in.   13. 2 ft

14. Suppose you roll two number cubes. List three outcomes that produce an even sum greater than 6.

15. Andrew spins the spinner shown at the right and gets an even number 15 times out of 36 spins. What are the experimental and theoretical probabilities of getting an odd number?

MODULE 1 TEST FORM Ⓐ

Use the line graph for Exercises 1–4.

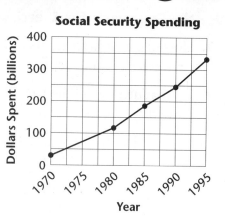

Social Security Spending

1. How much was spent on Social Security in 1980?

2. In what year was the Social Security spending approximately $250 billion?

3. During which five-year period did Social Security spending increase the most?

4. Estimate Social Security spending in the year 1975.

5. Twenty people were asked how many hours a week they spend exercising. Make a frequency table of the resulting data: 2, 3, 3, 6, 0, 2, 1, 4, 6, 2, 3, 0, 2, 6, 5, 3, 3, 2, 0, 4.

6. Use the data in Exercise 5 to make a bar graph.

7. Look at the shape sequence shown below. Each small cube is a unit cube. Notice that the side lengths of the large cubes are doubled as you go from left to right.

Term number	1	2	3	...
Term				...

a. Make a table for the number sequence that shows how many unit cubes are in the large cubes of the shape sequence. In the table for the number sequence, include the fourth term.

b. Write the first four terms of the number sequence in exponential form. Describe the pattern.

c. Use the pattern you identified in part (b) to find the fifth term. Write it in both exponential and standard form.

d. Predict the 20th term in the number sequence. Use exponential notation to help write the answer.

MODULE 1   TEST   FORM **A**

8. Make a table, draw a graph, and write an equation for the sequence 5, 16, 27, 38, ... Then predict the 150th term.

9. Find the volume of a cube when the length of an edge is 17 cm.

Refer to the spinner shown at the right for Exercises 10–12.

10. Terry spun the spinner 48 times. Her results are shown in the table below. Find the experimental probability of each outcome.

Outcome	Frequency
blue	20
yellow	12
green	16

11. Find the theoretical probability of each outcome.

12. Suppose you spin the spinner 360 times. About how many times would you expect it to land on blue?

13. Use the 4-step approach to solving problems to find the total number of triangles in the shape shown at the right. Explain your solution.

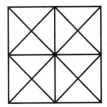

14. Assess your work in Exercise 13 using the problem solving scale on page 49 of the text.

For Exercises 15–17, evaluate each expression without using a calculator.

15. $16 \div 2 + 12 \cdot 2 - 10$ 16. $35 - 4^2 + 2 \cdot 3$ 17. $18 - (2 + 7) \div 3$

18. A driver wants to go to a store that is directly north of where he is. To avoid a traffic jam, he drives 5 blocks east, 2 blocks north, 1 block west, 6 blocks north, and 4 blocks west. How many fewer blocks would he have driven if there had been no traffic jam?

MODULE 1 TEST   **FORM B**

Use the line graph for Exercises 1–4.

1. What was the average amount spent on health care per person in 1975?

2. In what year was health care spending approximately $350 per person?

3. During which five-year period did per capita health care spending increase the most?

4. Estimate health care spending per capita in the year 2000.

Average Amount Spent on Health Care per Person

(line graph: Amount Spent (dollars) on the vertical axis from 0 to 4000; Year on the horizontal axis: 1970, 1975, 1980, 1985, 1990, 2000)

5. Eighteen people were asked how many hours a week they spend reading. Make a frequency table of the resulting data: 4, 6, 7, 3, 1, 0, 6, 7, 9, 8, 10, 2, 1, 4, 7, 15, 4, 6.

6. Use the data in Exercise 5 to make a bar graph.

7. Look at the shape sequence shown below. Notice that a new border of squares is added to get each new term.

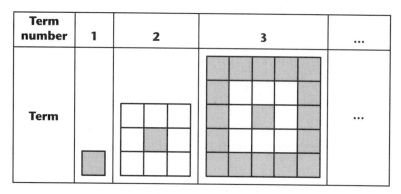

Term number	1	2	3	...
Term				...

a. Make a table for the number sequence that shows how many small squares are in each shape. In the table for the number sequence, include the fourth term.

b. Write the first four terms of the number sequence in exponential form. Describe the pattern.

c. Use the pattern you identified in part (b) to find the fifth term. Write it in both exponential and standard form.

d. Predict the 20th term in the number sequence.

8. Make a table, draw a graph, and write an equation for the sequence 5, 12, 19, 26 ... . Then predict the 150th term.

9. Find the volume of a cube when the length of an edge is 15 cm.

MODULE 1 TEST   FORM **B**

Refer to the spinner shown at the right for Exercises 10–12.

10. Tom spun the spinner 60 times. Her results are shown in the table below. Find the experimental probability of each outcome.

Outcome	Frequency
blue	12
yellow	34
green	14

11. Find the theoretical probability of each outcome.

12. Suppose you spin the spinner 150 times. About how many times would you expect it to land on yellow?

13. Use the 4-step approach to solving problems to find the total number of squares in the shape shown at the right. Explain your solution.

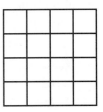

14. Assess your work in Exercise 13 using the problem solving scale on page 49 of the text.

For Exercises 15–17, evaluate each expression without using a calculator.

15. $(5^2 + 2 \cdot 4 - 17) \div 8$ 16. $7 \cdot 5 + 10 \div 2 - 20$ 17. $120 \div 3 + 5 - 2 \cdot 10$

18. A treasure map instructs the finder to walk 50 paces west, 10 paces north, 15 paces east, 20 paces north, and 35 paces east. A person who takes a minute to draw a diagram will discover a faster way to the treasure. How many paces should you take and in what direction to claim the treaure with as little walking as possible?

MODULE 1 STANDARDIZED ASSESSMENT

1. When did the value of the stock decrease?

Value of a Share of Stock

Price per Share (dollars)

Month

a. January
b. February
c. March
d. April

2. Which data would be better represented by a line graph than a bar graph?
a. high temperatures in ten cities
b. distances of planets from the sun
c. the weight of a kitten as it grows
d. favorite kinds of ice cream

3. Find the frequency of two pets in this data about number of pets per household:
0, 4, 1, 3, 2, 0, 1, 13, 2, 4, 0, 1, 2, 5
a. 2
b. 3
c. 4
d. 5.5

4. Predict the 75th term of the sequence 2, 9, 16, 23, ...
a. 518
b. 520
c. 525
d. 527

5. Write $2 \cdot 2 \cdot 2 \cdot 2$ in exponential form.
a. $4 \cdot 2$
b. 2^4
c. 4^2
d. $4 \cdot 2^4$

6. Anne tosses a coin 80 times and gets heads 45 times. Which of the following expressions represents the experimental probability of getting tails?
a. $80 - 45$
b. $\dfrac{45}{80}$
c. $\dfrac{45}{80 - 45}$
d. $\dfrac{80 - 45}{80}$

7. What is the theoretical probability of this spinner landing on white?

a. $\dfrac{1}{2}$
b. $\dfrac{1}{3}$
c. $\dfrac{1}{4}$
d. $\dfrac{2}{3}$

8. When n is the term number, which expression describes the nth term of the sequence 6, 12, 24, 48, ... ?
a. $3 \cdot 2^{n-1}$
b. $3 \cdot 2^n$
c. $3 \cdot 2(n - 1)$
d. $3 \cdot 2n$

9. Suppose you roll three number cubes. Which of the following outcomes produces an odd sum greater than 11?
a. 2, 6, 5
b. 1, 6, 3
c. 4, 2, 5
d. 4, 4, 4

10. What is the volume of a cube with side lengths of 21 in.?
a. 441 in.^{3}
b. 603 in.^{3}
c. 4860 in.^{3}
d. 9261 in.^{3}

11. Evaluate $25 \cdot 3 - 20 + 60 \div 15$.
a. 7
b. 35
c. 59
d. 65

12. On Monday, you have quizzes in both math and spelling. You will have a math quiz every 3rd day and a spelling quiz every 4th day. How many times in 10 weeks will you have both quizzes on the same day?
a. 3
b. 5
c. 7
d. 12

MODULE 1   **MODULE PERFORMANCE ASSESSMENT**

Step 1: Write numbers to represent the first 3 terms of sequence A shown below:

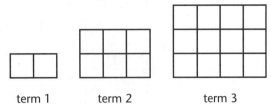

term 1   term 2   term 3

Step 2: Make a table showing the term number, term, and shape sequence for the first 3 terms of sequence A. Then predict what the fourth and fifth terms of the sequence will be. Explain your reasoning.

Step 3: Sequence B is defined by the following number pattern: 1, 4, 9, 16, 25 ... . Write an equation relating the term number n with the value of the term t for sequence B.

Step 4: Construct a visual representation that compares the first five terms of sequence A with the first five terms of sequence B. Explain which type of graph you used and why.

Step 5: Compare the results shown in your graph. Then write an equation relating the term number n with the value of the term t for sequence A. Explain how you determined the equation.

Step 6: Use your equation to find the 39th term of sequence A.

Answers

PRACTICE AND APPLICATIONS

Module 1, Section 1
1. a. 126 athletes **b.** favorite sources of protein for 126 athletes
2. a. chicken **b.** beans
3. the percent of athletes who chose each source of protein as their favorite
4. about $\frac{1}{2}$; about $\frac{1}{4}$
5. 126 athletes
6. more than
7. The bar for fish is 1.5 times the bar for beans.
8. The bar for chicken is about 4 times the bar for beans.
9. The percent of athletes who prefer beef is about twice that of the percent who prefer beans.
10. about 63 athletes
11. Answers may vary.
12. Answers may vary.
13. Answers may vary.
14. Sample Response: There were enough spaces to let each space represent one person.
15. Sample Response: I found the greatest number of tally marks; I found the longest bar.
16. Answers may vary.

Module 1, Section 2
1. Each term in the number sequence gives the number of squares in the corresponding term of the shape sequence.
2. a. 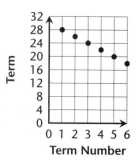 **b.** 10

3. a. Sample Response: Add 2 squares to the top row of the preceding term. **b.** 12 **c.** 20; 180
4. a. $t = 7n$ **b.** $t = n - 2$ **c.** $t = n + 6$ **d.** $t = \frac{n}{4}$
5. a.

Term number	Term
1	6
2	12
3	18
4	24
5	30
6	36

$t = 6n$; 60

b.

Term number	Term
1	28
2	26
3	24
4	22
5	20
6	18

$t = 30 - 2n$; 10

6. a. 27 in.^{3} **b.** 9 in.^{2}
7. a. 2^5 **b.** 3^3 **c.** 8^2 **d.** 5^4 **e.** 9^2 **f.** 4^3 **g.** $6^3 \cdot 2$ **h.** $8 \cdot 3^2$ **i.** $7 \cdot 2^4$
8. a. 49 **b.** 125 **c.** 32 **d.** 144 **e.** 0 **f.** 100,000,000 **g.** 1436 **h.** 256 **i.** 1
9. a. 300^2 **b.** 200^5
10. a. 1 ft^3 **b.** 27 in.^{3} **c.** 512 m^3 **d.** 3375 ft^3 **e.** 64,000 cm^3 **f.** 8,000,000 m^3 **g.** 216,000 cm^3 **h.** 512 ft^3 **i.** 2744 mm^3 **j.** $\frac{1}{64}$ ft^3 **k.** 29.791 cm^3
l. $15\frac{5}{8}$ m^3

11. a.

Side length (cm)	5	10	15	20
Area of a square (cm^2)	25	100	225	400

b.

Edge length (cm)	5	10	15	20
Volume of a cube (cm^3)	125	1000	3375	8000

12. 324 ft^2

Module 1, Section 3
1. a–d. Answers may vary.
2. a. $\frac{16}{38}$ or $\frac{8}{19}$ **b.** Sample Response: The spinner stops on a number less than 8; the spinner stops on a number greater than 8.
3. 1, 2, 3, 4, 5, or 6
4. Answers may vary, but the experimental probability for both outcomes should be about $\frac{1}{2}$.
5. Sample Responses are given. **a.** 4 and 6, 3 and 5, 2 and 4 **b.** 4 and 4, 3 and 3, 2 and 2 **c.** 3 and 5, 4 and 4, 2 and 6 **d.** 2 and 4, 2 and 6, 1 and 3
6. a. $\frac{24}{100}$ or $\frac{6}{25}$ **b.** $\frac{30}{100}$ or $\frac{3}{10}$ **c.** $\frac{26}{100}$ or $\frac{13}{50}$ **d.** $\frac{20}{100}$ or $\frac{1}{5}$
e. $\frac{80}{100}$ or $\frac{4}{5}$ **f.** $\frac{50}{100}$ or $\frac{1}{2}$ **g.** $\frac{76}{100}$ or $\frac{19}{25}$ **h.** $\frac{0}{100}$ or 0
i. $\frac{70}{100}$ or $\frac{7}{10}$
7. $\frac{1}{6}, \frac{1}{6}, \frac{1}{6}$

8.

Spinner 2	Spinner 1			
	1	**2**	**3**	**4**
1	2	3	4	5
2	3	4	5	6
3	4	5	6	7
4	5	6	7	8
5	6	7	8	9
6	7	8	9	10

a. $\frac{1}{24}$ **b.** $\frac{4}{24}$ or $\frac{1}{6}$ **c.** 0 **d.** $\frac{3}{24}$ or $\frac{1}{8}$ **e.** $\frac{2}{24}$ or $\frac{1}{12}$
f. $\frac{4}{24}$ or $\frac{1}{6}$ **g.** $\frac{7}{24}$ **h.** $\frac{12}{24}$ or $\frac{1}{2}$ **i.** 0

9. a. A, B **b.** No; A covers a larger area. **c.** $\frac{2}{3}$, $\frac{1}{3}$;
The area covered by A is twice that covered by B.
d. Sample Response: A: 20; B: 10; No; theoretical and experimental probabilities are usually not the same.
10. a. **b.**

Module 1, Section 4

1. a. 6 min **b.** 150 min
2. 32 sales
3. 32 in.
4. 2 horses
5. 99
6. October
7. 123 parents
8. 4 boards

Module 1, Section 5

1. a. Sample Response: 4; He made a plan and used it to solve the problem, but he didn't verify his work.
b. There are 29 squares; no. **c.** Answers may vary.
2. a. 3 quarters, 3 dimes, and 3 pennies or 1 quarter, 8 dimes, and 3 pennies **b.** Answers may vary.
3. a. 2 mysteries, 2 fantasy books, and 1 of each of the other books **b.** Answers may vary.

Module 1, Section 6

1. a. 16 **b.** 75 **c.** 34 **d.** 11 **e.** 16 **f.** 150 **g.** 14 **h.** 4
i. 3.2 **j.** 10 **k.** 29 **l.** 30
2. 3(50) + 3(25) + 8(5) + 4(10) + 2(1) = 307
3. a. (25 − 8) · 3 = 51 **b.** 9 + 4 · (5 − 3) = 17
c. (9 + 9) ÷ 3 · (5 − 3) = 12 **d.** (6 · 5) − (5² + 2) = 3
4. about 4500 students
5. 1997
6. Sample Response: There was a sharp decrease in the number of students in Middlevale who played baseball between 1994 and 1995. Overall, the numbers decreased from 1990 to 1997.

7. b; The diagram shows 8 objects divided into 4 groups and 3 out of the 4 groups are clearly identified.

Module 1, Sections 1–6

1. $2000
2. a. 1994 **b.** $11,000
3. a. more than **b.** less than **c.** less than **d.** more than
4.

	Tally	Frequency
6	III	3
7	II	2
8	JHT	5
9	III	3
10	II	2

5. a. **b.** perimeter = 4 · length
c. 16, 20 **d.** $P = 4s$; 80 cm **e.** For the table and graph, check students' work; 60.
6. a. $\frac{3}{12}$ or $\frac{1}{4}$ **b.** $\frac{3}{12}$ or $\frac{1}{4}$ **c.** $\frac{9}{12}$ or $\frac{3}{4}$ **d.** $\frac{6}{12}$ or $\frac{1}{2}$
e. $\frac{9}{12}$ or $\frac{3}{4}$ **f.** 0 **g.** $\frac{3}{12}$ or $\frac{1}{4}$ **h.** $\frac{6}{12}$ or $\frac{1}{2}$ **i.** $\frac{9}{12}$ or $\frac{3}{4}$
7. 6 h
8. a. Yes; if a teenager exercises about $2\frac{1}{2}$ h a week, then the teenager will exercise about 130 h in a year.
b. Answers may vary.
9. a. 26 **b.** 31 **c.** 4900 **d.** 3 **e.** 4 **f.** 5 **g.** 14 **h.** 19
10. a. (28 − 10) ÷ 6 = 3 **b.** (8 + 2) · 7 = 70
c. 18 ÷ (2 + 4) = 3 **d.** (4² + 2²) ÷ 4 = 5

STUDY GUIDE

Module 1, Section 1

1. the number of students enrolled at North Middle School in the years 1996, 1997, 1998, and 1999
2. The vertical axis has an interval of 5 students and the horizontal axis has an interval of $\frac{1}{2}$ year.
3. Sample Response: The enrollment for the year 2000 will be higher than the previous years.
4. No; 20% of 315 is 63, but the 1997 enrollment was only 20 students higher than the 1996 enrollment.
5.

Scores on an English Grammar Test

Score	Tally	Frequency
91–100	JHT III	8
81–90	JHT III	8
71–80	JHT I	6
61–70	II	2

6. Favorite Color of Cross Country Team Members

Color	Tally	Frequency
Blue	III	3
Red	III	3
Yellow	III	3
Green	III	3
Orange	I	1

7. 25 ft^2

8. 540 in.^2

9. 12

10. 12

11. 10

12. 44

13. 45 squares

Module 1, Section 2

1. $t = 4n$

2. $t = n - 2$

3. $t = 6 + 2n$ or $t = 2n + 6$

4.

Sequence Table

Term number	Term
1	6
2	12
3	18
4	24

Sequence Graph:

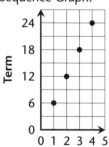

Term Number

Sequence Equation: $t = 6 \cdot n$, or $t = 6n$

The 100th term of the sequence is 6(100), or 600.

5.

6. 7^6

7. 12^8

8. 512

9. 81

10. 50

11. 0

12. 64 mm^3

13. 512 in.^3

14. 1000 km^3

15. $27,000 \text{ ft}^3$

16. Yes; the volume of a cube is the area of one of its faces multiplied by its height.

17. 50%

18. 115 blooms

19–22. Sample Responses are given.

19. $\frac{8}{10}$

20. $\frac{3}{5}$

21. $\frac{3}{9}$

22. $\frac{1}{15}$

Module 1, Section 3

1. $\frac{15}{25}$ or $\frac{3}{5}$

2. Sample Responses: P(spinning a number less than 5) = 1; P(spinning a 5) = 0

3. 1, 2, 3, 4, 5, 6

4. Check students' work.

5. $\frac{1}{4}$

6. $\frac{1}{4}$

7. $\frac{1}{2}$

8. $\frac{1}{2}$

9. A, B, C

10. No; the three sectors are not the same size.

11. $\frac{1}{4}; \frac{1}{2}; \frac{1}{4}$

12. Sample Response: Spin A about 5 times, B about 10 times, and C about 5 times. No; theoretical and experimental probabilities are often not the same.

13.

14.

Sequence Table

Term number	Term
1	3
2	4
3	5
4	6

Sequence Graph:

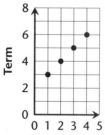

Term number

Sequence Equation: $t = n + 2$
The 100th term of the sequence is $100 + 2$, or 102.

15.

Sequence Table	
Term number	**Term**
1	4
2	7
3	10
4	13

Sequence Graph:

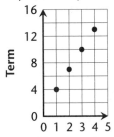

Term number

Sequence Equation: $t = 3n + 1$
The 100th term of the sequence is $3(100) + 1$, or 301.

16. 2.77

17. 84.43

18. 14.82

19. 24.84 s

Module 1, Section 4

1. 4 min

2. 5400 words

3. $33\frac{1}{3}$ h

4. No; both methods of payment would have a ratio of \$1 per 180 words.

5. 44 people

6. No; even if she scored a 100, her mean score would only be 89.5.

7. 4 times (on the 6th, 12th, 18th, and 24th days after today)

8. 5, 6, 7, and 8

9. $P(5) = \frac{2}{8}$ or $\frac{1}{4}$, $P(6) = \frac{2}{8}$ or $\frac{1}{4}$, $P(7) = \frac{1}{8}$, $P(8) = \frac{3}{8}$

10. 24 times

11. about 30

12. about 2

13. about 3

Module 1, Section 5

1. A and B; Check students' work.

2. Sample Response: 1; I did not understand the problem well enough to get started.

3. Sample Response: 3; I understood the problem well enough to make a plan and use it, but not well enough to extend the solution to other cases.

4. 11; Sample Response: The numbers in the pattern are modeled by the equation $n = 2t + 1$, where $n =$ the number and $t =$ the position of the number; the 200th number is $2(200) + 1$, or 401; I would rate my work a 5 on the scale.

5. 25, 30, and 45; Eliminate 15 because this score can only be achieved if all three darts land in the same scoring region. Eliminate 70 because the highest possible score for this situation is 45. The other scores are possible: $10 + 10 + 5 = 25$; $5 + 5 + 10 = 30$; and $20 + 20 + 5 = 45$.

6. 300

7. 216

8. 64

9. 15

10. 5

11. 28,800

12–17. Sample Responses are given.

12. about 13,000; $325(40) = 13,000$

13. about 60; $3600 \div 60 = 60$

14. about 1000; $150 + 800 + 50 = 1000$

15. about 8100; $9000 - 900 = 8100$

16. about 14,000; $100(143) = 14,300$

17. about 400; $200 + 75 + 125 = 400$

Module 1, Section 6

1. 6

2. 92

3. 8

4. 24

5. 32

6. 6

7. 4

8. 9

9. 8

10. $3(100) + 2(50) + 7(10) + 4(5) + 8(1) = 498$

11. $[2^3 + (6^2 - 4^2) \div 4] - 2 \cdot 3 = 7$

12. a.

Number of insects	Number of spiders	Number of legs
0	5	40
1	4	38
2	3	36
3	2	34

Jeremy has 3 insects and 2 spiders.

b. Answers may vary.

13. $\frac{1}{5}$

14. $\frac{3}{10}$

15. $\frac{2}{5}$

16. $\frac{1}{10}$

17. Sample Response: 2 A's, 3 B's, 4 C's, and 1 D; Using the experimental probabilities, 1 out of 5 or 2 out of 10 sectors are labeled A, 3 out of 10 sectors are labeled B, 2 out of 5 or 4 out of 10 sectors are labeled C, and 1 out of 10 sectors is labeled D.

18–21. Check students' work.

TECHNOLOGY

Module 1

1. a. 12.5%   **b.** The chance of throwing a 1 is 1 out 8, and $\frac{1}{8} = 0.125$.

2. =C13/80

3. =C13+C14

4. =C22/80

5. $\frac{3}{8}$ or 0.375

6. =(C14+C16+C18+C20)/80 or =C24/80

ASSESSMENT

Mid-Module 1 Quiz

1. about $275 billion

2. 1950s

3. 1960s

4. about $290 billion

5.

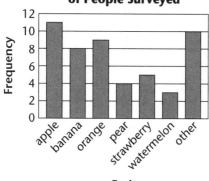

Favorite Fruit of People Surveyed

6.

Number of TV's	Tally	Frequency
0	II	2
1	JHT I	6
2	JHT I	6
3	III	3
4	I	1
5	II	2

7.

Term number	Term
1	3
2	9
3	27
4	81
5	243
6	729

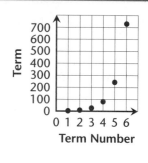

Term Number

$t = 3^n$, where t is the term and n is the term number; 3^{50}

8. 12^4

9. 7^3

10. 5^5

11. 4096 cm^3

12. 27,000 in.^{3}

13. 8 ft^3

14. Sample Response: 4 and 6; 3 and 5; 5 and 5

15. $\frac{7}{12}$, $\frac{1}{2}$

Module 1 Test (Form A)

1. Sample Response: about $120 billion

2. 1990

3. from 1990 to 1995

4. Sample Response: about $75 billion

5.

Number of hours	Tally	Frequency
0	III	3
1	I	1
2	JHT	5
3	JHT	5
4	II	2
5	I	1
6	III	3

6.

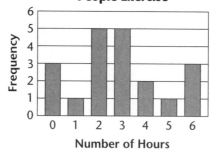

Amount of Time People Exercise

7. a.

Term number	Term
1	8
2	64
3	512
4	4096

b. 2^3, 4^3, 8^3, 16^3; Each term has double the base of the previous term, and the exponent is 3 in each term. **c.** $32^3 = 32{,}768$ **d.** $(2^{20})^3$

8.

Term number	Term
1	5
2	16
3	27
4	38
5	49
6	60

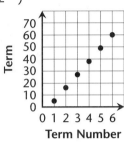

$t = 5 + 11(n - 1)$, where t is the term and n the term number; 1644

9. 4913 cm^3

10. The experimental probabilities are $\frac{5}{12}$ for blue, $\frac{1}{4}$ for yellow, and $\frac{1}{3}$ for green.

11. $P(\text{blue}) = \frac{2}{3}$, $P(\text{yellow}) = \frac{1}{6}$, $P(\text{green}) = \frac{1}{6}$

12. about 240 times

13. 40 triangles; In the figure, 16 triangles consist of 1 small triangle, 16 of 2 small triangles, 4 of 4 small triangles, and 4 of 8 small triangles.

14. Answers may vary.

15. 22

16. 25

17. 15

18. 10 blocks

Module 1 Test (Form B)

1. Sample Response: about $600

2. 1970

3. from 1985 to 1990

4. Sample Response: about $4000

5.

Number of hours	Tally	Frequency
0	I	1
1	II	2
2	I	1
3	I	1
4	III	3
6	III	3
7	III	3
8	I	1
9	I	1
10	I	1
15	I	1

6.

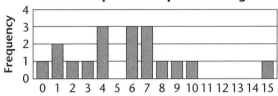

Hours per Week Spent Reading

7. a.

Term number	Term
1	1
2	9
3	25
4	49

b. 1^2, 3^2, 5^2, 7^2; The numbers in the sequence are the squares of the odd numbers. **c.** 9^2, 81 **d.** 39^2

8.

Term number	Term
1	5
2	12
3	19
4	26
5	33
6	40

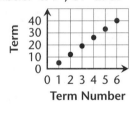

$t = 5 + 7(n - 1)$, where t is the term and n is the term number; 1048

9. 3375 cm^3

10. The experimental probabilities are $\frac{1}{5}$ for blue, $\frac{17}{30}$ for yellow, and $\frac{7}{30}$ for green.

11. $P(\text{blue}) = \frac{1}{4}$, $P(\text{yellow}) = \frac{1}{2}$, $P(\text{green}) = \frac{1}{4}$

12. about 75 times

13. 30 squares; In the figure, 16 squares consist of 1 small square, 9 of 4 small squares, 4 of 9 small squares, and 1 of 16 small squares.
14. Answers may vary.
15. 2
16. 20
17. 25
18. 30 paces north

STANDARDIZED TEST

Module 1
1. c
2. c
3. b
4. b
5. b
6. d
7. b
8. b
9. a
10. d
11. c
12. b

MODULE PERFORMANCE ASSESSMENT

Module 1
Step 1: 2, 6, 12, …
Step 2:

Term number	1	2	3	4	5
Term value	2	6	12	?	?
Shape sequence	☐☐ (1×2)	☐ (2×3)	☐ (3×4)	?	?

Using the progression of shape sequences shown in the table, the 4th and 5th terms can be predicted. The 4th and 5th shapes will be 4×5 and 5×6, so the 4th term = 20 and the 5th term = 30.

Step 3: $t = n^2$
Step 4: Graph sequences A and B on the same coordinate grid to compare the sequences, as shown below.

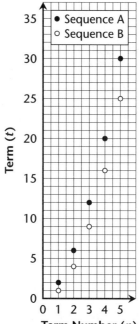

Step 5: By comparing terms with the same term number in the graph for sequences A and B, one can see that the value of each term of sequence A is greater than the corresponding term of sequence B by the amount of the term number. Term 1 of sequence A is 1 greater than term 1 of sequence B; Term 2 of sequence A is 2 greater than term 2 of sequence B, and so on. Since the equation for sequence B is $t = n^2$, where t is the term and n is the term number, the equation for sequence A is $t = n^2 + n$, where t is the term and n is the term number.
Step 6: $39^2 + 39 = 1521 + 39 = 1560$

TEACHER'S RESOURCES FOR MODULE 2

MIDDLE GRADES

MATH*Thematics*

MODULE 2 **Search and Rescue**

- **Planning and Teaching Suggestions, p. 2-8**
- **Labsheets, p. 2-47**
- **Extended Explorations, p. 2-59**
- **Blackline Masters, p. 2-62**

MODULE 2

SEARCH and RESCUE

Module Overview

A young boy's experience surviving a plane crash sets the stage for investigating how algebra topics such as coordinate graphing, integers, variables, functions, and equations can play important roles in rescue operations. Work with angles and angle relationships is also included.

Module Objectives

Section	Objectives	NCTM Standards
1	◆ Name rays and angles with symbols. ◆ Use a protractor to measure and draw angles. ◆ Classify angles as acute, obtuse, right, or straight. ◆ Recognize and find the measures of complementary and supplementary angles. ◆ Estimate the measure of an angle, including angles greater than 180°.	1, 2, 3, 4, 12, 13
2	◆ Use integers to represent real-life situations. ◆ Compare integers. ◆ Find the opposite and the absolute value of an integer. ◆ Recognize parallel and perpendicular lines in a plane. ◆ Use coordinates to identify and plot points in a coordinate plane.	1, 2, 3, 4, 5, 9, 12
3	◆ Model moves on a number line with integers. ◆ Add integers. ◆ Apply addition properties of 0 and opposites to integer addition. ◆ Apply the commutative and associative properties to integer addition. ◆ Subtract integers by writing a related addition problem.	1, 2, 3, 4, 7, 9
4	◆ Evaluate a variable expression involving integer addition and subtraction and whole number operations. ◆ Model a function with a table or an equation. ◆ Model a function with a graph. ◆ Use graphs to compare linear functions.	1, 2, 3, 4, 8, 9
5	◆ Write an addition or subtraction equation to model a situation. ◆ Solve addition equations using an algebra tile model. ◆ Solve addition and subtraction equations with integer solutions using inverse operations, and check a solution of an equation by substitution.	1, 2, 3, 4, 9

MODULE 2

Topic Spiraling

Section	Connections to Prior and Future Concepts
1	Section 1 reviews naming, measuring, and classifying angles from Modules 1 and 6 of Book 1, and introduces complementary and supplementary angles. Angles are applied to rotations in Module 4, polygons and intersecting lines in Module 6, and tessellations in Module 8.
2	Section 2 expands integer concepts begun in Module 7 of Book 1. Number lines and inequality symbols are used to compare integers, absolute value is introduced, and integers are graphed in a coordinate plane. Integer operations are explored in Section 3 and in Module 4.
3	Section 3 uses a number line model to explore addition and subtraction of integers, which are explored using a chip model in Module 8 of Book 1. The commutative and associative properties are introduced. Multiplication and division of integers are explored in Module 4.
4	Section 4 covers evaluating expressions. Functions and their representations in tables, equations, and coordinate graphs are introduced. Graphs are used to compare functions. The groundwork for functions was laid in Module 4 of Book 1 through work with input/output rules. Linear, exponential, and quadratic functions are explored in Module 7 of Book 3.
5	Section 5 covers addition and subtraction equations and related problems. Balance scale and algebra tile models are used to model and solve equations. Inverse operations are also used to solve equations, building on informal methods used in Module 7 of Book 1 based on number fact families. Equation solving is explored further in Modules 3, 4, and 7.

Integration

Mathematical Connections	1	2	3	4	5
algebra (including patterns and functions)	85	**88–100**	**101–116**	**117–129**	**130–143**
geometry	**76–87***	92, 94, 97, 98, 100		125	139, 140
data analysis, probability, discrete math	85	98, 99		127, 128	
Interdisciplinary Connections and Applications					
social studies and geography	85	88–90, 92, 96, 97	112	126	138
reading and language arts	76				
science		96, 98	106, 108, 111, 112		133
health, physical education, and sports			111	128	139
emergency rescue	76–77, 80, 86	88, 99	101, 114, 116	117–118	130–131, 134, 143
money, recreation			110–111	125, 127	140

*** Bold page numbers** *indicate that a topic is used throughout the section.*

Guide for Assigning Homework

Regular Scheduling (45 min class period)

Section/ P&A Pages	Core Assignment	Extended Assignment	Additional Practice/Review	Open-ended Problems	Special Problems
			exercises to note		
1 pp. 84–87	**Day 1:** 1–9, 12, SR 31–33	1–9, 12, SR 31–33	EP, p. 87; PA 10, 11, 13, 14		
	Day 2: 15, 16, 18–20, 22–28 (even), *ROS 30, SR 34–36	15, 16, 18–20, 22–28 (even), Chal 29, *ROS 30, SR 34–36	PA 17, 21–27 (odd)	St Sk, p. 87	Mod Proj 1–4
2 pp. 95–100	**Day 1:** 2–4, 6–10, 12–14, 16–20, 24, 26–31, 38–40, 42, 44, 45, 48	2–4, 6–10, 12–14, 16–20, 24, 26–31, 38–40, 42, 44, 45, 48	EP, p. 100; PA 1, 5, 11, 15, 21–23, 25, 32–37, 41, 43, 46, 47, 49, 50		
	Day 2: 51–56, ROS 59, SR 60–67	51–56, Chal 57–58, ROS 59, SR 60–67		PA 54; Mod Proj 7–8; Std Test, p. 100	Mod Proj 5–8
3 pp. 110–116	**Day 1:** 1–5, SR 48–53	1–5, SR 48–53	EP, p. 115		
	Day 2: 6–12, 15, 16, 19–23	6–12, 15, 16, 19–23	PA 13, 14, 17, 18		
	Day 3: 24–28, 30–32, 37–42, *ROS 47	24–28, 30–32, 37–42, *Chal 46, *ROS 47, Ext 54–55	PA 29, 33–36, 43–45	E^2, p. 116	E^2, p. 116; Mod Proj 9–10
4 pp. 125–129	**Day 1:** 2–4, 8–12, 14, 16–18, 22, 24, SR 37–39	2–4, 8–12, 14, 16–18, 22, 24, SR 37–39	EP, p. 129; PA 1, 5–7, 13, 15, 19–21, 23		
	Day 2: 25, 27, 30, 32, 34, *ROS 36, SR 40–43, Career 44	25, 27, 30, 32, Chal 33, 34, *ROS 36, SR 40–43, Career 44	PA 26, 28, 29, 31	PA 28	PA 35
5 pp. 138–143	**Day 1:** 2–8, 10–12, 16, SR 47–52	2–8, 10–12, 16, SR 47–52	EP, p. 142; PA 1, 9, 13–15, 17	PA 3, 4	
	Day 2: 20–28, 30, 36–44 (even), 45, *ROS 46, SR 53–57	20–28, 30, Chal 31, 36, 40, 44, 45, *ROS 46, SR 53–57, *Ext 58–63	TB, p. 581; PA 18, 19, 29, 32–35, 37–43 (odd)	ROS 46; Mod Proj 12	Mod Proj 11–12
Review/ Assess	Review and Assess (PE), Quick Quizzes (TRB), Mid-Module Quiz (TRB), Module Tests— Forms A and B (TRB), Standardized Assessment (TRB), Cumulative Test (TRB)				Allow 5 days
Enrich/ Assess	E^2 (PE) and Alternate E^2 (TRB), Module Project (PE), Module Performance Assessment (TRB)				
Yearly Pacing	**Mod 2:** 16 days	**Mods 1–2:** 34 days	**Remaining:** 106 days		**Total:** 140 days

Key: PA = Practice & Application; ROS = Reflecting on the Section; SR = Spiral Review; TB = Toolbox; EP = Extra Skill Practice; Ext = Extension; *more time

Block Scheduling (90 min class period)

	Day 1	Day 2	Day 3	Day 4	Day 5	Day 6	
Teach	Sec 1	Sec 2	Sec 3 Expl 1–2	Sec 3 Expl 3	Sec 4	Sec 5	
Apply/ Assess (P&A)	Sec 1: 2, 4–9, 12, 15, 16, 18, 19, 22, 26, *ROS 30, SR 31–36	Sec 2: 2–12 (even), 13, 14, 16, 20–28 (even), 31, 39, 42, 44, 48, 51–53, 55, 56, ROS 59, SR 60–67	Sec 3: 1–6, 10, 12, 15, 16, 20–23, SR 48–53	Sec 3: 24–32, 38, 42, *ROS 47	Sec 4: 2–24 (even), 25, 26, 30, 32, 34, *ROS 36, SR 37–43	Sec 5: 4–7, 10–12, 16, 20, 24, 28, 30, 36, 40, 44, 45, *ROS 46, SR 47–57	Allow 2 days review/assess/projects
Yearly Pacing	**Mod 2:** 8 days		**Mods 1–2:** 17 days		**Remaining:** 53 days		**Total:** 70 days

Materials List

Section	Materials
1	Labsheets 1A–1C, protractor, ruler, Project Labsheet A
2	Graph paper, Project Labsheet B
3	Labsheets 3A–3C, scissors, 3 paper clips, data from Question 4, Project Labsheet C
4	Labsheet 4A, ruler
5	Algebra tiles; for R and A: protractor, graph paper

Support Materials in this Resource Book

Section	Practice	Study Guide	Assessment	Enrichment
1	Section 1	Section 1	Quick Quiz	
2	Section 2	Section 2	Quick Quiz	
3	Section 3	Section 3	Quick Quiz Mid-Module Quiz	Alternate Extended Exploration
4	Section 4	Section 4	Quick Quiz	Technology Activity
5	Section 5	Section 5	Quick Quiz	
Review/ Assess	Sections 1–5		Module Tests Forms A and B Standardized Assessment Module Performance Assessment Cumulative Test Modules 1–2	

Classroom Ideas

Bulletin Boards:
- different types of maps (contour, topographic, street, nautical, etc.)
- search and rescue articles from newspapers or magazines with maps
- pictures and maps of cities built on a grid

Student Work Displays:
- homework and television watching data displays
- data displays used for phone chain in the E^2
- labsheets and newspaper articles from the module project

Interest Center:
- books and magazines on backpacking with samples of equipment and food

Visitors/Field Trips:
- search and rescue personnel, orienteering expert, cartographer

Technology:
- Module 2 Technology Activity in TRB for PE p. 123
- *McDougal Littell Mathpack Geometry Inventor* CD-ROM/disks Mac/Win

The Math Gazette
Search and Rescue

Sneak Preview!

Over the next three weeks in our mathematics class, we will be developing geometry, coordinate graphing, and pre-algebra concepts while completing a thematic unit on Search and Rescue. Some of the topics we will be discussing are:

✗ the techniques and skills necessary for planning a search

✗ weather and geographic conditions

✗ preparation for searches—clothing, food, and so on

We will look at how mathematics can be used in a variety of search and rescue situations.

Ask Your Student

How do pilots and ship captains navigate their vessels to make certain they reach their destinations? (Sec. 1)

In what ways is mathematics used to describe the weather? (Sec. 2 and Sec. 3)

If you are planning to take a hike in the wilderness, what would

you bring along in case you get lost? (Sec. 6)

Connections

Literature:
Students will read excerpts from *Hatchet*, by Gary Paulsen. In the story, a boy is forced to fly a plane after the pilot has a heart attack. You may enjoy reading this novel together.

Science:
Students will read about extreme weather conditions encountered by missing people and searches. Discuss with your student how weather affects your daily lives. Your student may also be interested in how a meteorologist attempts to predict the weather.

Geography:
Maps will be used throughout this module and map reading skills such as determining headings, using scale, and locating points with coordinates will be discussed. Look for different types of maps in newspapers, magazines, or around the house and discuss them with your student.

How are they read? What do they show? What is the scale?

E² Project

Following Section 3, students will have approximately one week to complete the E^2 project, *A Phone Chain.* Students will use drawings, charts, diagrams, or tables to determine how long it may take for members of a search and rescue team to be notified of a missing plane or person by way of a phone chain.

Students may use the following material for the project:

✗ large sheets of blank paper for drawing diagrams

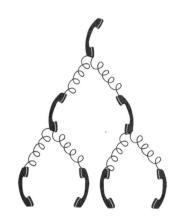

Search and Rescue

Section Title	Mathematics Your Student Will Be Learning	Activities
1: Heading Out	◆ naming, measuring, and classifying angles ◆ using supplementary and complementary angles	◆ use a protractor and compass to measure angles ◆ use a map to devise a search plan for a missing plane
2: Searching for Integers	◆ comparing integers ◆ using opposites and absolute values of integers ◆ identifying and plotting points in a coordinate plane	◆ use a map to devise a search plan for a missing person
3: A Call for Help	◆ adding and subtracting integers	◆ perform addition and subtraction of integers by "hiking" on a number line ◆ use a revised search grid to continue a search for a missing person
4: Urban Rescue	◆ modeling functions with tables, equations, and graphs ◆ evaluating variable expressions	◆ use a location table to determine how long it takes to transport an injured person to a hospital ◆ use graphing technology to find the intersection for the graphs of two linear functions
5: Searching for a Solution	◆ writing addition and subtraction equations ◆ solving addition and subtraction equations	◆ model equations using a balance scale ◆ model and solve equations using algebra tiles

Activities to do at Home

◆ Plan a dream vacation across the United States. Choose several places you would like to visit and use a map to estimate the headings a plane would have to follow and the distances if you traveled by airplane. (After Sec. 1)

◆ Does the weather seem unusually hot or cold this year? Track the high and low temperatures reported in your newspaper for several weeks. Make a chart to compare the temperatures in your town or city to several other places in the country or world. (After Sec. 2)

◆ Look for articles in newspapers or magazines for search and rescue missions. Discuss the conditions and adversities faced by the missing people and the searchers. (After Sec. 3)

Related Topics

You may want to discuss these related topics with your student:

 Navigation and orienteering

 Meteorology

 Cartography

 Camping and survival in the wilderness

Section ① Looking at Angles

Section Planner

DAYS FOR MODULE 2

1 2 3 4 5 6 7 8 9 10 11

SECTION 1

First Day
Setting the Stage, *p. 76*
Exploration 1, *pp. 77–79*

Second Day
Exploration 2, *pp. 80–82*
Key Concepts, *p. 83*

Block Schedule

Day 1
Setting the Stage, Exploration 1,
Exploration 2, Key Concepts

RESOURCE ORGANIZER

Teaching Resources
• Practice and Applications, Sec. 1
• Study Guide, Sec. 1
• Warm-Up, Sec. 1
• Quick Quiz, Sec. 1

Section Overview

Students begin the lesson in Section 1 by identifying the parts of an angle. They will also study the classification of angles by their measures in this section. Degrees and complete rotations will be discussed and students will practice drawing angles using a protractor. New vocabulary includes *ray, angle, vertex, degree, right angle, straight angle, acute angle,* and *obtuse angle.* A discussion of the mathematics used by search and rescue teams will lead students to an exploration of the relationship between angles and compass headings. They will draw rays using the principal directions of a compass (north, south, east, and west) in order to estimate other headings. Students will extend their study of compass headings to the measures of *supplementary* and *complementary angles.* They will use the relationships between complementary angles and between supplementary angles to estimate compass headings.

In the Beginning the Module Project on page 86, students will use mathematical skills to help a search and rescue team plan a rescue.

SECTION OBJECTIVES

Exploration 1
• name rays and angles with symbols
• use a protractor to measure angles
• use a protractor to draw angles
• classify angles as acute, obtuse, right, or straight

Exploration 2
• recognize and find the measures of complementary and supplementary angles
• estimate the measure of an angle, including angles greater than 180°

ASSESSMENT OPTIONS

Checkpoint Questions
• Question 6 on p. 78
• Question 11 on p. 79
• Question 16 on p. 81
• Question 19 on p. 82

Embedded Assessment
• For a list of embedded assessment exercises see p. 2-13.

Performance Task/Portfolio
• Exercise 30 on p. 85 (oral report)
★ Module Project on p. 86

★ = a problem solving task that can be assessed using the Assessment Scales

SECTION 1 MATERIALS

Exploration 1
◆ Labsheet 1A
◆ protractor
◆ ruler

Exploration 2
◆ Labsheets 1B and 1C
◆ protractor
◆ ruler

Module Project on page 86
◆ Project Labsheet A
◆ protractor

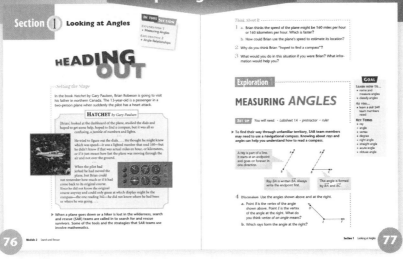

Setting the Stage

MOTIVATE

Initiate a class discussion on flying. Have students relate their flying experiences, discussing what types of airplanes they have flown on. Allow those students who have flown on a small airplane to describe their experience in more detail. Have students list the advantages/disadvantages of flying on a small airplane. Encourage students to read the book *Hatchet*.

Exploration 1

PLAN

Classroom Management
Exploration 1 can best be performed working individually. In answering *Question 1(a)*, make sure that students understand that a kilometer is approximately $\frac{2}{3}$ of a mile; therefore,

160 km/hour is not as fast as 160 mi/hour. Each student will need a copy of Labsheet 1A, a protractor, and a straightedge. Students may work in groups of two if there are not enough protractors. However, each student will still need a copy of Labsheet 1A.

GUIDE

Developing Math Concepts In the discussion for *Question 4*, students should conclude that the vertex of an angle is the shared endpoint of two rays. It is important that students understand that a 360-degree revolution is made when rotating a ray around a point. After completing *Question 10* on page 79, students should be able to name the degree range of an acute angle and an obtuse angle.

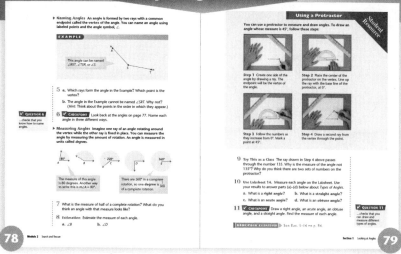

Exploration 1 continued

Classroom Examples
Name the angle below in three ways.

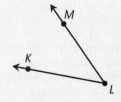

Answer: ∠KLM, ∠MLK, or ∠L

Common Error When using protractors, students will often line up the bottom of the protractor with the ray rather than placing the center of the protractor on the vertex. Check to make sure that students are using the protractor correctly. An overhead example in the use of the protractor would be beneficial.

Question 9 points out the use of a protractor that has two sets of numbers. Be sure students have a good feel for right angles, thus knowing which set of numbers to use.

Checkpoint Have several angles on the overhead and have students name the angles. Students should conclude that when naming an angle using three points, the vertex is always the middle point listed.
Question 11 checks to see if students know the definitions of various angles.

Writing Have students write the definitions of the various angles in their journals, providing a drawing with each definition.

HOMEWORK EXERCISES

See the Suggested Assignment for Day 1 on page 2-13. For Exercise Notes, see page 2-13.

Customizing Instruction

Alternative Approach Have each student use two pencils to demonstrate angles with various measures. Students can use the eraser ends of the pencils as endpoints of the rays forming the angles. As you orally call out various angle measures, have students form the angles with their pencils.

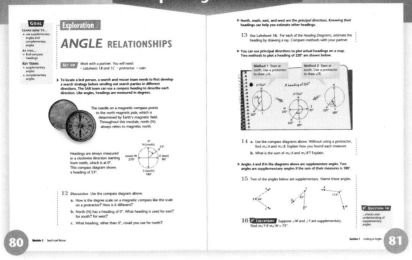

Exploration 2

PLAN

Classroom Management
Exploration 2 is best performed working in groups of two. Each student will need a protractor, a ruler, and a copy of Labsheets 1B and 1C. Students can share protractors if there are not enough available. It would be beneficial to have direction compasses available for students to view, especially for those students who may have never seen one.

GUIDE

Developing Math Concepts In *Question 12*, make sure that students understand that a heading of 0 degrees and a heading of 360 degrees are the same. When determining angle measures greater than 180 degrees, it is important to let students choose the method that is easiest for them. As students are defining complementary and supplementary angles, an easy way to keep from getting them mixed up is to remind students that *c* comes before *s* in the alphabet, and 90 comes before 180 when counting. Therefore, complementary angles have a sum of 90 degrees, and supplementary angles have a sum of 180 degrees.

Common Error Students will have a tendency to use the horizontal ray or east heading as the starting point for measuring rays. Reinforce that when working with compasses and direction headings, the North heading is 0 degrees. Some students will have difficulty naming headings between 270 degrees and 360 degrees. Provide extra practice involving these angle measures.

Checkpoint *Questions 16* and *19* check to see that students understand the definition of complementary and supplementary angles. Have students verbalize strategies they use to distinguish between the two types of angles.

Customizing Instruction

Alternative Approach Working with partners, have each person write a series of directions. For example: a heading of 90 degrees, take three steps; a heading of 100 degrees, take five steps; a heading of 210 degrees, take two steps. After students have completed their directions, have them exchange directions with their partner and have each student carry out the directions. This activity can best be done outside or in a larger area than the classroom. Prior to stepping off the directions, have students predict where they will end up.

Career Information If your area has a Search and Rescue Team, invite someone from the team to speak to the students. Have them outline for the students their strategies for carrying out a search, the coordination involved, numbers of people and support members needed, etc. If there has been a recent search in the area, ask the member to give highlights of the search.

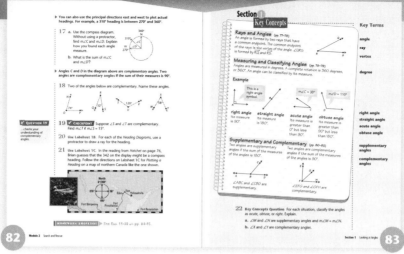

Exploration 2 continued

Writing Have students write in their Journals using their own words the definitions of complementary and supplementary angles, using diagrams to support their definitions.

Classroom Examples
Draw and label an angle that is complementary to the angle below. Then draw and label an angle that is supplementary to the angle below.

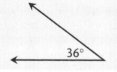

Answer: complementary angle:

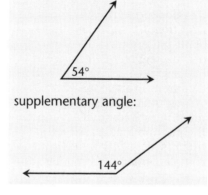

supplementary angle:

HOMEWORK EXERCISES

See the Suggested Assignment for Day 2 on page 2-13. For Exercise Notes, see page 2-13.

CLOSE

Closure Question How are individual angles classified and how are pairs of angles related?

Sample Response: Individual angles are classified by determining whether their measures are between 0° and 90°, equal to 90°, between 90° and 180°, or equal to 180°. Pairs of angles are classified as complementary or supplementary by determining whether the sum of their measures is 90° or 180°.

Customizing Instruction

Home Involvement Those helping students at home will find the Key Concepts on page 83 a handy reference to the key ideas, terms, and skills for Section 1.

Absent Students For students who have been absent for all or part of this section, the blackline Study Guide for Section 2 may be used to present the ideas, concepts, and skills of Section 1.

Extra Help For students who need additional practice, the blackline Practice and Applications for Section 1 provides additional exercises that may be used to confirm the skills of Section 1. The Extra Skill Practice on page 87 also provides additional exercises.

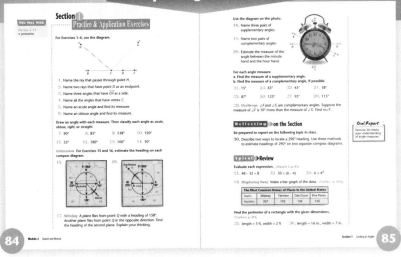

SUGGESTED ASSIGNMENT

Core Course
Day 1: Exs. 1–9, 12, 31–33
Day 2: Exs. 15, 16, 18–20,
22–28 even, 30, 34–36

Extended Course
Day 1: Exs. 1–9, 12, 31–33
Day 2: Exs. 15, 16, 18–20,
22–28 even, 29, 30,
34–36

Block Schedule
Day 1: Exs. 2, 4–9, 12, 15, 16,
18, 19, 22, 26, 30–36

EMBEDDED ASSESSMENT

These section objectives are
tested by the exercises listed.

**Name rays and angles with
symbols.**
Exercises 2, 4, 6

**Use a protractor to mea-
sure angles.**
Exercises 5, 6

**Use a protractor to draw
angles.**
Exercises 8, 9

**Classify angles as acute,
obtuse, right, or straight.**
Exercises 7–9, 12

**Recognize and find the
measures of complemen-
tary and supplementary
angles.**
Exercises 18, 19, 22, 26

**Estimate the measure of
an angle, including angles
greater than 180°.**
Exercises 15, 16

Practice & Application

EXERCISE NOTES

Developing Math Concepts
Exs. 7–14 and *Exs. 21–28*
require that students know the
definitions presented in this section. Check to be sure that students know the definitions. In
having students draw the heading in *Ex. 17*, it is important
that they first draw a ray to represent the North heading.

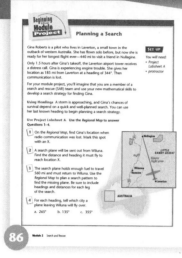

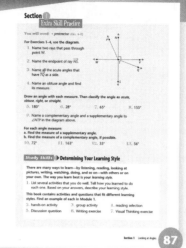

Each student will need a copy of Project Labsheet A and a protractor. As students plan the rescue, encourage them to be precise in their measuring and plotting. It is very helpful for students to draw in the North heading each time there is a change in direction.

Closing the Section

While learning how a Search and Rescue Team operates, students have explored angles. They have learned how to measure and classify angles. They have been presented numerous definitions pertaining to angles in order to be able to classify angles. Students have made real world connections in applying angles and angle measures to determining headings. *Reflecting on the Section Exercise 30* allows students to apply their knowledge of angle measure in more than one way.

The Study Skills on page 87 allows students to examine their learning style. This provides students with the knowledge to develop those learning style areas in which they may be weak.

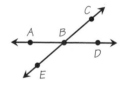

QUICK QUIZ ON THIS SECTION

1. Name two acute angles in the figure below.

2. Name two supplementary angles in the figure above.

3. What is the measure of an angle complementary to 40°? supplementary to 40°?

4. Draw the three angles in question 3.

5. Measure the heading.

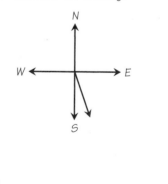

For answers, see Quick Quiz blackline on p. 2-62.

Section ② Integers and Coordinates

Section Planner

DAYS FOR MODULE 2

1 2 **3** **4** 5 6 7 8 9 10 11

SECTION 2

First Day
Setting the Stage, p. 88
Exploration 1, pp. 89–91

Second Day
Exploration 2, pp. 92–93
Key Concepts, p. 94

Block Schedule

Day 2
Setting the Stage, Exploration 1,
Exploration 2, Key Concepts

RESOURCE ORGANIZER

Teaching Resources
• Practice and Applications, Sec. 2
• Study Guide, Sec. 2
• Warm-Up, Sec. 2
• Quick Quiz, Sec. 2

Section Overview

In Section 2, students will extend the discussion of the mathematics used in a search and rescue operation to integers and the coordinate plane. Students will use familiar models such as temperature to compare integers. They will use familiar everyday models such as feet above sea level to discuss the *opposite* of an integer. In this context, they will explore the meaning of *absolute value*. By extending the number line to a coordinate grid, students will be able to discuss location in terms of *latitude* and *longitude*. They will also use the coordinate grid to investigate *intersecting*, *parallel*, and *perpendicular* lines. Students will identify the coordinates of a point on the coordinate grid and will learn to plot points on the grid. *Coordinate plane*, *origin*, and *ordered pair* are all defined in this section.

In the Module Project on page 99, students will plan a search. They will define their search area based on a grid of probability zones that help predict where a lost person might be found.

SECTION OBJECTIVES

Exploration 1
• use integers to represent real-life situations
• compare integers
• find the opposite of an integer
• find the absolute value of an integer

Exploration 2
• recognize parallel and perpendicular lines in a plane
• use coordinates to identify and plot points in a coordinate plane

ASSESSMENT OPTIONS

Checkpoint Questions
• Question 9 on p. 90
• Question 12 on p. 91
• Question 14 on p. 91
• Question 25 on p. 93

Embedded Assessment
• For a list of embedded assessment exercises see p. 2-20.

Performance Task/Portfolio
• Exercises 57–58 on p. 98 (challenge)
• Exercise 59 on p. 98 (visual thinking)
★ Module Project on p. 99
• Standardized Testing 1–5 on p. 100

★ = a problem solving task that can be assessed using the Assessment Scales

SECTION 2 MATERIALS

Exploration 2
◆ graph paper

Module Project on page 99
◆ Project Labsheet B

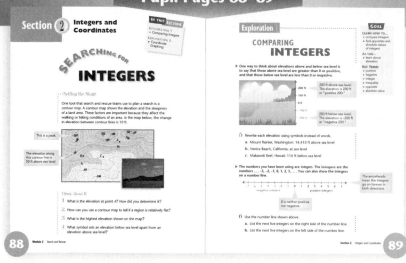

88 Module 2 Search and Rescue

Section 2 Integers and Coordinates **89**

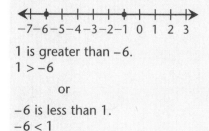

Setting the Stage

MOTIVATE

Have a topography map of the local area or state available for students to view. Ask them to determine the highest and lowest points in the area/state. Initiate a discussion as to why some of the contour lines are close to each other and others are a great distance apart. It would be helpful to bring in a three-dimensional model of an area, showing the contour lines for those students who are visual learners. If a model is not available, a simple model can be made by using cardboard. Have students check their geography books for contour maps.

Exploration 1

PLAN

Classroom Management
Exploration 1 is best performed working individually. It is helpful to have a horizontal and a vertical integer number line visible throughout the section. Adding machine tape can be used to make a number line that can be displayed.

GUIDE

Developing Math Concepts
Students need to understand that the set of integers contains the set of whole numbers and their opposites. Fractions and decimals are not included in the set of integers. However, students should be aware that positive and negative fractions and decimals do exist. Reinforce that zero is the only neutral point on the number line and all points to the right of zero are positive, while all points to the left of zero are negative.

Classroom Examples
Write two inequalities to compare −6 and 1. Use a number line to explain your answer.

Answer:

$$\longleftarrow \overset{\bullet}{\underset{-7\ -6\ -5\ -4\ -3\ -2\ -1\ \ \ 0\ \ \ 1\ \ \ 2\ \ \ 3}{|\!\!-\!\!|\!\!-\!\!|\!\!-\!\!|\!\!-\!\!|\!\!-\!\!|\!\!-\!\!|\!\!-\!\!\overset{\bullet}{|}\!\!-\!\!|\!\!-\!\!|}} \longrightarrow$$

1 is greater than −6.
1 > −6

            or

−6 is less than 1.
−6 < 1

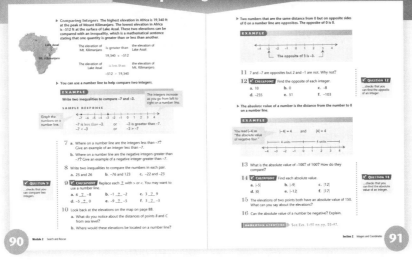

Exploration I continued

Developing Math Concepts

Question 7 develops the concept that when a point is picked on the number line, all points to the right of the point have values that are greater than that point and all points to the left of the point have a lesser value. When discussing the concept of absolute value, explain to students that they are measuring the distance a number is from zero. Distance is measured in positive values, therefore the absolute value of a number will be positive.

Classroom Examples

Use a number line to find the opposite of −6.

Answer:

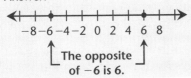

The opposite of −6 is 6.

Common Error When comparing integers, students often assume that the larger the digit (without regard to sign), the greater the value. For example, they would say that −8 is greater than −2. Have them refer back to the number line to see that −8 would lie to the left of −2. Therefore, −8 is less than −2.

Checkpoint *Question 9* checks students' understanding of comparing two integers. If students are having difficulty, encourage them to refer to the number line. As students do *Question 9*, have them write the integers, not just the greater than or less than symbol. This will help reinforce the meaning of the *greater than* and *less than* symbols.

Question 12 checks to see if students can find the opposite of an integer. Students should be able to verbalize that opposites have to be an equal distance from zero on the number line. Therefore, the digits will be the same, with one being positive and one being negative.

Question 14 checks to see if students understand the concept of absolute value. Students should be able to verbalize that absolute value determines the *distance* from zero on the number line. Therefore, it is always positive.

Classroom Examples

Use a number line to find |−2| and |2|.

Answer:

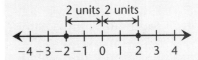

Since −2 is two units from 0, |−2| = 2. Since 2 is two units from 0, |2| = 2.

Visual Learners Have a horizontal and a vertical number line displayed for students to use as a reference.

HOMEWORK EXERCISES

See the Suggested Assignment for Day 1 on page 2-20. For Exercise Notes, see page 2-20.

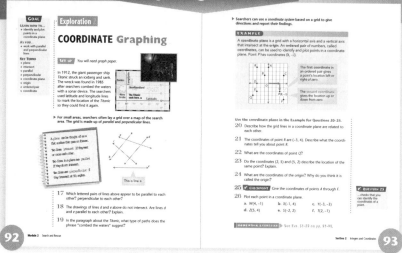

Exploration 2

PLAN

Classroom Management

Exploration 2 is best performed working individually. Each student will need graph paper. Graph paper can be cut in halves or fourths to save on paper.

GUIDE

Developing Math Concepts

Questions 17 and *18* check to see that students understand the definitions given. Have students give examples from the real world where intersecting, parallel, and perpendicular lines can be found. In graphing on a coordinate plane, students should understand that the coordinate plane is formed by the intersection of two number lines, one horizontal (the *x*-axis) and one vertical (the *y*-axis). Because the coordinate plane is two-dimensional, it takes two coordinates to name one point. In contrast, only one coordinate is needed to name a point on a number line.

Classroom Examples

Draw a coordinate plane with a horizontal axis and a vertical axis. Then plot and label the points *A*(−4, 3), *B*(5, 1), *C*(−3, −3), *D*(1, 0), and *E*(2, −5). Explain how you plotted each point.

Answer:

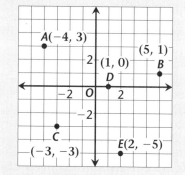

To plot point *A*, move 4 units left and 3 units up.
To plot point *B*, move 5 units right and 1 unit up.
To plot point *C*, move 3 units left and 3 units down.
To plot point *D*, move 1 unit right.
To plot point *E*, move 2 units right and 5 units down.

Common Error

When giving ordered pairs, students often mix up the *x*- and *y*-coordinates. Reinforce that *x* always comes before *y*, just as in the alphabet. Also make sure that each time students draw a coordinate plane, they label the *x*- and *y*-axis to reinforce which is which.

Visual Learners

When discussing the definitions of intersecting, parallel, and perpendicular lines, have students use two pencils to give examples of each.

Checkpoint

Question 25 checks to see if students can give the coordinates of a point. Reinforce that *x* is listed first in an ordered pair and is the distance right or left from zero; *y* is listed second and is a vertical distance. Check to make sure that when students are listing ordered pairs they place them in parentheses.

HOMEWORK EXERCISES

See the Suggested Assignment for Day 2 on page 2-20. For Exercise Notes, see page 2-20.

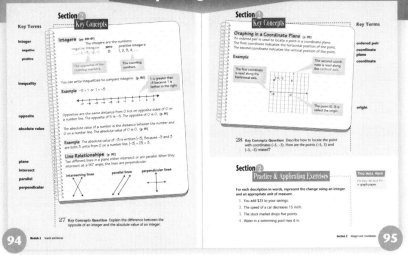

CLOSE

Closure Question How do perpendicular and parallel lines help you determine the coordinates of a point in a coordinate plane?

Sample Response: The axes of a coordinate plane are perpendicular lines. One is horizontal and the other is vertical. First move parallel to the horizontal axis to determine how far to the left or right of the vertical axis the point is. This tells you the first coordinate of the point. Then move parallel to the vertical axis to determine how far above or below the horizontal axis the point is. This tells you the second coordinate of the point.

Customizing Instruction

Home Involvement Those helping students at home will find the Key Concepts on pages 94–95 a handy reference to the key ideas, terms, and skills for Section 2.

Absent Students For students who were absent for all or part of this section, the blackline Study Guide for Section 2 may be used to present the ideas, concepts, and skills of Section 2.

Extra Help For students who need additional practice, the blackline Practice and Applications for Section 2 provides additional exercises that may be used to confirm the skills of Section 2. The Extra Skill Practice on page 100 also provides additional exercises.

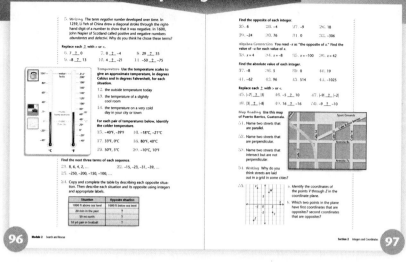

SUGGESTED ASSIGNMENT

Core Course

Day 1: Exs. 2–4, 6–10, 12–14,
16–20, 24, 26–31,
38–40, 42, 44, 45, 48

Day 2: Exs. 51–56, 59–67

Extended Course

Day 1: Exs. 2–4, 6–10, 12–14,
16–20, 24, 26–31,
38–40, 42, 44, 45, 48

Day 2: Exs. 51–67

Block Schedule

Day 2: Exs. 2–12 even, 13, 14,
16, 20–28 even, 31, 39,
42, 44, 48, 51–53, 55,
56, 59–67

EMBEDDED ASSESSMENT

These section objectives are tested by the exercises listed.

Use integers to represent real-life situations.

Exercises 2–4, 12–14

Compare integers.

Exercises 6, 8, 10, 16, 20

Find the opposite of an integer.

Exercises 24, 26, 28, 31

Find the absolute value of an integer.

Exercises 39, 42, 44, 48

Recognize parallel and perpendicular lines in a plane.

Exercises 51–53

Use coordinates to identify and plot points in a coordinate plane.

Exercises 55, 56

Practice & Application

EXERCISE NOTES

Background Information

Exs. 12–20 deal with two temperature scales. Discuss with students that the Fahrenheit scale is the one most generally used in everyday life in this country, while the Celsius scale is a metric scale and is used extensively throughout the rest of the world.

Developing Math Concepts

For *Exs. 33–36* point out to students that it is helpful to read $-x$ as the *opposite of x*. This concept is very important later when students will be doing integer operations. As students compare numbers, reinforce the importance of writing the numbers with the inequality symbols to avoid mistakes.

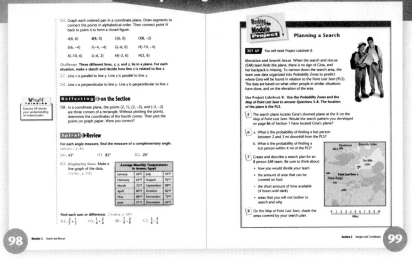

When answering *Questions 5–8* on page 99, have students work in groups of two. Each group of two will need a copy of Project Labsheet B. Students will need Project Labsheet A to answer *Question 5*. Have students present their search plan to the whole class, justifying the decisions they made. Discuss similarities and differences between various plans. If time permits, have students discuss how the search plans may vary due to different Point Last Seen locations.

Closing the Section

Students have used the real world connection of geography, land contour, and mapping to explore integers and coordinates. They have reinforced and formalized concepts while developing strategies for a search plan in a given area. *Reflecting on the Section Exercise 59* allows students to use their knowledge of the coordinate plane and ordered pairs to find a missing point.

QUICK QUIZ ON THIS SECTION

1. Represent this temperature change using an integer and an appropriate unit of measure: The temperature dropped 29°F.

2. Find the next three terms in the sequence 14, 8, 2, ...

3. What is the opposite of 18,942?

4. Is |−11| greater than or less than 10?

5. Graph (−2, −4), (3, −1), and (−5, 2) in a coordinate plane.

For answers, see Quick Quiz blackline on p. 2-63.

Section ③ Integer Addition and Subtraction

Section Planner

DAYS FOR MODULE 2

| 1 | 2 | 3 | 4 | 5 | 6 | 7 | 8 | 9 | 10 | 11 |

SECTION 3

First Day
Setting the Stage, p. 101
Exploration 1, pp. 102–103

Second Day
Exploration 2, pp. 103–105

Third Day
Exploration 3, pp. 106–108
Key Concepts, p. 109

Block Schedule

Day 3
Setting the Stage, Exploration 1,
Exploration 2

Day 4
Exploration 3, Key Concepts

RESOURCE ORGANIZER

Teaching Resources
• Practice and Applications, Sec. 3
• Study Guide, Sec. 3
• Mid-Module Quiz
• Warm-Up, Sec. 3
• Quick Quiz, Sec. 3

Section Overview

The rescue theme of this module continues in Section 3. The need of the search and rescue team to identify a location will introduce students to addition and subtraction of integers. Students will take hikes along a number line to model the integers. Then they will use their hikes along the number line to model integer addition and subtraction. Students will learn to add integers by making an initial move on the number line to represent the first addend. Then they will face the positive direction and move either forward or backward depending on the sign of the second addend. To model subtraction, students will face the negative direction before they move on the number line to model the integer being subtracted. Students will formulate rules for adding and subtracting integers. The number line models will help them see a related addition problem for each subtraction of integers problem. Their hikes will also model the *commutative* and *associative properties of addition*, which are the only new vocabulary words for this section.

SECTION OBJECTIVES

Exploration 1
• model moves on a number line with integers

Exploration 2
• add integers
• apply addition properties of 0 and opposites to integer addition
• apply the commutative and associative properties to integer addition

Exploration 3
• write subtraction of integers as a related addition problem
• subtract integers

ASSESSMENT OPTIONS

Checkpoint Questions
• Question 11 on p. 104
• Question 16 on p. 105
• Question 28 on p. 108

Embedded Assessment
• For a list of embedded assessment exercises see p. 2-28.

Performance Task/Portfolio
• Exercise 46 on p. 112 (challenge)
• Exercise 47 on p. 113 (journal)
• Module Project on p. 114
★ Extended Exploration on p. 116

★ = a problem solving task that can be assessed using the Assessment Scales

SECTION 3 MATERIALS

Exploration 1
◆ Labsheets 3A, 3B, and 3C
◆ scissors
◆ three paper clips

Exploration 2
◆ Labsheet 3C with data from Question 4

Module Project on page 114
◆ Project Labsheet C

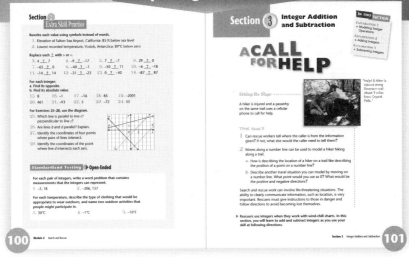

Setting the Stage

MOTIVATE

As students enter the classroom, give each student a card with an integer written on it. As soon as all students are in the classroom, have them form a human number line by ordering themselves from least to greatest using the integer card they were given. This will be a quick review of ordering integers, while getting the students ready for the Hiking activity.

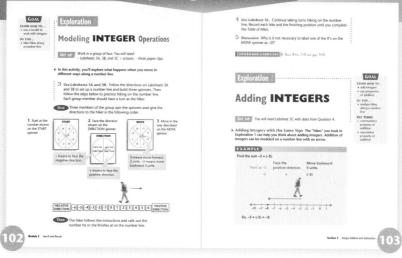

MODULE 2 ◆ SECTION 3

Exploration 1

PLAN

Classroom Management
Exploration 1 can best be performed by working in groups of four. Each group of four will need a copy of Labsheets 3A and 3B, a pair of scissors, and three paper clips. Each student will need a copy of Labsheet 3C. Have students construct their number line and spinners. Additional space may be necessary for all groups to place their number line on the floor. Keep the integers approximately one foot apart in order to facilitate students hiking along the number line. In answering *Question 1*, answers will vary based on whether students assume the trail passes by the waterfall or it ends at the waterfall.

GUIDE

Managing Time
If class time is short, have students cut out Labsheet 3A and construct the spinners the previous day. Allow ample time for students to complete Labsheet 3C.

Developing Math Concepts
In hiking along the number line, students should be able to verbalize that a positive three indicates a forward move, while a negative three indicates moving backward. Moving forward and backward are independent of the direction the hiker is facing. Check with each group to ensure they are "hiking" correctly.

Classroom Examples
Suppose 2 is spun on the START spinner, a – (minus sign) is spun on the DIRECTION spinner, and 3 is spun on the MOVE spinner. Describe what you would do to move the hiker to model this problem. Then give the hiker's finishing position.

Answer: Start at 2, face the negative direction, and move 3 units forward. The finishing position is –1.

▌HOMEWORK EXERCISES

See the Suggested Assignment for Day 1 on page 2-28. For Exercise Notes, see page 2-28.

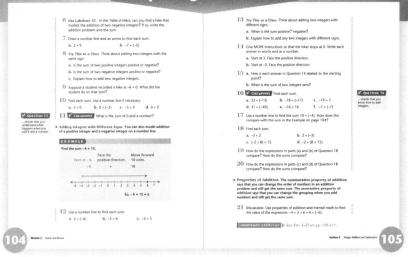

104 Module 2 Search and Rescue

Section 3 Integer Addition and Subtraction 105

Exploration 2

PLAN

Classroom Management
Exploration 2 can best be performed working individually. Each student will need Labsheet 3C. It would be helpful to students to have a paper with several integer number lines on it.

GUIDE

Developing Math Concepts
Students will be adding integers involving three different situations: adding a positive and a positive; a negative and a negative; and a positive and a negative, or a negative and a positive. Students should be able to verbalize that a positive plus a positive will always result in a positive sum; a negative plus a negative will always result in a negative sum; and a positive plus a negative or a negative plus a positive can result in either a positive or negative sum. Students should develop the concept that when adding a positive and a negative number, the sum is the difference of the absolute values of the numbers. Stress to students that anytime a number is added to it's opposite, the sum is zero. Students should formalize the concept that two numbers can be added in any order and the sum will be the same (Commutative Property). Students

should also formalize that when adding more than two numbers, numbers can be grouped differently in order to add, but the sum remains the same (Associative Property). As students become familiar with the addition properties, they should be able to apply them to facilitate solving problems such as in *Question 21*.

Classroom Examples
Find the sum −4 + (−2).

Answer:

Start at −4.	Face the positive direction.	Move backward 2 units.
− 4	+	(−2)

So, −4 + (−2) = −6.

Find the sum 7 + (−9).

Answer:

Start at 7.	Face the positive direction.	Move backward 9 units.
7	+	(−9)

So, 7 + (−9) = −2.

Checkpoint *Question 11* checks to see if students know the additive property of zero. This is a natural concept for them to understand and should be easy for them to explain. Have students give several examples. *Question 16* checks to see if students understand how to add integers. Should any student have problems with adding integers, you may wish to refer them to the Toolbox on pages 589–590 which uses an integer chip model. Students should be able to formalize and verbalize the rules for adding integers.

Writing Have students write in their journals the addition rules for integers, encouraging them to use mathematics shorthand: pos + pos = pos; neg + neg = neg; pos + neg or neg + pos = neg or pos. Have students give an example of each on a number line. Have students write definitions of the Commutative and Associative Properties in their own words, providing examples.

HOMEWORK EXERCISES

See the Suggested Assignment for Day 2 on page 2-28. For Exercise Notes, see page 2-28.

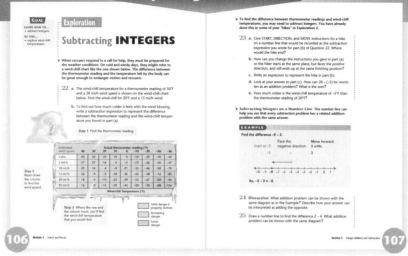

Exploration 3

PLAN

Classroom Management
Exploration 3 can best be performed working in groups of
two. It would be beneficial to
have an overhead of a wind chill
chart in order to demonstrate to
students how they are used.

GUIDE

Developing Math Concepts
After students have modeled
several integer subtraction problems on the number line, they
should begin to formalize the
concept that subtraction is the
inverse of addition. Give students a list of addition problems
and their corresponding subtraction problems. Students should
be able to conclude that subtracting an integer is the same as
adding that integer's opposite.
Students should understand that
addition and subtraction are
inverse operations.

Classroom Examples
Find the difference $-1 - (-4)$.

Answer:

Start at -1.	Face the negative direction.	Move backward 4 units.
-1	$-$	(-4)

So, $-1 - (-4) = 3$.

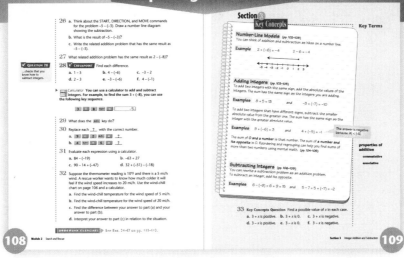

Exploration 3 continued

Common Error When subtracting integers, students will often rewrite the subtraction problem as an addition problem and take the opposite of both integers. Reinforce to students that when reading a subtraction problem such as $-5 - 10$ it is the same as a -5 plus the opposite of ten, which is $-5 + (-10)$. Once the integer subtraction problem is changed to an addition problem, students can apply the rules for integer addition that developed in Exploration 2.

Checkpoint *Question 28* checks to see if students can subtract integers. Should any student have problems with subtracting integers, you may wish to refer them to the Toolbox on pages 589–590 which uses an integer chip model. Have students orally give the related addition problem for each subtraction problem given.

Writing Have students write a rule for subtracting integers.

■ **HOMEWORK EXERCISES** ▶

See the Suggested Assignment for Day 3 on page 2-28. For Exercise Notes, see page 2-28.

CLOSE

Closure Question How does absolute value help you to add two integers?

Answer: Absolute value is helpful if the numbers you are adding have different signs. The sum will have the same sign as the number with the greater absolute value. If the numbers have different signs and equal absolute values, then they are opposites and their sum is 0, which is neither positive nor negative.

MODULE 2 ◆ SECTION 3

Customizing Instruction

Home Involvement Those helping students at home will find the Key Concepts on page 109 a handy reference to the key ideas, terms, and skills for Section 3.

Absent Students For students who were absent for all or part of this section, the blackline Study Guide for Section 3 may be used to present the ideas, concepts, and skills of Section 3.

Extra Help For students who need additional practice, the blackline Practice and Applications for Section 3 provides additional exercises that may be used to confirm the skills of Section 3. The Extra Skill Practice on page 115 also provides additional exercises.

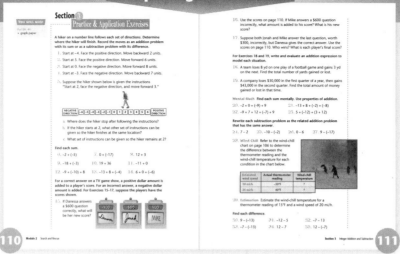

SUGGESTED ASSIGNMENT

Core Course
Day 1: Exs. 1–5, 48–53
Day 2: Exs. 6–12, 15, 16, 19–23
Day 3: Exs. 24–28, 30–32,
    37–42, 47

Extended Course
Day 1: Exs. 1–5, 48–53
Day 2: Exs. 6–12, 15, 16, 19–23
Day 3: Exs. 24–28, 30–32,
    37–42, 46, 47, 54, 55

Block Schedule
Day 3: Exs. 1–5, 6, 10, 12, 15,
    16, 20–23, 48–53
Day 4: Exs. 24–32, 38, 42, 47

EMBEDDED ASSESSMENT

These section objectives are
tested by the exercises listed.

**Model moves on a number
line with integers.**
Exercises 1–5

Add integers.
Exercises 6, 10, 12, 15, 16

**Apply addition properties
of 0 and opposites to integer addition.**
Exercises 20–23

**Apply the commutative
and associative properties
to integer addition.**
Exercises 20–23

**Write subtraction of inte-
gers as a related addition
problem.**
Exercises 24–27

Subtract integers.
Exercises 28, 30, 32, 38, 42

Practice & Application

EXERCISE NOTES

Visual Learners For *Exs. 6–14*
and *Exs. 30–35*, encourage students to use number lines if
they are having difficulty in
adding and subtracting integers.

Developing Math Concepts
For *Exs. 30–35* and *Exs. 39–44*
have students change each subtraction problem to the related
addition problem and apply the
rules they developed for addition to arrive at an answer.

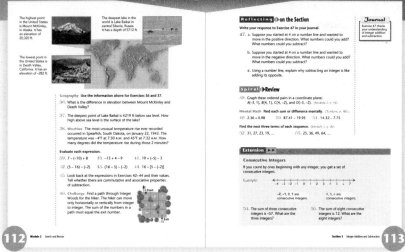

Practice & Application

Research For *Exs. 36* and *37*, you may wish to have students research Mount McKinley, Death Valley, and Lake Baikal. You may also wish to have students research the difference in elevation between the highest and lowest points on all seven continents.

Common Error In *Ex. 44* students may forget to work inside the parentheses first and do the exercise as 16 – 5 –(–2). Remind students that any operations inside parentheses must be done first. You may wish to have students work more exercises of this type to help solidify this point.

Developing Math Concepts Some students may think that since addition is commutative and associative, subtraction is also. *Ex. 45* should help dispel this incorrect notion.

Developing Math Concepts If your students have some familiarity with variables and equations you may wish to show them how to solve *Exs. 54* and *55* by using equations.

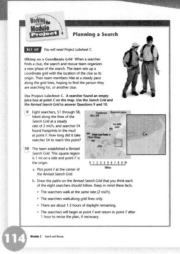

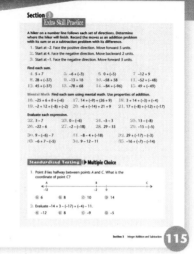

Each student will need a copy of Project Labsheet C. After students complete *Questions 9* and *10*, have them compare their results with a partner. Stress to students that searchers can only walk along the grid, thus traveling only horizontally or vertically on the grid, not diagonally.

Closing the Section

While examining wind-chill temperatures, students developed and formalized rules for the addition and subtraction of integers. In writing subtraction problems as addition problems, students made the mathematical connection that subtraction is the inverse of addition. *Reflecting on the Section Exercise 47* on page 113 allows students to demonstrate the modeling of addition and subtraction of integers on the number line, showing that the operations are inverses of each other.

QUICK QUIZ ON THIS SECTION

1. Find the sum −12 + 8.

2. Rewrite 2 − (−3) as the related addition problem that has the same answer. Solve.

3. Find the difference −20 − 41.

4. From −6°F at 6:00 A.M. the temperature rose 28°, then fell 35° by 9:00 P.M. Write and evaluate an addition expression to model the situation.

5. Find three possible values of x so that 5 − (−x) is negative, zero, and positive.

For answers, see Quick Quiz blackline on p. 2-64.

Section ④ Function Models

Section Planner

DAYS FOR MODULE 2

1 2 3 4 5 6 7 **8 9 10 11**

SECTION 4

First Day
Setting the Stage, p. 117
Exploration 1, pp. 118–120

Second Day
Exploration 2, pp. 121–122
Key Concepts, p. 124

Block Schedule

Day 5
Setting the Stage, Exploration 1,
Exploration 2, Key Concepts

RESOURCE ORGANIZER

Teaching Resources
• Practice and Applications, Sec. 4
• Study Guide, Sec. 4
• Technology Activity, Sec. 4
• Warm-Up, Sec. 4
• Quick Quiz, Sec. 4

Section Overview

In Section 4, students will explore how functions are used to understand search and rescue situations and to make decisions. Students will begin the section by using a table to model distance as a function of time. They will evaluate a variable expression to find the distance for a given time. Then, using a table of input and output values based on the distance formula, students will learn the meaning of a function. Key terms in the section are *evaluate*, *equation*, and *function*. Students will work with functions involving one or two operations. In Exploration 2, students will plot values on a location grid to represent a rescue vehicle's location in relation to its traveling time. After graphing two functions on the same grid, students will discuss how the graphs help them to compare and analyze the functions.

If graphing calculators are available to students, the technology page will show them how to use the calculators to study their graphs from Exploration 2. They will use the TRACE feature to estimate values for the function, or the INTERSECTION or TABLE features to find exact values.

SECTION OBJECTIVES

Exploration 1
• evaluate a variable expression involving integer addition and subtraction and whole number operations
• model a function with a table or an equation

Exploration 2
• model a function with a graph
• use graphs to compare linear functions

ASSESSMENT OPTIONS

Checkpoint Questions
• Question 9 on p. 120
• Question 12 on p. 120
• Question 17 on p. 122

Embedded Assessment
• For a list of embedded assessment exercises see p. 2-36.

Performance Task/Portfolio
• Exercise 25 on p. 126 (social studies)
• Exercise 28 on p. 127 (open-ended)
★ Exercise 32 on p. 127 (writing)
• Exercise 36 on p. 128 (discussion)
• Exercise 44 on p. 128 (career)
★ Standardized Testing on p. 129

★ = a problem solving task that can be assessed using the Assessment Scales

SECTION 4 MATERIALS

Exploration 2
◆ Labsheet 4A
◆ ruler

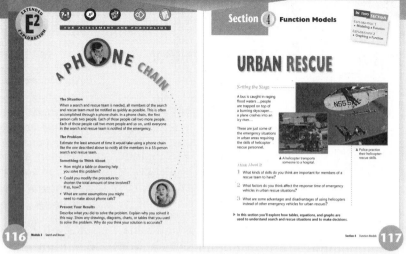

Setting the Stage

MOTIVATE

As students begin Section 4, display an overhead of a local or state newspaper clipping involving a situation in which a rescue team performed rescue operations. If your area has an emergency situation office, invite a guest speaker from that office or an Emergency Medical Technician to talk to your class about procedures they use when implementing a rescue plan or going on an ambulance call. Have students discuss the numbers of people involved and the equipment required to perform various rescue operations.

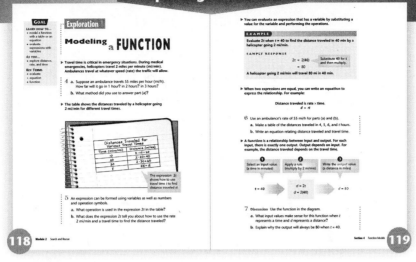

Exploration 1

PLAN

Classroom Management
Exploration 1 can best be performed working in groups of
two. Allow enough time for students to share their answers for
Questions 1 and *2* with the
whole class. Students like to discuss disasters. Therefore, monitor the amount of time allowed.
It will be beneficial for students
to have a quick review of order
of operations before beginning
Exploration 1.

GUIDE

Developing Math Concepts
Students will be using tables to
set up and evaluate functions.
Draw the mathematical connection between the table and the
function machines that were
used in Book 1. Students should
be able to verbalize the difference
between an expression and an
equation. Review the concept
that when a variable has a
numerical coefficient, the operation of multiplication is present.
Anytime a variable is written
with a numeral in front of it,
multiplication is to be performed.

Classroom Examples
Evaluate 2t when $t = 15$ to find
the distance traveled in 15 min
by a helicopter going 2 mi/min.

Answer: Substitute 15 for t and
then multiply.

$$2t = 2(15)$$
$$= 30$$

A helicopter going 2 mi/min will
travel 30 mi in 15 min.

Common Error When substituting for a variable in a multiplication expression, students will
sometimes forget to perform the
multiplication and simply write
the number in place of the variable. For example, in substituting
4 in the expression 2t, students
may write 24. Stress to students to
remember to do the multiplication. When working with expressions involving two operations
such as the **Example** on page
120, students will have a tendency to do the subtraction first,
then do the substitution, and
finally do the multiplication.
Encourage students to always
show the substitution first, then
perform the indicated operations
using the order of operations rule.

MODULE 2 ◆ SECTION 4

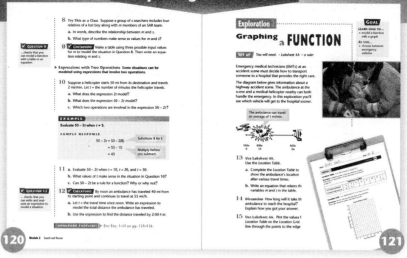

Exploration 1 continued

Developing Math Concepts

Make sure that students understand what *Question 8* is explaining to them. Students may come up with different representations, for example, $s = m + 4$, $s - m = 4$, or $s - 4 = m$. Discuss various representations and have students verbalize how they are similar.

Checkpoint *Question 9* checks to see if students can model a function with a table or use an equation to describe a function.

Ongoing Assessment Have students do *Question 9* in their journal. Check to see that they are setting up the table correctly, including a title, and identifying what each variable represents. Have students explain why they think the variables s and m were chosen.

Classroom Examples

Evaluate $76 + 2t$ when $t = 12$.

Answer: Substitute 12 for t and follow the order of operations.

$$76 + 2t = 76 + 2(12)$$
$$= 76 + 24$$
$$= 100$$

Checkpoint *Question 12* checks that students can write and evaluate an expression that models a situation. If students are having trouble evaluating expressions, make sure they are showing the substitution and using the order of operations.

▌ HOMEWORK EXERCISES ▶

See the Suggested Assignment for Day 1 on page 2-36. For Exercise Notes, see page 2-37.

Exploration 2

PLAN

Classroom Management

Exploration 2 can best be performed working in groups of two. Each person will need a copy of Labsheet 4A and a ruler. Have students fill out the Location Table working together and then individually graph the ordered pairs. Have partners compare their graphs to assure that they did not mix up the x- and y-coordinates.

GUIDE

Developing Math Concepts

As students plot the values from their function tables in *Questions 15* and *17*, they should conclude that in both cases a line was formed. These functions are linear equations. Therefore, students should understand that if the plotting of their ordered pairs doesn't form a line, they have made an error in completing the Location Table or in graphing the ordered pairs.

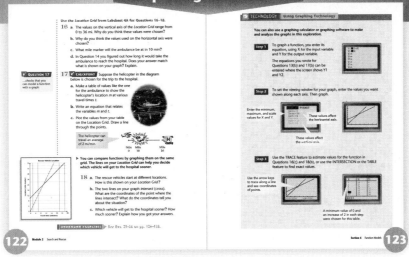

Exploration 2 continued

Classroom Examples

A number y is 2 more than 3 times another number x. Make a table, write an equation, and draw a graph of the equation.

Answer:

Input x	Output y
−2	−4
−1	−1
0	2

Equation: $y = 3x + 2$

Graph:

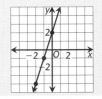

Checkpoint *Question 17*

checks to see that students can set up a function table, complete the table from the given information, plot the values on a graph, and draw conclusions from the information. Have students discuss how a function graph gives them information that may not be present in the function table.

HOMEWORK EXERCISES

See the Suggested Assignment for Day 2 on page 2-36. For Exercise Notes, see page 2-37.

CLOSE

Closure Question Suppose you are graphing a function and that you are using the first coordinates to represent input values. Can two different points have the same first coordinates? Explain.

Answer: No. For a function, there is only one output value for each input value.

MODULE 2 ♦ SECTION 4

Customizing Instruction

Background Information Almanacs usually contain much information on great disasters. You might want to have students consult an almanac to determine information about some of these disasters.

Technology Graphing calculators or graphing software can be used to set up function tables and graph functions. The information on page 123 explains how to use technology to analyze the graphs in Section 4. The screens displayed are those for a graphing calculator, but graphing software is similar. In Step 3, the Y_1 values are for the equation $Y_1 = 10 + X$. The Y_2 values are for the equation $Y_2 = 2X$.

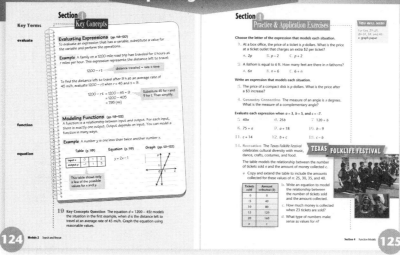

SUGGESTED ASSIGNMENT

Core Course

Day 1: Exs. 2–4, 8–12, 14, 16–18, 22, 24, 37–39

Day 2: Exs. 25, 27, 30, 32, 34, 36, 40–44

Extended Course

Day 1: Exs. 2–4, 8–12, 14, 16–18, 22, 24, 37–39

Day 2: Exs. 25, 27, 30, 32–34, 36, 40–44

Block Schedule

Day 5: Exs. 2–24 even, 25, 26, 30, 32, 34, 36–43

EMBEDDED ASSESSMENT

These section objectives are tested by the exercises listed.

Evaluate a variable expression involving integer addition and subtraction and whole number operations.

Exercises 8, 12, 16, 18, 22

Model a function with a table or an equation.

Exercises 14, 24

Model a function with a graph.

Exercises 25, 30

Use graphs to compare linear functions.

Exercises 32, 34

Customizing Instruction

Home Involvement Those helping students at home will find the Key Concepts on page 124 a handy reference to the key ideas, terms, and skills of Section 4.

Absent Students For students who were absent for all or part of this section, the blackline Study Guide for Section 4 may be used to present the ideas, concepts, and skills of Section 4.

Extra Help For students who need additional practice, the blackline Practice and Applications for Section 4 provides additional exercises that may be used to confirm the skills of Section 4. The Extra Skill Practice on page 129 also provides additional exercises.

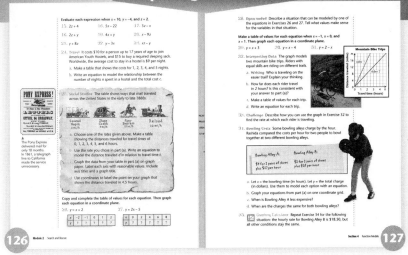

Practice & Application

Managing Time For *Exs. 25–27, 29–31*, and *34*, have graph paper and rulers available.

Research For *Ex. 25*, you may wish to have students do research on the Pony Express and the first transcontinental railroad.

Developing Math Concepts

For *Exs. 26–27* and *Exs. 29–31*, students should be aware that all the equations are linear equations. Therefore, if their graphs do not form lines, they have made a computational or a plotting error.

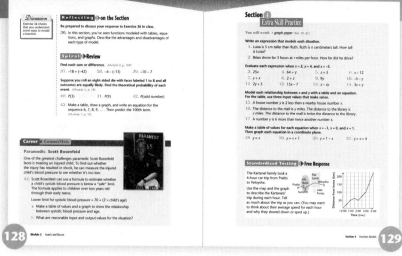

Practice & Application

Writing For *Ex. 36*, have students write the answer in their Journal, describing the advantages and disadvantages of each method. This will demonstrate their understanding of functions.

Closing the Section

Students have used their knowledge of equations, functions, and graphing to compare various rescue options. They have applied functions to the real world in order to make real-world and sometimes life-deciding decisions. They have formalized their understanding of how a graph can be used to obtain information not found in a function table and also to predict. *Reflecting on the Section Exercise 36* allows students to refine the knowledge they have obtained in this section, determining what display of information they feel is most useful as they examine real-world situations.

QUICK QUIZ ON THIS SECTION

1. Emily spends d dollars for dinner and m dollars for a movie. How much does she spend in all?

2. Evaluate $a^2 + b$ when $a = 4$ and $b = -5$.

3. It costs $5 for admission to an amusement park and $1.50 per ride. Write an equation to model the relationship between n, the number of rides taken, and c, the total cost.

4. Copy and complete the table of values for $y = 3x + 1$. Then graph the equation in a coordinate plane.

x	y
−2	
−1	
0	
1	
2	
3	

5. The speed limit on a stretch of highway is x mi/h. If a policeman travels 15 mi/h above the speed limit, how far will he go in 3 h?

For answers, see Quick Quiz blackline on p. 2-65.

Section ⑤ Addition and Subtraction Equations

Section Planner

DAYS FOR MODULE 2

1 2 3 4 5 6 7 8 9 **10** **11**

SECTION 5

First Day
Setting the Stage, p. 130–131
Exploration 1, pp. 131–134

Second Day
Exploration 2, pp. 134–136
Key Concepts, p. 137

Block Schedule

Day 6
Setting the Stage, Exploration 1,
Exploration 2, Key Concepts

RESOURCE ORGANIZER

Teaching Resources
• Practice and Applications, Sec. 5
• Study Guide, Sec. 5
• Module Tests Forms A and B
• Standardized Assessment
• Module Performance Assessment
• Cumulative Test Modules 1–2
• Warm-Up, Sec. 5
• Quick Quiz, Sec. 5

Section Overview

Students will begin their work in Section 5 by comparing the weights of the supplies that rescuers carry on rescues during different seasons of the year. The comparison will serve as a model for an equation. Using their models, they will discuss how rescuers can substitute supplies of equal weight and maintain the same total weight. Their models will help students to visualize an equation and see how the expressions on either side of an equation must be equal. They will then investigate the solutions of addition and subtraction equations with algebra tiles. *Solution of an equation, solving an equation* and *inverse operations* are key concepts of this section. Once students have solved equations with algebra tiles, they will learn to solve the equations algebraically using inverse operations. The importance of checking the solution to an equation will be discussed.

Students will also examine how they can solve equations such as $n + (-2) = 5$ using both addition and subtraction. If students will benefit from a review of adding and subtracting integers before they solve these equations, refer them to page 109 in Section 3.

SECTION OBJECTIVES

Exploration 1
• write an addition or subtraction equation to model a situation
• solve addition equations using an algebra tile model

Exploration 2
• solve addition and subtraction equations with integer solutions using inverse operations
• check a solution of an equation by substitution

ASSESSMENT OPTIONS

Checkpoint Questions
• Question 10 on p. 133
• Question 14 on p. 134
• Question 18 on p. 136
• Question 23 on p. 136

Embedded Assessment
• For a list of embedded assessment exercises see p. 2-44.

Performance Task/Portfolio
• Exercises 3–4 on p. 138 (open-ended)
• Exercise 46 on p. 140 (research)
• Exercises 58–63 on p. 141 (extension)
★ Standardized Testing on p. 142
★ Module Project on p. 143

★ = a problem solving task that can be assessed using the Assessment Scales

SECTION 5 MATERIALS

Exploration 1
◆ algebra tiles

Review and Assessment on p. 144
◆ protractor
◆ graph paper

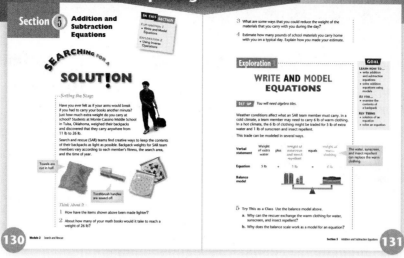

Setting the Stage

MOTIVATE

At the beginning of Section 5, have a balance scale available to demonstrate to students how a balance scale works. Use items that can be found in your classroom to show two different items or groups of items that have the same weight and then ask students to exchange the items on one side of the scale with alternative items. Base ten blocks can be used. Packaged food items also work well.

Exploration I

PLAN

Classroom Management

Exploration 1 can best be performed working individually. Each student will need a set of algebra tiles. If there are not enough algebra tiles, have students work in groups of two or three. If algebra tiles are available for student use, it is very helpful to have an overhead set of algebra tiles for demonstration purposes and for students to present their solutions to the class. If algebra tiles are not available, you can substitute beans and a cup, colored rods, or chips. Be sure to allow time for class discussion on *Question 5*.

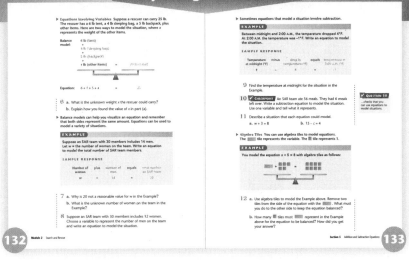

GUIDE

Developing Math Concepts

The **Example** on page 132 gives a sample of an equation that models the situation involved. Prompt students to model the situation using different equations than the one given. Students should make the connection between the different equations and the fact families they learned in elementary school. As students begin to solve equations it is beneficial that they remember two key ideas: (1) The goal in solving any equation is to get the variable by itself on one side of the equal sign with a positive one as its numerical coefficient; (2) Whenever working with equations, whatever you do on one side of the equal sign, you must do the exact same thing on the other side of the equal sign.

Classroom Examples

Suppose an SAR team carries 15 pieces of equipment that include 8 flares. Let s = the number of other pieces of equipment. Write an equation to model the total number of pieces of equipment that the SAR team carries.

Answer:

Number of other equipment plus number of flares equals

$$s + 8 = 15$$

total number of pieces of equipment

While searching, an SAR rescue team had to travel 50 ft down a hill to avoid an obstacle. When they finished their descent, they were at an elevation of 1350 ft. Write an equation to model the situation.

Sample Answer:

Elevation at the top of the hill minus descent equals

$$e - 50 = 1350$$

elevation at bottom of hill

Model the equation $x + 4 = 9$ with algebra tiles.

Answer:

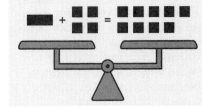

Visual Learners For those student having difficulty solving equations, provide ample opportunities for them to use the algebra tiles to solve equations. As students use the algebra tiles, have them verbalize what they are doing in each step and then record on paper what mathematics is occurring at each step.

Checkpoint *Question 10* checks that students can use equations to model situations. Insist that when students use a variable they always write what the variable represents. Students should understand that various equations can model the same situation. *Question 14* on page 134 checks that students can use a model to solve an addition equation. Using overhead algebra tiles, have various students model solving an addition equation for the class. Students should explain what mathematics they are using as they solve the equation.

HOMEWORK EXERCISES

See the Suggested Assignment for Day 1 on page 2-44. For Exercise Notes, see page 2-44.

MODULE 2 ◆ SECTION 5

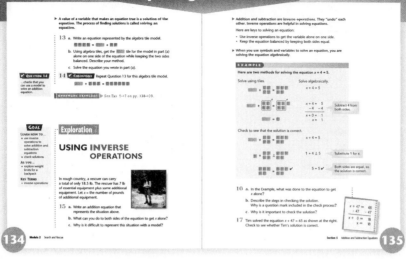

Exploration 2

PLAN

Classroom Management
Exploration 2 is best performed working individually. Have algebra tiles available for those students who may need them. Review with students the mathematical concept that any number plus its opposite is equal to zero.

GUIDE

Developing Math Concepts
As students solve equations, it is essential that they understand that an equal sign in an equation means that quantities on each side of the equal sign have the same value. Therefore, whatever operation is performed on one side of the equal sign, the exact same operation must be performed on the other side in order that the equal sign remains valid. Remind students they have been exposed to the concept of inverse operations in Section 3 when they changed subtraction problems to addition problems while subtracting integers.

For most of the examples given in Exploration 2, average and above average students will be able to simply look at the equation and mentally substitute for the variable to arrive at a solution for the equation. Provide more difficult exercises for those students in order that they practice the procedure for solving an equation. It is important to always have students substitute their solution into the equation to check if it is correct.

Common Error When solving subtraction problems students will often disregard the subtraction sign in the equation, and thus subtract the number given from each side of the equation. It is helpful to have students change the subtraction problems to addition problems and then use the additive inverse to obtain the sum of zero on the side of the equation with the variable.

Checkpoint *Question 18* on page 136 checks that students understand how inverse operations can be used to solve equations. Have students be prepared to discuss how the equations are solved. *Question 23* checks to see if students understand how to substitute their solution into the original equation to see if it is a correct solution. Require students to check each equation they solve in this section.

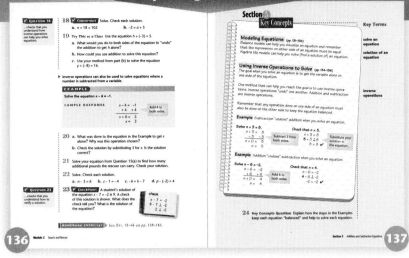

Exploration 2 continued

Classroom Examples

Use algebra tiles and algebra to solve the equation $x + 6 = 10$.

Answer:
Solve using tiles.

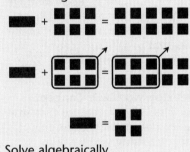

Solve algebraically.

$$x + 6 = 10 \quad \text{Subtract 6 from}$$
$$\underline{-6 \quad -6} \quad \text{both sides.}$$
$$x + 0 = \quad 4$$
$$\qquad x = \quad 4$$

Solve the equation $x - 7 = -11$.

Answer:
$$x - 7 = -11$$
$$\underline{+ 7 \quad + 7} \quad \text{Add 7 to both}$$
$$x + 0 = \quad -4 \quad \text{sides}$$
$$\qquad x = \quad -4$$

▶ HOMEWORK EXERCISES

See the Suggested Assignment for Day 2 on page 2-44. For Exercise Notes, see page 2-44.

CLOSE

Closure Question Describe how to choose an operation to solve an addition or subtraction equation.

Answer: Choose the inverse operation. If a number is added to the variable on one side of the equation, then subtract that number from both sides. If a number is subtracted from the variable on one side of the equation, then add that number to both sides.

Customizing Instruction

Home Involvement Those helping students at home will find the Key Concepts on page 137 a handy reference to the key ideas, terms, and skills of Section 5.

Absent Students For students who were absent for all or part of this section, the blackline Study Guide for Section 5 may be used to present the ideas, concepts, and skills of Section 5.

Extra Help For students who need additional practice, the blackline Practice and Applications for Section 5 provides additional exercises that may be used to confirm the skills of Section 5. The Extra Skill Practice on page 142 also provides additional exercises.

MODULE 2 ◆ SECTION 5

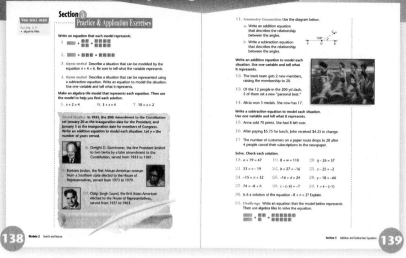

SUGGESTED ASSIGNMENT

Core Course
Day 1: Exs. 2–8, 10–12, 16, 47–52

Day 2: Exs. 20–28 even, 30, 36–44 even, 45, 53–57

Extended Course
Day 1: Exs. 2–8, 10–12, 16, 47–52

Day 2: Exs. 20, 24, 28, 30, 31, 36, 40, 44–46, 53–63

Block Schedule
Day 6: Exs. 4–7, 10–12, 16, 20, 24, 28, 30, 36, 40, 44–57

EMBEDDED ASSESSMENT

These section objectives are tested by the exercises listed.

Write an addition or subtraction equation to model a situation.

Exercises 4, 10–12, 16

Solve addition equations using an algebra tile model.

Exercises 5–7

Solve addition and subtraction equations with integer solutions using inverse operations.

Exercises 24, 28, 36, 40, 45

Check a solution of an equation by substitution.

Exercises 20, 24, 28, 30

Practice & Application

EXERCISE NOTES

Social Studies For *Ex. 8*, point out that the longest term in office for a U.S. President was that of Franklin D. Roosevelt. He served for 12 years from 1933 to 1945. The shortest term in office was that of William Henry Harrison who only served 32 days in 1841.

Developing Math Concepts For *Exs. 12–17*, require that students always list the variable they are using and write in words what the variable represents. Students should understand that various variables can be used to represent the same thing as long as the variable is identified.

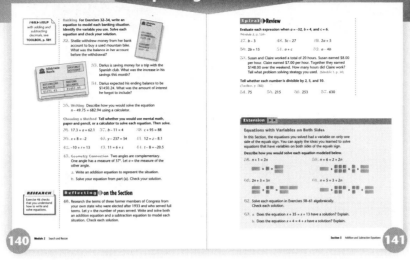

Practice & Application

Review For *Exs. 32–44*, a review of decimal addition and subtraction would be beneficial to students.

Developing Math Concepts In solving equations with variables on both sides such as those in *Exs. 58–61*, students should conclude that inverse operations can be used to get all of the variables on one side of the equal sign in the same way they used inverse operations to get the just one variable alone on one side of the equal sign. It is extremely helpful to use algebra tiles to model this situation.

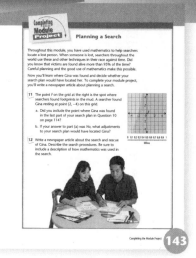

Closing the Section

While examining different search and rescue techniques, studying contour maps and elevations, using wind-chill tables, and exploring backpack weights, students have expanded their knowledge of integers, functions, and solving equations. They have used algebra tiles to model equation solving and formalize steps in solving equations. They have used graphs and technology to develop function concepts and to show how graphs of functions can provide information. They have formalized rules for addition and subtraction of integers. *Reflecting on the Module in Exercise 38* on page 145 has students summarizing the concepts and mathematics they learned in the module. All students should be prepared to report orally on the concepts learned in Module 2.

QUICK QUIZ ON THIS SECTION

1. Write an equation represented by the algebra tile model.

2. Write an addition or subtraction equation to model the following situation. Use one variable and tell what it represents.

   During a flu epidemic 14 students were absent, leaving only 11 in the class.

3. Solve $-20 + n = 32$.

4. Is 21 a solution of $-24 = m - 3$?

5. Two angles are supplementary. One angle has a measure of 82°. Let d = the measure of the other angle. Write and solve the related addition equation.

For answers, see Quick Quiz blackline on p. 2-66.

Completing the Module Project

Have students be prepared to discuss their answer for *Question 11(b)*. After students have finished *Question 11*, discuss as a class *Question 12*. Make sure that students understand they will be writing an article about Gina's rescue. Encourage students to use diagrams if it helps in their explanation. Have students be prepared to read their articles to the class. Provide bulletin board space to display various student newspaper articles.

MODULE 2 LABSHEET **1A**

Types of Angles (Use with Question 10 on page 79.)

Directions Use a protractor to measure each angle.

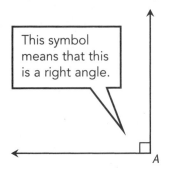

This symbol means that this is a right angle.

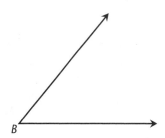

a. _____ degrees
a *right* angle

b. _____ degrees
an *acute* angle

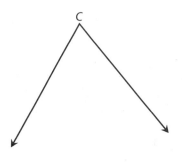

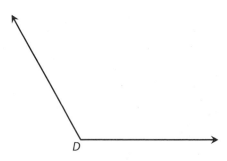

c. _____ degrees
an *acute* angle

d. _____ degrees
an *obtuse* angle

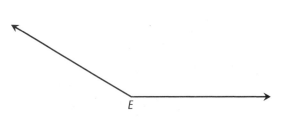

e. _____ degrees
an *obtuse* angle

f. _____ degrees
a *straight* angle

Name _____   Date _____

Heading Diagrams (Use with Questions 13 and 20 on pages 81–82.)

Directions Draw rays on these diagrams to represent headings.

a. 20° heading

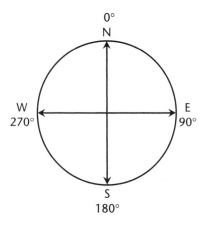

b. 120° heading

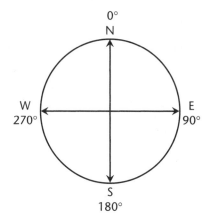

c. 225° heading

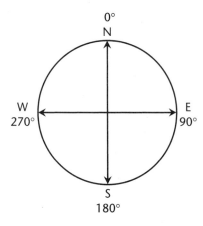

d. 345° heading

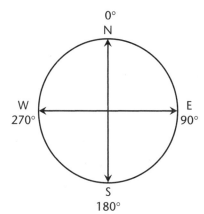

MODULE 2   **LABSHEET** **1C**

Plotting a Heading (Use with Question 21 on page 82.)

Directions In the reading from *Hatchet* in your textbook, Brian guesses that the 342 on the display might be a compass heading. Suppose Brian's plane is at the center of the compass diagram on the map below.

a. Estimate a heading of 342° by drawing a dashed ray on the compass diagram.

b. Use a protractor to measure a heading of 342°. Use a solid ray to plot the heading. How do the two rays compare?

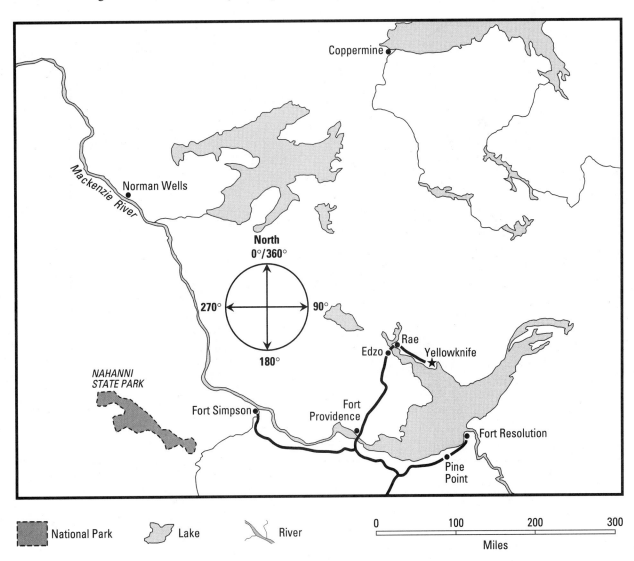

MODULE 2

PROJECT LABSHEET **A**

Regional Map (Use with Questions 1–4 on page 86.)

Directions Use headings to plan your initial search strategy.

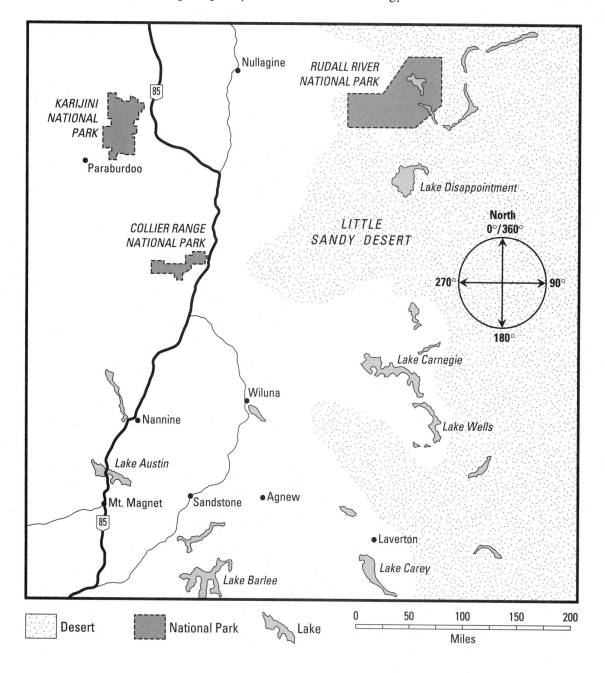

MODULE 2   **PROJECT LABSHEET** ⒝

Map of Point Last Seen (Use with Questions 5, 7, and 8 on page 99.)

Directions Use the *Map of Point Last Seen* as you refine your search plan.

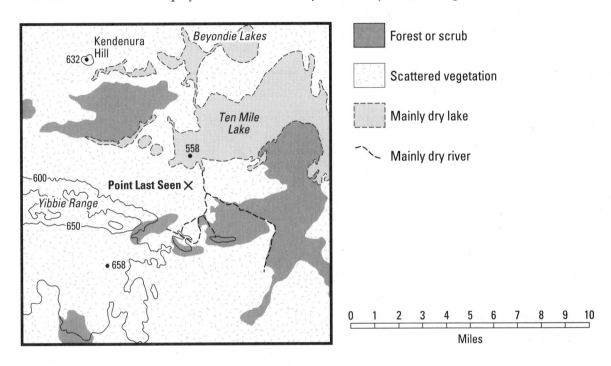

Probability Zones (Use with Questions 6–7 on page 99.)

Directions Use the chart of *Probability Zones* to help you predict where Gina will be found relative to the Point Last Seen (PLS).

9% of victims are found uphill from the PLS and within 1 mi of the PLS.

Probability Zones					
	Within 1 mi	Between 1 and 2 mi	Between 2 and 3 mi	Between 3 and 4 mi	Beyond 4 mi
Walk uphill	9%	10%	9%	0%	0%
Walk downhill	14%	18%	2%	2%	4%
Walk on same level	7%	16%	9%	0%	0%

Example: The probability that a victim will be found within 2 mi of the
PLS is as follows: 9% + 10% + 14% + 18% + 7% + 16% = 74%.

MODULE 2   LABSHEET 3A

Number Line Markers   (Use with Question 3 on page 102.)

Directions Cut out these number line markers. Arrange the markers on the floor from least to greatest to create a number line. Place them about 1 ft apart.

−6	**−5**	**−4**	**−3**
−2	**−1**	**0**	**1**
2	**3**	**4**	**5**
6	**POSITIVE DIRECTION**		
	NEGATIVE DIRECTION		

MODULE 2 **LABSHEET** **3B**

Spinner for Hiking   (Use with Question 3 on page 102.)

Directions

• Cut out each spinner along the rectangular border.

• Unfold three paper clips to use as pointers for the spinners.

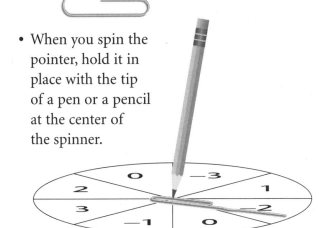

• When you spin the pointer, hold it in place with the tip of a pen or a pencil at the center of the spinner.

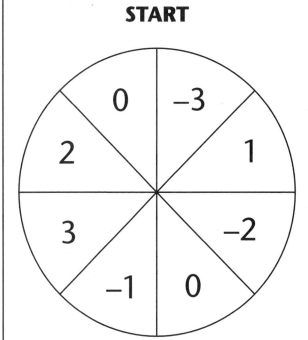

START

0	–3
2	1
3	–2
–1	0

DIRECTION

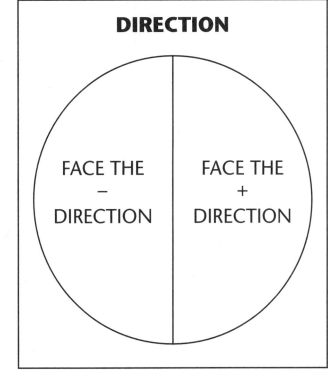

FACE THE – DIRECTION

FACE THE + DIRECTION

MOVE

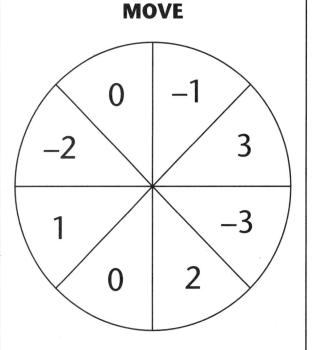

0	–1
–2	3
1	–3
0	2

MODULE 2 ——————————————————————————————— **LABSHEET** **3C**

Table of Hikes (Use with Question 4 on page 103, and Question 6 on page 104.)

Directions Take turns hiking on your number line as described on page 102. Record each hike and the finishing position in the table. Continue until the table is full.

Hiker's name	Started at	Direction faced	Moved		Finishing position
Example	2 The starting position of the hike is 2.	– – tells the hiker to face the negative direction.	–3 –3 tells the hiker to move backward 3 units.	=	5
				=	
				=	
				=	
				=	
				=	
				=	
				=	
				=	
				=	
				=	
				=	
				=	

MODULE 2   **PROJECT LABSHEET**

Search Grid (Use with Question 9 on page 114.)

Directions Use the grid to find how long it took searcher S4 to find footprints in the mud at point *F*.

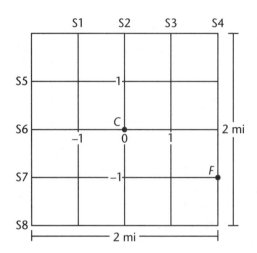

....

Revised Search Grid (Use with Question 10 on page 114.)

Directions Plot point *F*, your starting point, at the origin in the center of the grid and draw the paths that you think the searchers should follow based on the information in Question 10.

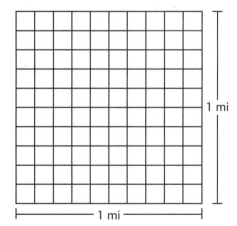

MODULE 2   **LABSHEET** (4A)

Location Table (Use with Question 13 on page 121.)

Directions Complete the table to show the ambulance's location
(mile marker) at various times. Use the information in the diagram
on page 121.

Ambulance Location								
Travel time (minutes)	0	4	8	12	16	20	24	t
Location (mile marker)	10	14						m

Location Grid (Use with Questions 15–18 on pages 121–122.)

Directions Plot the values from the table above on the grid below.
Draw a line through the points to the edge of the grid.

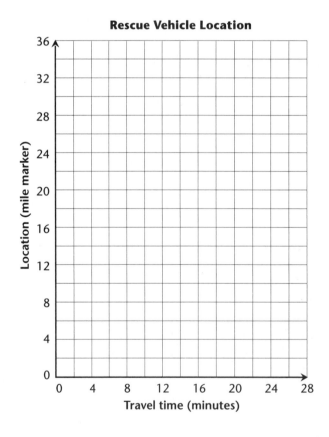

Rescue Vehicle Location

Name _____ Problem _____

☆ *The star indicates that you excelled in some way.*

Problem Solving

|———1———2———3———4———5———→☆→|

① You did not understand the problem well enough to get started or you did not show any work.

③ You understood the problem well enough to make a plan and to work toward a solution.

⑤ You made a plan, you used it to solve the problem, and you verified your solution.

Mathematical Language

|———1———2———3———4———5———→☆→|

① You did not use any mathematical vocabulary or symbols, or you did not use them correctly, or your use was not appropriate.

③ You used appropriate mathematical language, but the way it was used was not always correct or other terms and symbols were needed.

⑤ You used mathematical language that was correct and appropriate to make your meaning clear.

Representations

|———1———2———3———4———5———→☆→|

① You did not use any representations such as equations, tables, graphs, or diagrams to help solve the problem or explain your solution.

③ You made appropriate representations to help solve the problem or help you explain your solution, but they were not always correct or other representations were needed.

⑤ You used appropriate and correct representations to solve the problem or explain your solution.

Connections

|———1———2———3———4———5———→☆→|

① You attempted or solved the problem and then stopped.

③ You found patterns and used them to extend the solution to other cases, or you recognized that this problem relates to other problems, mathematical ideas, or applications.

⑤ You extended the ideas in the solution to the general case, or you showed how this problem relates to other problems, mathematical ideas, or applications.

Presentation

|———1———2———3———4———5———→☆→|

① The presentation of your solution and reasoning is unclear to others.

③ The presentation of your solution and reasoning is clear in most places, but others may have trouble understanding parts of it.

⑤ The presentation of your solution and reasoning is clear and can be understood by others.

Content Used: _____ **Computational Errors:** Yes ☐ No ☐

Notes on Errors: _____

Name _____ Problem _____

 STUDENT | **SELF-ASSESSMENT SCALES**

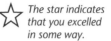 If your score is in the shaded area, explain why on the back of this sheet and stop.

☆ The star indicates that you excelled in some way.

 Problem Solving

❶   ❷   ❸   ❹   ❺   ☆

I did not understand the problem well enough to get started or I did not show any work.

I understood the problem well enough to make a plan and to work toward a solution.

I made a plan, I used it to solve the problem, and I verified my solution.

 Mathematical Language

❶   ❷   ❸   ❹   ❺   ☆

I did not use any mathematical vocabulary or symbols, or I did not use them correctly, or my use was not appropriate.

I used appropriate mathematical language, but the way it was used was not always correct or other terms and symbols were needed.

I used mathematical language that was correct and appropriate to make my meaning clear.

 Representations

❶   ❷   ❸   ❹   ❺   ☆

I did not use any representations such as equations, tables, graphs, or diagrams to help solve the problem or explain my solution.

I made appropriate representations to help solve the problem or help me explain my solution, but they were not always correct or other representations were needed.

I used appropriate and correct representations to solve the problem or explain my solution.

 Connections

❶   ❷   ❸   ❹   ❺   ☆

I attempted or solved the problem and then stopped.

I found patterns and used them to extend the solution to other cases, or I recognized that this problem relates to other problems, mathematical ideas, or applications.

I extended the ideas in the solution to the general case, or I showed how this problem relates to other problems, mathematical ideas, or applications.

 Presentation

❶   ❷   ❸   ❹   ❺   ☆

The presentation of my solution and reasoning is unclear to others.

The presentation of my solution and reasoning is clear in most places, but others may have trouble understanding parts of it.

The presentation of my solution and reasoning is clear and can be understood by others.

A Phone Chain (E² on textbook page 116)

Solutions to this problem will vary depending on the amount of time students estimate each phone call will take and how the calls are made. All of the *Math Thematics* Assessment Scales can be used to assess students' solutions, but the problem does not provide much opportunity to use mathematical vocabulary, so you may not want to score them on the Mathematical Language Scale.

Each sample response below shows part of a student's solution.

Partial Solution

I decided a call would last about 30 seconds. I got 30 seconds by having my friend call me and give directions about where to meet and stuff. It took about 27 seconds, so I rounded to 30. My approach was to draw a diagram.

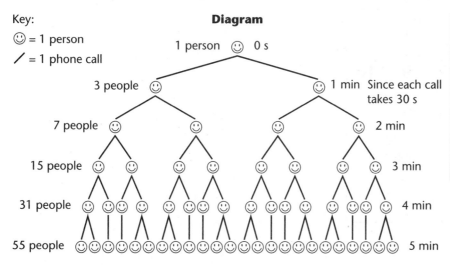

Key:
☺ = 1 person
╱ = 1 phone call

Level	Total number called	Total time
1	1	0 s
2	3	1 min
3	7	2 min
4	15	3 min
5	31	4 min
6	55	5 min

My solution to this problem is that it takes 5 minutes for the phone chain to finish.

Partial Solution

I decided a call would take about 30 seconds and that people would start making their calls as soon as they were called. I drew a diagram of the calls.

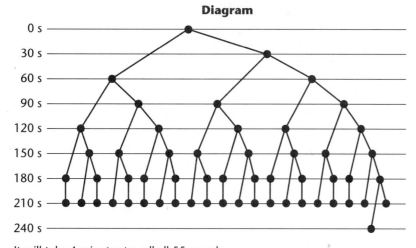

Time	People called	Total number called
0	1	1
30 s	1	2
1 min	2	4
90 s	3	7
2 min	5	12
150 s	8	20
3 min	13	33
210 s	21	54
4 min	1	55

It will take 4 minutes to call all 55 people.

MODULE 2   **ALTERNATE E²**

A Calendar Problem

The Situation

Take the calendar page for any month of the year and choose any 3 by 3 array of dates on it as shown below. What is the sum of the numbers in the array?

\begin{array}{c} \textbf{\textit{January}} \end{array}						
Sun.	*Mon.*	*Tues.*	*Wed.*	*Thurs.*	*Fri.*	*Sat.*
				1	2	3
4	5	6	7	8	9	10
11	12	13	14	15	16	17
18	19	20	21	22	23	24
25	26	27	28	29	30	31

The Problem

How is the sum of the numbers in any 3 by 3 array on a month of a calendar page related to the middle number in the array?

Something to Think About

- How is each number in a calendar related to the number in the row above it?
- How is each number in a calendar related to the number to its left?

Present Your Results

Tell how the sum of the numbers in any 3 by 3 array on the calendar page for any month is related to the middle number in the array. Explain how you know this is always true.

A Calendar Problem

There is only one solution to this problem, but students' approaches and reasoning will vary. All of the *Math Thematics* Assessment Scales can be used to assess students' solutions, but the problem does not provide much opportunity to use mathematical terms, so you may not want to score students on the Mathematical Language Scale.

Each sample response below shows part of a student's solution.

Partial Solution

I tried several 3 by 3 arrays on different pages of a calendar, and in every one of them the sum of the numbers in the array was 9 times the middle number. I decided this must always be true, but I wasn't sure why. After studying the example for a while, it hit me.

Pick a number on a calendar page. The number to its left is one less than the number and the number to its right is one more than the number so the three numbers must add up to 3 times the number you started with. In the example:

$$12 + 13 + 14 = (13 - 1) + 13 + (13 + 1)$$
$$= 13 + 13 + 13 - 1 + 1$$
$$= 3 \cdot 13$$

Also, each number in the top row of the array is 7 less than the number below it and each number in the bottom row is 7 more than the number above it. So the sum of the numbers in the top row is 21 less than the sum of the numbers in the middle row and the sum of the numbers in the bottom row is 21 more. In the example:

$$5 + 6 + 7 = (12 - 7) + (13 - 7) + (14 - 7) \quad \text{and} \quad 19 + 20 + 21 = (12 + 7) + (13 + 7) + (14 + 7)$$
$$= (12 + 13 + 14) - 7 - 7 - 7 \qquad\qquad\qquad = (12 + 13 + 14) + 7 + 7 + 7$$
$$= (12 + 13 + 14) - 21 \qquad\qquad\qquad\qquad = (12 + 13 + 14) + 21$$

That means that if you add the numbers in the top row and the numbers in the bottom row, the sum will be twice the sum of the numbers in the middle row. When you add the numbers in the middle row to the sum, the result is 3 times the sum of the numbers in the middle row or 3 times 3 times the middle number or 9 times the middle number.

Partial Solution

The numbers in a 3 by 3 array on a calendar page are related as shown below.

$n-8$	$n-7$	$n-6$
$n-1$	n	$n+1$
$n+6$	$n+7$	$n+8$

Sum $= (n + 8) + (n + 7) + (n + 6) + (n + 1) + n + (n - 8) + (n - 7) + (n - 6) + (n - 1)$
$= (n + n + n + n + n + n + n + n + n) + (8 + 7 + 6 + 1) - (8 + 7 + 6 + 1)$
$= 9n + 0$
$= 9n$

So the sum of the numbers in the array will always be 9 times the middle number.

Other Considerations

• Students may also extend the solution to 5 by 5 arrays, 7 by 7 arrays, etc.

Illustrate each term with a drawing and state its dimension.

1. point   **2** line   **3.** plane   **4.** cube

MODULE 2 SECTION 1   **QUICK QUIZ**

1. Name two acute angles in the figure below.

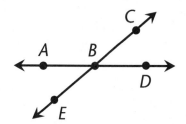

2. Name two supplementary angles in the figure above.

3. What is the measure of an angle complementary to 40°? supplementary to 40°?

4. Draw the three angles in question 3.

5. Measure the heading.

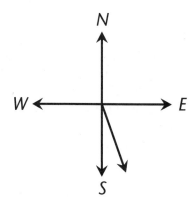

ANSWERS

Warm-Ups: 1. •; no dimension   **2.** ⟷; 1 dimension

3. ⟋‾‾‾⟍; 2 dimensions   **4.** ◻; 3 dimensions

Quick Quiz: 1. ∠ABE and ∠CBD   **2.** Sample Response: ∠ABC and ∠CBD   **3.** 50°; 140°

4. 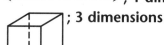 40°   50°   140°   **5.** 160°

MODULE 2 SECTION 2 — WARM-UPS

Compare the two given numbers. Use <, >, or =.

1. 21 ___?___ 12
2. 8 ___?___ 6
3. 6 ___?___ 8
4. 4.00 ___?___ 4
5. 0.09 ___?___ 0.0900
6. 0 ___?___ 0.1

MODULE 2 SECTION 2 — QUICK QUIZ

1. Represent this temperature change using an integer and an appropriate unit of measure: *The temperature dropped 29°F.*
2. Find the next three terms in the sequence 14, 8, 2, … .
3. What is the opposite of 18,942?
4. Is $|-11|$ greater than or less than 10?
5. Graph (–2, –4), (3, –1), and (–5, 2) in a coordinate plane.

ANSWERS

Warm-Ups: **1.** > **2.** > **3.** < **4.** = **5.** = **6.** <

Quick Quiz: **1.** –29° **2.** –4, –10, –16 **3.** –18,942 **4.** greater than **5.**

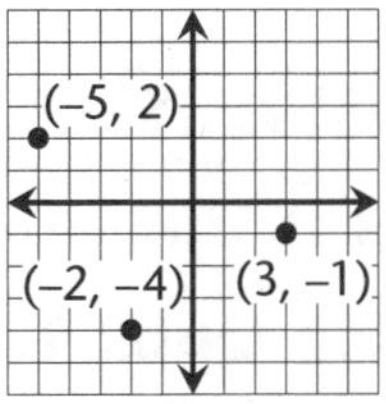

Use mental math to add or subtract.

1. 14 + 9   **2.** 5 + 15 + 10

3. 8 + 3 + 17   **4.** 16 – 4

5. 27 – 16   **6.** 38 – 19

MODULE 2 SECTION 3   **QUICK QUIZ**

1. Find the sum –12 + 8.

2. Rewrite 2 – (–3) as the related addition problem that has the same answer. Solve.

3. Find the difference –20 – 41.

4. From –6°F at 6:00 A.M. the temperature rose 28°, then fell 35° by 9:00 P.M. Write and evaluate an addition expression to model the situation.

5. Find three possible values of x so that 5 – (–x) is negative, zero, and positive.

ANSWERS

Warm-Ups: 1. 23 **2.** 30 **3.** 28 **4.** 12 **5.** 11 **6.** 19

Quick Quiz: 1. –4 **2.** 2 + 3 = 5 **3.** –61 **4.** –6 + 28 + (–35) = –13
5. Sample Response: –10, –5, 10

Find each sum or difference when $x = -5$.

1. $5 + x$ 2. $x - 2$

3. $x + 3$ 4. $10 - x$

5. $1 + x$

MODULE 2 SECTION 4   **QUICK QUIZ**

1. Emily spends d dollars for dinner and m dollars for a movie. How much does she spend in all?

2. Evaluate $a^2 + b$ when $a = 4$ and $b = -5$.

3. It costs $5 for admission to an amusement park and $1.50 per ride. Write an equation to model the relationship between n, the number of rides taken, and c, the total cost.

4. Copy and complete the table of values for $y = 3x + 1$. Then graph the equation in a coordinate plane.

x	y
-2	
-1	
0	
1	
2	
3	

5. The speed limit on a stretch of highway is x mi/h. If a policeman travels 15 mi/h above the speed limit, how far will he go in 3 h?

ANSWERS

Warm-Ups: 1. 0 **2.** -7 **3.** -2 **4.** 15 **5.** -4

Quick Quiz: 1. $d + m$ **2.** 11 **3.** $c = 5 + 1.5 \cdot n$ **4.** -5, -2, 1, 4, 7, 10; Check students' graphs. **5.** $3 \cdot (x + 15)$ mi

Math Thematics, Book 2 **2-65**

MODULE 2 SECTION 5 — WARM-UPS

Use mental math to solve each equation.

1. $n + 6 = 10$

2. $27 - p = 14$

3. $r \times 7 = 42$

4. $44 \div y = 4$

5. $9 \cdot b = 72$

6. $\frac{x}{4} = 20$

MODULE 2 SECTION 5 — QUICK QUIZ

1. Write an equation represented by the algebra tile model.

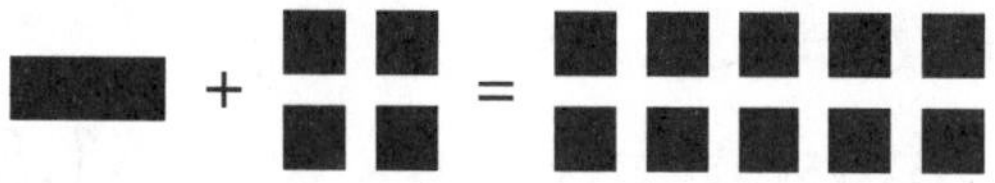

2. Write an addition or subtraction equation to model the following situation. Use one variable and tell what it represents.

During a flu epidemic 14 students were absent, leaving only 11 in the class.

3. Solve $-20 + n = 32$.

4. Is 21 a solution of $-24 = m - 3$?

5. Two angles are supplementary. One angle has a measure of 82°. Let d = the measure of the other angle. Write and solve the related addition equation.

ANSWERS

Warm-Ups: 1. $n = 4$ **2.** $p = 13$ **3.** $r = 6$ **4.** $y = 11$ **5.** $b = 8$ **6.** $x = 80$

Quick Quiz: 1. $x + 4 = 10$ **2.** $n - 14 = 11$, where n is the number of students enrolled in the class **3.** $n = 52$ **4.** No. **5.** $82 + d = 180$; $d = 98$

MODULE 2 SECTION 1   **PRACTICE AND APPLICATIONS**

For use with Exploration 1

For Exercises 1–6, use the diagram.

1. Name three angles that have point *R* as a vertex.

2. Name all the angles that have $\overrightarrow{SA}$ as a side.

3. Name two straight angles.

4. Name an acute angle that has *S* as its vertex and find its measure.

5. Name a right angle.

6. Name three obtuse angles and find their measures.

Draw an angle with each measure. Then classify each angle as *acute*, *right*, *obtuse*, or *straight*.

7. 155°   8. 25°   9. 180°   10. 90°

11. Two cuts have already been made in a pizza, as shown in the diagram at the right. Is it possible to make one more cut from the center *C* so that the three pieces of pizza will be the same size? Explain your thinking.

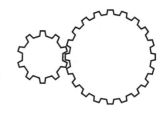

12. How many times from 3 P.M. to 6 P.M. do the minute hand and hour hand of a clock form a right angle?

13. Refer to the diagram at the right. If the gear on the right makes one full revolution, then the gear on the left makes two revolutions. Suppose the gear on the right is turned through an obtuse angle. Will the gear on the left make a full turn?

(continued)

For use with Exploration 2

14. Plane 1 is flying from point *A* at a heading of 50°. Plane 2 is flying from point *A* at a heading of 140°. What is the measure of the angle formed by the flight paths of the two planes?

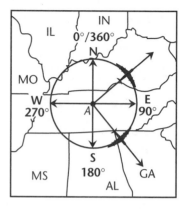

For each angle measure:
a. Find the measure of a supplementary angle.
b. Find the measure of a complementary angle, if possible.

15. 25°   **16.** 172°   **17.** 72°   **18.** 90°

19. 43°   **20.** 20°   **21.** 146°   **22.** 108°

For Exercises 23 and 24, refer to the map at the right.

23. A private plane and a jumbo jet both leave from Cary, but in opposite directions. The private plane is flying toward Jasper at a heading of 223°. What is the heading for the jumbo jet?

24. Morris is located due north of Jasper. Measure on the map with a protractor to find what heading should be used for a flight from Morris to Cary.

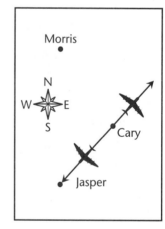

Name _____   Date _____

For use with Exploration 1

1. Write each quantity using symbols instead of words.

   a. New Orleans, Louisiana is 8 ft below sea level.

   b. Big Stone Lake in South Dakota is 966 ft above sea level.

   c. For the first big drop on a roller coaster ride, the speed of Kim's car increased 60 miles per hour.

   d. Maurice lost 480 points on a quiz show.

2. Refer to the number line.

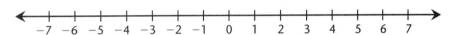

   a. Where on the number line are the integers less than –2?

   b. List all the negative integers that are greater than – 4.

   c. List all the positive integers that are less than 6.

   d. List all the integers that are less than 3 but greater than –7.

3. Replace each ___?___ with > or <.

   a. –8 __?__ –5   **b.** 0 __?__ –2   **c.** –9 __?__ 9

   d. 12 __?__ 7   **e.** –13 __?__ –17   **f.** –25 __?__ 14

4. Find the opposite of each integer.

   a. –12   **b.** 53   **c.** –42

   d. 26   **e.** 0   **f.** –84

5. Find each absolute value.

   a. $|-8|$ **b.** $|23|$ **c.** $|-95|$

   d. $|95|$ **e.** $|-16|$ **f.** $|44|$

6. Replace each ___?___ with > or <.

   a. 6 __?__ $|-15|$ **b.** –8 __?__ $|-8|$ **c.** $|-21|$ __?__ $|-3|$

(continued)

| MODULE 2 SECTION 2 | PRACTICE AND APPLICATIONS |

For use with Exploration 2

For Exercises 7–11, refer to the grid shown below.

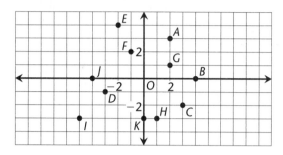

7. a. Name a point on the horizontal axis.

 b. Name a point on the vertical axis.

 c. Is the line through A and G horizontal or vertical?

 d. Is the line through H and I horizontal or vertical?

 e. How many horizontal lines go through point D?

 f. How many vertical lines go through point D?

8. Write the coordinates of each point.

 a. C **b.** E **c.** A

 d. I **e.** J **f.** K

9. Name two points that have the same first coordinate.

10. Name three points that have the same second coordinate.

11. Plot each point in a coordinate plane. Use the grid shown above.

 a. $M(6, -3)$ **b.** $N(-7, 0)$ **c.** $P(-8, 4)$

 d. $Q(7, 2)$ **e.** $R(-8, -4)$ **f.** $S(0, 1)$

12. How can you draw axes on a flat, rectangular table top so that the points on the table top can be located without using any negative coordinates? Can you do this for a mathematical plane? Explain your thinking.

Name _____   Date _____

For use with Exploration 1

A hiker on a number line follows each set of directions. Determine where the hiker will finish. Record the moves as an addition problem with its sum or as a subtraction problem with its difference.

   1. Start at –6. Face the negative direction. Move backward 2 units.

   2. Start at 4. Face the positive direction. Move backward 6 units.

   3. Start at 3. Face the negative direction. Move forward 7 units.

   4. Start at –3. Face the positive direction. Move forward 5 units.

For use with Exploration 2

Use a number line to find each sum. Then write the addition problem with its sum.

   5. –4 + 8

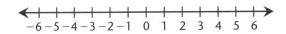

   6. 3 + (–5)

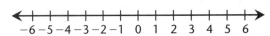

   7. –2 + (–3)

   8. 0 + (–2)

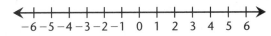

Find each sum.

   9. 3 + (–9)   **10.** –7 + 2   **11.** –5 + (–4)

   12. –8 + 8   **13.** 12 + (–6)   **14.** –11 + 7

   15. 16 + (–10)   **16.** –9 + (–5)   **17.** –13 + 4

For Exercises 18–20, write and evaluate an addition expression to model each situation.

   18. The temperature at 2 P.M. was –3°F. By 5 P.M., the temperature had risen 12°F.

   19. In the first round of a game, Gabriela lost 500 points. In the second round, she gained 900 points.

   20. A weather balloon was released from the top of a hill 250 ft above sea level. The balloon rose 830 ft and was later found floating in the ocean a few miles away.

(continued)

Name _____ Date _____

For use with Exploration 3

Use a number line to find each difference. Then write the subtraction problem with its difference.

21. −1 − (−6)

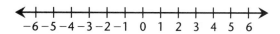

22. 5 − 8

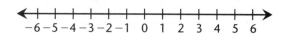

23. −3 − 3

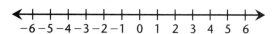

24. 2 − (−4)

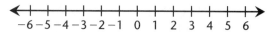

Write the related addition problem that has the same result.

25. −17 − 2   **26.** 8 − (−4)   **27.** 5 − 10

28. −15 − (−6)   **29.** 30 − 42   **30.** −9 − (−25)

Find each difference.

31. 7 − 11   **32.** −3 − 8   **33.** 5 − (−4)

34. −20 − (−10)   **35.** −35 − 16   **36.** −29 − (−15)

Evaluate each expression using a calculator.

37. 3 + (−7) −12   **38.** −42 + 6 − 15   **39.** (8 − 14) − (−3)

40. −2 − (4 − 29)   **41.** (8 − 3) − (3 − 8)   **42.** −6 + (−9) − (−2)

43. The greatest known depth in the Pacific Ocean is 36,198 ft. The greatest known depth in the Atlantic Ocean is 30,246 ft. What is the difference between the deepest point in the Atlantic Ocean and the deepest point in the Pacific Ocean?

44. A diver from a seaside cliff went a vertical distance of 67 ft before coming up to the surface of the water. If the elevation of the cliff is 49 ft, to what depth did he go in the sea?

45. A quiz show contestant starts her second day on the show with 500 points. On the first round, she loses 700 points. On the second round, she gains 850 points. How many points does she have after the second round?

MODULE 2 SECTION 4   **PRACTICE AND APPLICATIONS**

For use with Exploration 1

1. a. Nita started at her home and has driven at a steady speed for 2 hours. She has driven 110 miles. What is Nita's rate of speed?

b. Suppose Nita keeps the same speed for the whole trip. Complete the table of the distances driven in 1, 2, 3, 4, and 5 hours.

Hours driven	Miles traveled
1	
2	
3	
4	
5	

c. Write an equation relating Nita's distance driven to her travel time.

d. Nita is going to Destin, which is 550 miles from her home. How many hours does it take her to drive from her home to Destin?

e. What does the expression $550 - 55t$ model?

f. What values of t make sense for the expression in part (e)?

Choose the letter of the expression that models each situation.

2. An amusement park charges \$3 to enter and \$2 for each ride. What is the price of going to the park and riding on k rides?

a. $2k$ **b.** $2k - 3$ **c.** $3 + 2k$

3. Mr. Anderson gets his brakes checked every 6 months. How many times does he get his brakes checked over a period of y years?

a. $2y$ **b.** $6y$ **c.** $2y - 6$

Evaluate each expression when $x = 5$, $y = -3$, and $z = 6$.

4. $10x$ **5.** $2z + y$ **6.** $y - x$

7. $60 \div x$ **8.** $y + 7x$ **9.** $5z - y$

10. $y + xz$ **11.** $y - xz$ **12.** $2x - 4z$

13. a. Describe a situation that can be modeled by the expression $25q$.

b. Make a table that shows the values of the expression $25q$ for $q = 1$, $q = 2$, $q = 3$, and $q = 4$.

(continued)

MODULE 2 SECTION 4   **PRACTICE AND APPLICATIONS**

For use with Exploration 2

Copy and complete the table of values for each equation.
Then graph each equation in a coordinate plane.

14. $y = x - 6$

x	−2	−1	0	1	2
y					

15. $y = x + 4$

x	−2	−1	0	1	2
y					

16. $y = 7 - x$

x	−2	−1	0	1	2
y					

17. $y = x + 5$

x	−2	−1	0	1	2
y					

Make a table of values for each equation. Then graph the
equation in a coordinate plane.

18. $y = 3 - x$ **19.** $y = x + 9$ **20.** $y = 8 - x$

21. Linda borrowed some money to buy new software for her
computer. Mike borrowed money for a CD player. The graph
shows how they paid back their loans.

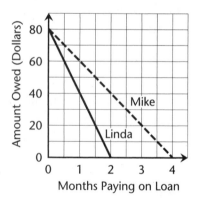

  a. How much did each person borrow? How does the graph
  show this information?

  b. How much did Linda pay back each month? How does
  the graph show this?

  c. How much did Mike pay back each month?

  d. Make tables to show how Linda and Mike paid back
  their loans.

  e. For each person, write an equation that describes how his
  or her loan was repaid. Tell what each variable represents.

Use each graph to make a table of values of *x* and *y*. Then
write an equation to model the relationship between *x* and *y*.

22.

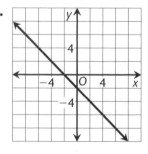

23.

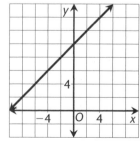

| MODULE 2 SECTION 5 | PRACTICE AND APPLICATIONS |

For use with Exploration 1

a. Write an equation that the model represents.

b. Solve the equation you wrote in part (a).

1. ▭ + ⬜⬜ / ⬜⬜⬜ = ⬜⬜⬜⬜⬜ / ⬜⬜⬜⬜⬜

2. ▭ + ⬜⬜⬜⬜ = ⬜⬜⬜⬜⬜⬜⬜

Write an addition equation to model each situation.

3. Sharlene has done 6 of her 10 homework problems.

4. Of the 23 mineral samples in Yoshi's collection, 4 are clear quartz.

Write a subtraction equation to model each situation.

5. The temperature dropped to –3°F after an afternoon high of 17°F.

6. A dentist sees only 36 patients, since 7 people cancelled appointments.

For use with Exploration 2

Solve. Check each solution.

7. $k - 19 = -80$ **8.** $a + 8 = 53$ **9.** $19 + m = 74$

10. $-15 + t = 24$ **11.** $n - 65 = 32$ **12.** $-17 = b + 50$

For Exercises 13–18, tell whether the number that follows the equation is or is not a solution of the equation.

13. $a - 14 = 30$; 16 **14.** $-9 + b = -4$; 5 **15.** $x - (-7) = 26$; 19

16. $w + 5 = -30$; –35 **17.** $k - 8 = -8$; 16 **18.** $51 + n = -61$; 112

Write an addition or subtraction equation to model each situation. Then solve and check the equation.

19. Two angles are supplementary. The larger has a measure of 139°.

20. After rising 55 m, a submarine was 63 m below sea level.

21. Andrew saved $85, but the CD player he plans to buy is $160.

Name _____   Date _____

For use with Section 1

1. Draw an angle with each measure. Then classify each angle as acute, obtuse, right, or straight.

    a. 90°   **b.** 25°   **c.** 160°

2. For each angle measure:
Find the measure of a supplementary angle.
Find the measure of a complementary angle, if possible.

    a. 75°   **b.** 98°   **c.** 112°

For use with Section 2

3. Rewrite each elevation using symbols instead of words.

    a. Gannett Peak, Wyoming: 13,804 ft above sea level   **b.** Bristol Bay, Alaska: at sea level

    c. New Orleans, Louisiana: 8 ft below sea level   **d.** Death Valley, California: 282 ft below sea level

4. Find the opposite and the absolute value of each integer.

    a. 0   **b.** 49   **c.** –68

    d. –235   **e.** –99   **f.** 400

5. Replace each ___?___ with > or <.

    a. 12 ___?___ 0   **b.** –6 ___?___ 6   **c.** $|-30|$ ___?___ $|-50|$

    d. $|14|$ ___?___ $|-11|$ **e.** $|-28|$ ___?___ $|45|$ **f.** –36 ___?___ –41

For use with Section 3

6. Find each sum or difference.

    a. 9 + (–16)   **b.** –17 – 3   **c.** –5 + 25

    d. –10 – (–4)   **e.** 5 + 28   **f.** 16 + (–5)

    g. 19 + (–19)   **h.** –15 – 9   **i.** –26 – (–60)

(continued)

MODULE 2 SECTIONS 1–5 · PRACTICE AND APPLICATIONS

For use with Section 4

7. Evaluate each expression when $x = 12$, $y = -4$, and $z = 6$.

a. $3z + 6$ **b.** $2x - 21$ **c.** $11z - x$

d. $y + 8z$ **e.** $y - 2x$ **f.** $xz - 20$

g. $5x - y$ **h.** $xz + y$ **i.** $4z - y$

8. Copy and complete the table of values for each equation. Then graph each equation in the coordinate plane.

a. $y = x - 5$

x	−10	−5	0	5	10
y	?	?	?	?	?

b. $y = 2x + 1$

x	−2	−1	0	1	2
y	?	?	?	?	?

9. A bus travels at an average rate of 50 mi/h.

a. Make a table showing the distance traveled for travel times of 0, 1, 2, 3, 4, 5, and 6 h.

b. Write an equation to model the distance traveled d in relation to travel time t.

For use with Section 5

10. Write an addition equation and a subtraction equation to model each situation. Use one variable and tell what it represents.

a. Diana has 38 marbles. She and her brother together have 75 marbles.

b. Ramon needs 5 points in the last quarter of the game to tie his high score of 23 points.

c. Spring spent $8 and has $9 remaining.

11. Solve. Check each solution.

a. $a + 19 = 7$ **b.** $15 + w = 32$ **c.** $r - 17 = -11$

d. $82 = v - 61$ **e.** $b + 26 = -49$ **f.** $k - 51 = -9$

g. $-14 = n + 22$ **h.** $-43 + d = 39$ **i.** $y - 8 = -62$

MODULE 2 SECTION 1   STUDY GUIDE

Heading Out   Looking at Angles

GOAL **LEARN HOW TO:** • name and measure angles
          • classify angles
          • use supplementary and complementary angles

AS YOU: • learn a skill SAR team members need
            • find compass headings

Exploration 1: Measuring Angles

Rays and Angles

A **ray** is a part of a line. It starts at an endpoint and goes on forever in one direction. Ray BC is written $\overrightarrow{BC}$. Always write the endpoint first.

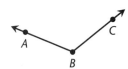

An **angle** is formed by two rays with a common endpoint called the **vertex** of the angle. The angle at the right, formed by $\overrightarrow{BA}$ and $\overrightarrow{BC}$, can be called $\angle ABC$, $\angle CBA$, or $\angle B$. Always write the vertex as the middle letter.

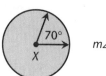

Measuring and Classifying Angles

The measure of an angle is the amount of rotation between its two rays. An angle is measured in units called *degrees*. There are 360° in a complete rotation, so one **degree** is $\frac{1}{360}$ of a complete rotation.

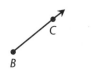

$m\angle X = 70°$

An angle can be classified by its measure.

The measure of an **acute angle** is between 0° and 90°.	The measure of a **right angle** is exactly 90°.	The measure of an **obtuse angle** is between 90° and 180°.	The measure of a **straight angle** is exactly 180°.

               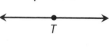

$m\angle Q = 50°$ $m\angle R = 90°$ $m\angle S = 105°$ $m\angle T = 180°$

MODULE 2 SECTION 1   **STUDY GUIDE**

Exploration 2: Angle Relationships

Supplementary and Complementary

Two angles are **supplementary angles** if the sum of the measures of the angles is 180°. $\angle P$ and $\angle Q$ at the right are supplementary angles.

Two angles are **complementary angles** if the sum of the measures of the angles is 90°. $\angle X$ and $\angle Y$ at the right are complementary angles.

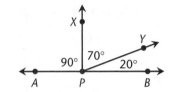

Example

Refer to the diagram.

a. Name two angles that are complementary.

b. Name two angles that are supplementary.

Sample Response

a. To identify two complementary angles, look for a *sum* of 90°.

Since $m\angle XPY = 70°$ and $m\angle YPB = 20°$, and $70° + 20° = 90°$, $\angle XPY$ and $\angle YPB$ are complementary angles.

b. To identify two supplementary angles, look for a *sum* of 180° or look for two angles that form a straight angle.

$\angle APB$ is a straight angle. One pair of angles that form $\angle APB$ is $\angle APY$ and $\angle YPB$.

Notice that $m\angle APY = 90° + 70°$, or 160°, $m\angle YPB = 20°$, and $160° + 20° = 180°$.

So, $\angle APY$ and $\angle YPB$ are one pair of supplementary angles.

Two other angles that are supplementary are $\angle APX$ and $\angle BPX$, whose measures are 90° and $70° + 20°$, or 90°, respectively.

Name _____   Date _____

Exploration 1

For Exercises 1–4, use the diagram.

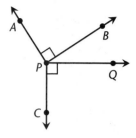

1. Name the ray that passes through point Q.

2. Name an acute angle and find its measure.

3. Name three angles that have $\overrightarrow{PB}$ as a side.

4. **Visual Thinking** Name all the angles that have vertex P.

5. What is the measure of an angle that is one quarter of a full rotation? By what special name is an angle of that measure called?

Exploration 2

For Exercises 6–8, use the diagram.

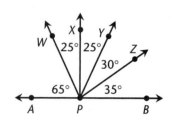

6. Name four pairs of supplementary angles.

7. Name five pairs of complementary angles.

8. **Writing** Are $\angle XPY$, $\angle YPZ$, and $\angle ZPB$ complementary angles? Explain.

9. Draw a pair of supplementary angles that are of equal measure. Classify these angles.

10. **Challenge** Find the measure of the angle whose complementary angle measures $\frac{1}{3}$ of its supplementary angle.

Spiral Review

11. **Patterning** Here are geometric models for the first four *triangular numbers.*

    Draw a geometric model for the fifth triangular number. What is the value of this number? **(Module 1, page 14)**

    ```
     •        •          •            •
             • •        • •          • • •
                       • • •        • • • •
     1        3          6            10
    ```

12. **Probability** There are 6 boys and 4 girls on a school committee. One of the members is chosen at random to serve as secretary. What is the probability that the member selected is a boy? **(Module 1, page 30)**

Name _____   Date _____

Searching for Integers   Integers and Coordinates

GOAL   **LEARN HOW TO:** • compare integers
                            • find opposites and absolute values of integers
                            • identify and plot points in a coordinate plane

        AS YOU: • learn about elevation
                    • work with parallel and perpendicular lines

Exploration 1: Comparing Integers

Integers

Numbers greater than zero are **positive**.

Numbers less than zero are **negative**.

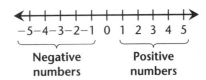

Integers are the counting numbers,
their opposites, and zero. Two numbers
are **opposites** if they are the same
distance from 0 on a number line
but on opposite sides of 0.

The opposite of 5 is –5.
The opposite of –8 is 8.
The opposite of 0 is 0.

The integers are the numbers …, –4, –3, –2, –1, 0, 1, 2, 3, 4, … .

An **inequality** is a mathematical sentence stating that one quantity is
greater than or less than another. You can write inequalities to compare
integers.

    –3 is greater than –6   or   –6 is less than –3
        $-3 > -6$ $-6 < -3$

Example

Write two inequalities to compare –9 and 7.

Sample Response

Graph the numbers on a number line. The integers increase as you go from left
to right.

$$\longleftarrow\!\!+\!\!+\!\!+\!\!+\!\!+\!\!+\!\!+\!\!+\!\!+\!\!+\!\!+\!\!+\!\!+\!\!+\!\!+\!\!+\!\!\longrightarrow$$
$$-9\,-8\,-7\,-6\,-5\,-4\,-3\,-2\,-1\ \ 0\ \ 1\ \ 2\ \ 3\ \ 4\ \ 5\ \ 6\ \ 7$$

$-9 < 7$ or $7 > -9$

MODULE 2 SECTION 2   STUDY GUIDE

The **absolute value** of a number is the distance from the number to 0 on a number line. You read $|-3|$ as "the absolute value of negative three."

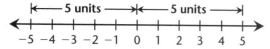

Example

Find the absolute value of –5 and 5.

■ Sample Response ■

$\longleftarrow$ 5 units $\longrightarrow$ $\longleftarrow$ 5 units $\longrightarrow$

$-5 \quad -4 \quad -3 \quad -2 \quad -1 \quad 0 \quad 1 \quad 2 \quad 3 \quad 4 \quad 5$

–5 is 5 units from 0, so $|-5| = 5$.

5 is 5 units from 0, so $|5| = 5$.

Exploration 2: Coordinate Graphing

Line Relationships

A **plane** can be thought of as a flat surface that goes on forever.

Two lines **intersect** if they meet or cross each other. Lines a and b intersect.

Two lines in a plane are **parallel** if they do not intersect. Lines c and d are parallel.

Two lines are **perpendicular** if they intersect at 90° angles. Lines e and f are perpendicular.

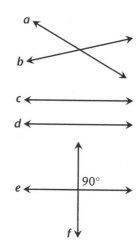

Graphing in a Coordinate Plane

The **coordinate plane** is a grid with a **horizontal axis** and a **vertical axis** that intersect at the **origin**.

An **ordered pair** of numbers, called **coordinates,** can be used to identify and plot points in a coordinate plane.

The *first coordinate* in an ordered pair gives a point's location to the left or right of zero on the horizontal axis. The *second coordinate* gives the point's location up or down from zero on the vertical axis.

The ordered pair for the **origin** is (0, 0).

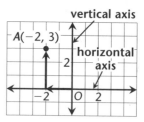

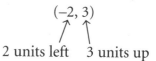

Point A has coordinates (–2, 3).

(–2, 3)

2 units left   3 units up

Name _____   Date _____

MODULE 2 SECTION 2 | PRACTICE & APPLICATION EXERCISES | STUDY GUIDE

Exploration 1

Replace each ___?___ with > or <.

1. 9 ___?___ 5   **2.** 0 ___?___ −5   **3.** 43 ___?___ −53

4. −16 ___?___ −20   **5.** −3 ___?___ −1   **6.** 8 ___?___ 11

Find the opposite of each integer.

7. 5   **8.** −30   **9.** 588   **10.** −19

Find the absolute value of each integer.

11. $|-10|$ **12.** $|50|$ **13.** $|-2|$ **14.** $|312|$

Exploration 2

15. a. Identify the coordinates of the points A through E in the coordinate plane.

   b. Graph the ordered pairs $(-3, 5)$ and $(-3, -3)$ in a coordinate plane. Draw a segment to connect the points.

   c. Graph the ordered pairs $(-1, 4)$ and $(-4, 1)$ in the coordinate plane for part (b). Draw a segment to connect the points.

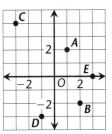

Spiral Review

For each angle measure in Exercises 16–18, find the measure of a complementary angle. (Module 2, p. 83)

16. 37°   **17.** 16°   **18.** 69°

19. **Displaying Data** Make a bar graph of the data below. (Toolbox, p. 594)

Total Miles Logged This Week by Members of The Walkers Club			
Monday...15	Tuesday...25	Wednesday...40	Thursday...42
Friday...22	Saturday...50	Sunday...19	

Find each sum or difference. (Toolbox, p. 587)

20. $\frac{2}{7} + \frac{3}{7}$ **21.** $\frac{7}{9} - \frac{4}{9}$ **22.** $\frac{3}{4} - \frac{2}{4}$ **23.** $\frac{1}{8} + \frac{6}{8}$

MODULE 2 SECTION 3 · STUDY GUIDE

A Call for Help   Integer Addition and Subtraction

GOAL **LEARN HOW TO:** • use a model to work with integers
• add integers
• use properties of addition
• subtract integers

AS YOU: • take and analyze hikes along a number line
• explore wind-chill temperatures

Exploration 1: Modeling Integer Operations

Number-Line Models

You can think of addition and subtraction as hikes on a number line.

> **Example**
>
> Find the sum $3 + (-5)$.
>
> **Sample Response**
>
> Start at 3, facing in the positive direction. Move backward 5 units.
>
>
> So, $3 + (-5) = -2$.

Exploration 2: Adding Integers

To add two integers with the *same sign*, add the absolute values of the integers. The sum has the same sign as the integers you are adding. For example, $9 + 3 = 12$ and $-5 + (-3) = -8$.

To add two integers that have *different signs*, subtract the lesser absolute value from the greater one. The sum has the same sign as the integer with the greater absolute value. For example, $2 + (-3) = -1$ and $-5 + 9 = 4$.

The sum of **0 and a number** is that number. For example, $0 + 6 = 6$ and $-3 + 0 = -3$.

The sum of **a number and its opposite** is 0. For example, $8 + (-8) = 0$.

MODULE 2 SECTION 3 STUDY GUIDE

Properties of Addition

The **commutative property of addition** says that you can change the order of numbers in an addition problem and still get the same sum.

> **Example**
>
> $8 + 3 = 11$ and $3 + 8 = 11$
>
> $-7 + 2 = -5$ and $2 + (-7) = -5$
>
> $-3 + (-4) = -7$ and $-4 + (-3) = -7$

The **associative property of addition** says that you can change the grouping when you add numbers and still get the same sum.

> **Example**
>
> $3 + (4 + 5) = 3 + 9 = 12$ and $(3 + 4) + 5 = 7 + 5 = 12$
>
> $-5 + [4 + (-3)] = -5 + 1 = -4$ and $[-5 + 4] + (-3) = -1 + (-3) = -4$

Exploration 3: Subtracting Integers

You can rewrite a subtraction problem as an addition problem. To subtract an integer, add its opposite.

> **Example**
>
> Find each difference.
>
> **a.** $4 - (-7)$ **b.** $3 - 9$
>
> ---
>
> **Sample Response**
>
> **a.** Rewrite the subtraction as an addition and then add.
>
> $4 - (-7) = 4 + 7$ ← Add the opposite of –7.
>
> $ = 11$
>
> **b.** Rewrite the subtraction as an addition and then add.
>
> $3 - 9 = 3 + (-9)$ ← Add the opposite of 9.
>
> $ = -6$

MODULE 2 SECTION 3 | PRACTICE & APPLICATION EXERCISES | STUDY GUIDE

Exploration 1

A hiker on a number line follows each set of directions. Determine where the hiker will finish. Record the moves as an addition problem with its sum or as a subtraction problem with its difference.

1. Start at –5. Face the positive direction. Move backward 2 units.

2. Start at 3. Face the negative direction. Move forward 4 units.

3. Start at –1. Face the negative direction. Move backward 2 units.

Exploration 2

Find each sum.

4. $-4 + (-2)$　　　　　**5.** $-5 + 0$　　　　　**6.** $7 + 5$

7. $-13 + (-18)$　　　　**8.** $-9 + 5 + (-3)$　　**9.** $5 + 0 + (-5)$

Mental Math **Find each sum mentally. Use properties of addition.**

10. $-7 + 0 + (-5) + 7$　　　　**11.** $9 + (-4) + (-3) + 4 + (-6)$

12. $-8 + 5 + 13 + 0 + (-2)$　　**13.** $3 + (-14) + (-8) + 5$

Exploration 3

For Exercises 14–17, rewrite each subtraction problem as the related addition problem that has the same answer. Then solve.

14. $9 - 5$　　　**15.** $-5 - (-8)$　　　**16.** $0 - (-3)$　　　**17.** $8 - (-2)$

18. Find the difference $-6 - (-5)$.

Spiral Review

19. Graph these ordered pairs in a coordinate plane:

$S(-2, 5)$, $T(3, 6)$, $U(2, -1)$, $V(-3, -5)$, $W(4, 0)$, and $X(0, 3)$
(Module 2, p. 95)

Mental Math **Find each sum or difference mentally.** (Toolbox, p. 581)

20. $1.46 + 0.95$　　　　**21.** $36.55 - 20.99$　　　　**22.** $12.18 - 9.2$

Find the next three terms of each sequence. (Module 1, p. 20)

23. $22, 27, 32, 37, \ldots$　　　　**24.** $100, 89, 78, 67, \ldots$

Name _____   Date _____

Urban Rescue   Function Models

GOAL   **LEARN HOW TO:** • model a function with a table or an equation
 • evaluate expressions with variables
 • model a function with a graph

AS YOU: • explore distance, rate, and time
 • choose between emergency vehicles

Exploration 1: Modeling a Function

Evaluating Expressions

To **evaluate** an expression that has a variable, substitute a value for the
variable and perform the operations. When two expressions are equal, you
can write an **equation** to express the relationship.

> **Example**
>
> A hiker on a 50 mi journey has traveled for t hours at r miles per hour. Find the
> distance left to hike after 12 h at an average rate of 2 mi/h.
>
> ▬ **Sample Response** ▬
>
> Distance, rate, and time are related by the formula *distance traveled = rate × time*. So,
> the distance traveled in t hours at r miles per hour is the product rt.
>
> Therefore, an expression for the distance left to hike is $50 - rt$. Evaluate this expression
> for $r = 2$ and $t = 12$.
>
> $$50 - rt = 50 - 2 \cdot 12 \quad \leftarrow \text{Substitute 2 for } r \text{ and 12 for } t.$$
> $$= 50 - 24$$
> $$= 26$$
>
> The hiker has 26 mi left to travel.

Modeling Functions

A **function** is a relationship between input and output. For each input,
there is exactly one output. You can model a function in many ways.
Making a table and writing an equation are two ways to model a function.

> **Example**
>
> A number y is 3 more than twice another number x. Model this function in two ways.
>
> Table:
>
> | Input x | 0 | 1 | 2 | 3 | 4 |
> |-----------|---|---|---|---|----|
> | Output y | 3 | 5 | 7 | 9 | 11 |
>
> **Equation:** $y = 2x + 3$

MODULE 2 SECTION 4   STUDY GUIDE

Exploration 2: Graphing a Function

A function can also be modeled using a graph.

Example

A festival sold tickets for a concert at $2.00 each. A local company has agreed to donate an additional $1.00 for each ticket sold. Model the relationship between the number of tickets sold and the amount of money collected using a table, an equation, and a graph. Then find out how much money is collected if 450 tickets are sold.

■ Sample Response ■

Make a table to show the relationship between the number of tickets sold (n) and the amount of money collected (c) for these values: 1, 2, 3, and n.

Tickets sold	Amount collected ($)
1	3
2	6
3	9
n	c

Write an equation to model the relationship between the number of tickets sold and the amount collected.

$c = 3n$

Make a graph of the equation using the values in the table.

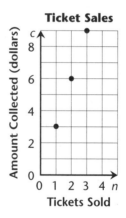

Use the equation to determine how much money is collected if 450 tickets are sold.

$c = 3n$
$ = 3(450)$ ← Replace n with 450.
$ = 1350$

For 450 tickets, $1350 is collected.

| MODULE 2 SECTION 4 | PRACTICE & APPLICATION EXERCISES | STUDY GUIDE |

Exploration 1

1. Choose the letter of the expression that models this situation. The price of a book is m dollars. What is the price after a $1.50 decrease?

    A. $m + \$1.50$ **B.** $m - \$1.50$ **C.** $\$1.50 \div m$

2. Write an expression that models this situation.
Larry is 2 years older than Fran. Fran is t years old. How old is Larry?

Evaluate each expression when $a = 2$, $b = -2$, and $c = 3$.

  3. $30a$ **4.** $6b$ **5.** $45 \div c$

  6. $4b + 5$ **7.** $-3a - 11$ **8.** $b + 3c + a$

Exploration 2

For Exercises 9 and 10, copy and complete the table of values for each equation. Then graph each equation in a coordinate plane.

  9. $y = x + (-2)$ **10.** $y = 2x - 1$

x	-2	-1	0	1	2
y	?	?	?	?	?

x	-10	-5	0	5	10
y	?	?	?	?	?

11. Describe a situation that can be modeled by the equation $y = x - 4$. Then make a table of values for the equation and graph the equation in a coordinate plane.

Spiral Review

Find each sum or difference. (Module 2, p. 109)

  12. $-12 + (-31)$ **13.** $-7 - (-5)$ **14.** $-11 - 17$

For Exercises 15–17, suppose you roll a nine-sided die with faces labeled 1 to 9 and all outcomes are equally likely. Find the theoretical probability of each event. (Module 1, p. 33)

  15. $P(8)$ **16.** $P(13)$ **17.** $P(\text{even number})$

18. Make a table, draw a graph, and write an equation for the sequence 11, 12, 13, 14, … . Then predict the 100th term. **(Module 1, p. 20)**

MODULE 2 SECTION 5   STUDY GUIDE

Searching for a Solution   Addition and Subtraction Equations

GOAL   **LEARN HOW TO:** • write addition and subtraction equations
                       • solve addition equations using models
                       • use inverse operations to solve addition and subtraction equations
                       • check solutions

            AS YOU: • examine the contents of a backpack
                     • explore weight limits for a backpack

Exploration 1: Write and Model Equations

Modeling Equations

A value of a variable that makes an equation true is a **solution of the equation**. The process of finding solutions is called **solving an equation**.

Balance models can help you visualize an equation and remember that both sides represent the same amount. *Algebra tile models* can help you solve (find a solution of) an equation.

Example

Model this situation: Derrick has 5 more colors of model paint than Sherry. Sherry has 11 colors. How many colors does Derrick have?

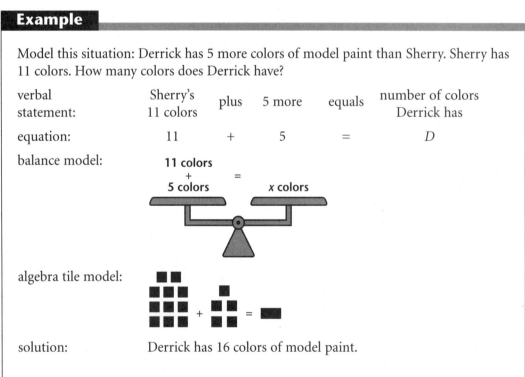

verbal statement:	Sherry's 11 colors	plus	5 more	equals	number of colors Derrick has
equation:	11	+	5	=	D

balance model:

algebra tile model:

solution: Derrick has 16 colors of model paint.

| MODULE 2 SECTION 5 | STUDY GUIDE |

Exploration 2: Using Inverse Operations

Using Inverse Operations to Solve

Addition and subtraction are **inverse operations**. They "undo" each other.

When you use symbols and variables to solve an equation, you are solving the equation *algebraically*.

To solve an equation, remember these ideas:

• The goal is to get the variable alone on one side of the equation.

• Use inverse operations to "undo" one another.

• Any operation done on one side of an equation must also be done on the other side to keep the equation balanced.

• Check that your solution is correct by substituting the value for the variable into the equation.

• If necessary, use tiles to model the equation.

Subtraction "undoes" addition when you solve an equation.

| **Example** |

Solve $n + 5 = 8$.

■ Sample Response ■

$$
\begin{aligned}
n + 5 &= 8 \\
-5 &= -5 \quad \leftarrow \text{Subtract 5 from both sides.} \\
\hline
n + 0 &= 3 \\
n &= 3
\end{aligned}
$$

Check:

$n + 5 = 8 \quad \leftarrow$ Substitute 3 for n.

$3 + 5 \stackrel{?}{=} 8$

$8 = 8$ ✔

Addition "undoes" subtraction when you solve an equation.

| **Example** |

Solve $n - 5 = 8$.

■ Sample Response ■

$$
\begin{aligned}
n - 5 &= 8 \\
+5 &= +5 \quad \leftarrow \text{Add 5 to both sides.} \\
\hline
n + 0 &= 13 \\
n &= 13
\end{aligned}
$$

Check:

$n - 5 = 8 \quad \leftarrow$ Substitute 13 for n.

$13 - 5 \stackrel{?}{=} 8$

$8 = 8$ ✔

Name _____   Date _____

Exploration 1

1. Write the equation represented by the model at the right.

2. Open-ended Describe a situation that can be modeled by the equation $x - 4 = 7$. Be sure to tell what the variable represents.

3. Make an algebra tile model that represents $x - 2 = 5$. Then use the model to help you find the solution.

4. Write an addition equation to model this situation: Dorothy enrolled 36 new newspaper customers raising her total subscriptions to 78. Use one variable and tell what it represents.

5. Write a subtraction equation to model this situation: After distributing 143 flyers, David had 7 left. Use one variable and tell what it represents.

Exploration 2

For Exercises 6–14, solve each equation. Check each solution.

6. $x - (-8) = -6$ **7.** $45 = 34 + t$ **8.** $y - 25 = -16$

9. $n + (-5) = 18$ **10.** $k - 19 = 13$ **11.** $49 = -5 + g$

12. $8 = 9 + c$ **13.** $0 = y - (-4)$ **14.** $w + 6 = 27$

15. Is 5 a solution of the equation $-9 + n = 4$? Explain.

Spiral Review

Evaluate each expression when $x = 5$, $y = 3$, and $z = -12$.
(Module 2, p. 124)

16. $x - 9$ **17.** $-3 + 2y$ **18.** $z - 6x$

For Exercises 19–22, tell whether each number is divisible by 2, 5, and 10. (Toolbox, p. 582)

19. 30   **20.** 130   **21.** 465   **22.** 123

23. James and Andy earned a total of $112. James worked 6 h and Andy worked 8 h. How much did each earn if they make the same amount per hour? Tell what problem solving strategy you used. **(Module 2, p. 44)**

MODULE 2   **TECHNOLOGY**

For Use with Section 4

Suppose Gabriel leaves his house on a bike ride at 9:00 A.M. He travels at an average speed of 20 mi/h. Two hours after he leaves, his mother discovers that he has forgotten his lunch. Immediately, she sets off after him in her car. She drives at an average speed of 45 mi/h. At what time will Gabriel's mother catch up with her son?

To solve this problem using a graphing calculator, enter the function Y1=20X on the Y= list. This function models the distance that Gabriel has traveled after riding for X hours. Since Gabriel's mother leaves 2 hours later, the function that models her distance traveled is Y2=45(X–2).

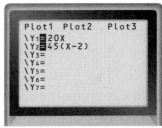

To find how far Gabriel or his mother is from home, you can use the Table feature of the calculator. Enter the Table Setup values shown on the screen at the right. Then display the table.

1. How far from home is Gabriel at noon? Explain how you arrived at your answer. _____

2. How far from home is Gabriel's mother at noon?

    _____

3. How much ahead of his mother is Gabriel after he has been riding 3.5 hours? _____

4. At what time does Gabriel's mother catch up with Gabriel?

    _____

5. Suppose that Gabriel was traveling at a speed of 15 mi/h and his mother at a speed of 35 mi/h. At what time would Gabriel's mother catch up with Gabriel? _____

Name _____   Date _____

For Exercises 1–5 use the diagram at the right.

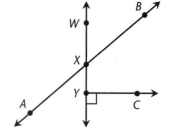

1. Name two rays that pass through point X.

2. Name an acute angle, an obtuse angle, a right angle, and a straight angle.

3. Find the measure of $\angle AXW$.

4. Name and find the measure of an angle supplementary to $\angle AXW$.

5. Draw an angle complementary to $\angle WXB$.

6. Use a protractor to find the heading shown in the compass diagram. What would the heading be if you were flying from town B to town A?

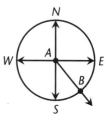

For each description in words, represent the change using an integer and an appropriate unit of measure.

7. You withdraw $48 from your savings account.

8. You scale a cliff 280 ft high.

Find the next three terms in each sequence.

9. $28, -2, -32, \ldots$ 10. $15, 7, -1, \ldots$ 11. $7, 4, 1, \ldots$

Find the opposite of each integer.

12. 27 13. -13 14. -199 15. 54

Find the absolute value of each integer.

16. $|-24|$ 17. $|81|$ 18. $|35|$ 19. $|-40|$

Replace each __?__ with >, <, or =.

20. -81 __?__ 22 21. $|-4|$ __?__ -5 22. $-|-3|$ __?__ -3

23. Plot each point in a coordinate plane: $A(4, -6)$, $B(2, 3)$, $C(-4, -4)$, $D(5, 0)$, $E(-1, 2)$.

24. In three plays, a football team gains 11 yd, loses 18 yd, and gains 3 yd. Write and evaluate an addition expression to model the situation.

Evaluate each expression.

25. $-90 + (-8)$ 26. $16 - 22$ 27. $38 - (-8)$

28. $-8 + (-6)$ 29. $-3 + 14$ 30. $5 + (-17)$

Name _____ Date _____

For Exercises 1–5, use the diagram at the right.

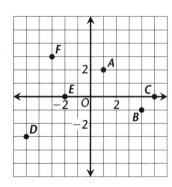

1. Name two obtuse angles.

2. Name two right angles.

3. Name three acute angles.

4. Name a straight angle.

5. Find the measure of a complementary angle and a supplementary angle to ∠YMH.

6. After heavy spring rains, a newspaper in a small town reported that the local river was within 4 ft of flood stage. Use integers to describe this situation. Be sure to indicate what positive integers, negative integers, and zero represent.

For Exercises 7 and 8, use the following integers: –19, 0, 4, –7, 12, –13.

7. Which list shows the integers in order from least to greatest?

   a. 0, 4, –7, 12, –13, –19   **b.** –7, –13, –19, 0, 4, 12

   c. –19, –13, –7, 0, 4, 12   **d.** –19, –13, 12, –7, 4, 0

8. Which integer has the least absolute value?

   a. –19   **b.** –7   **c.** 0   **d.** 4

9. A swing is built for a playground that is situated on a level field. Describe the relationship between the ropes that support the flat wooden seat of the swing. Then describe the relationship between each of the ropes and the seat.

For Exercises 10–15, refer to the coordinate plane at the right. Write the coordinates of each point.

10. point A   11. point B

12. point C   13. point D

14. point E   15. point F

Math Thematics, Book 2 **2-95**

Name _____   Date _____

Evaluate each expression.

16. $9 + (-7)$ **17.** $-4 + 12$ **18.** $-7 + (-3)$ **19.** $0 - (-3)$

20. $-8 - 17$ **21.** $5 - 14$ **22.** $6 + (-3) - 10$ **23.** $-9 + 20 - 11$

Evaluate each expression when $m = 7$, $a = -3$, $b = -4$, and $n = 12$.

24. $2m + a$ **25.** $b - 3n$ **26.** $7 - a$

27. $n - 3m$ **28.** $2m - a$ **29.** $4m - 4n$

30. A contractor is going to purchase steel pipe and plastic tubing for a building project. The steel pipe weighs 5 lb/ft and the plastic tubing weighs 2 lb/ft.

    a. Copy and complete the table to show the weights of the different lengths of pipe and plastic tubing the contractor needs.

    b. Write an equation that shows the relationship between L, the length of the pipe or tubing, and w, the weight.

Length (ft)	Weight (lb)	
	Steel pipe	Plastic tubing
10		
20		
40		
50		
60		

    c. Graph your equations from part (b) on the same coordinate grid. Draw lines connecting the points for each item.

    d. Use your graph to find out which item would weigh more if the contractor buys a piece 45 ft long. How much more would it weigh?

Solve and check.

31. $k + 20 = 13$ **32.** $-6 + a = 10$ **33.** $y - (-8) = 27$

34. $45 + x = 52$ **35.** $-18 + m = -25$ **36.** $30 = v + 40$

37. Elsa has 47 CDs. Last week she gave 9 CDs to a friend. Write an equation to model the situation. Identify the variable you use. Then solve the equation.

MODULE 2 TEST   FORM **B**

For Exercises 1–5, use the diagram at the right.

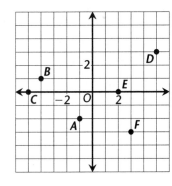

1. Name two obtuse angles.

2. Name two right angles.

3. Name three acute angles.

4. Name a straight angle.

5. Find the measure of a complementary angle and a supplementary angle to ∠*XME*.

6. After heavy spring rains, a newspaper in a small town reported that the local river was within 7 ft of flood stage.

   Use integers to describe this situation. Be sure to indicate what positive integers, negative integers, and zero represent.

For Exercises 7 and 8, use the following integers: –25, 0, 7, –9, 12, –13.

7. Which list shows the integers in order from least to greatest?

   a. 0, 7, –9, 12, –13, –25   **b.** –9, –13, –25, 0, 7, 12

   c. –25, –13, –9, 0, 7, 12   **d.** –25, –13, 12, –9, 7, 0

8. Which integer has the least absolute value?

   a. –25   **b.** –9

   c. 0   **d.** 7

9. Describe the relationship between the lines on a piece of notebook paper. Then describe the relationship between the left edge and the bottom edge.

For Exercises 10–15, refer to the coordinate plane at the right. Write the coordinates of each point.

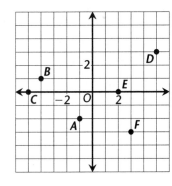

10. point *A*   **11.** point *B*

12. point *C*   **13.** point *D*

14. point *E*   **15.** point *F*

MODULE 2 TEST   FORM **B**

Evaluate each expression.

16. $8 + (-7)$ **17.** $-3 + 11$ **18.** $-6 + (-4)$ **19.** $0 - (-5)$

20. $-8 - 16$ **21.** $6 - 14$ **22.** $5 + (-3) - 11$ **23.** $-9 + 13 - 8$

Evaluate each expression when $m = 7$, $a = -3$, $b = -4$, and $n = 12$.

24. $6m + a$ **25.** $b - 2n$ **26.** $7 - b$

27. $n - 3m$ **28.** $2n + a$ **29.** $4m - 4n$

30. A contractor is going to purchase steel pipe and plastic tubing for a building project. The steel pipe weighs 15 lb/yd and the plastic tubing weighs 6 lb/yd.

   a. Copy and complete the table to show the weights of the different lengths of pipe and plastic tubing the contractor needs.

   b. Write an equation that shows the relationship between L, the length of the pipe or tubing, and w, the weight.

Length (yd)	Weight (lb)	
	Steel pipe	**Plastic tubing**
30		
60		
120		
150		
180		

   c. Graph your equations from part (b) on the same coordinate grid. Draw lines connecting the points for each item.

   d. Use your graph to find out which item would weigh more if the contractor buys a piece 45 yd long. How much more would it weigh?

Solve and check.

31. $a + 20 = 17$ **32.** $-3 + x = 12$ **33.** $y - (-8) = 15$

34. $15 + x = 39$ **35.** $-17 + m = -40$ **36.** $16 = v + 30$

37. Elsa has 39 cassettes. Last week she gave 5 cassettes to a friend. Write an equation to model the situation. Identify the variable you use. Then solve the equation.

Name _____ Date _____

1. Which of the following statements is false?

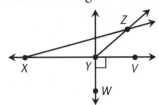

   a. ∠YXZ is obtuse.
   b. ∠XYV is straight.
   c. ∠ZYV is acute.
   d. ∠WYV is right.

2. ∠A and ∠B are complementary. The measure of ∠A is 20°. What is the measure of an angle that is supplementary to ∠B ?
   a. 70°   **b.** 110°
   c. 140°   **d.** 160°

3. The deepest point in the world's oceans is 35,797 ft below sea level. Mt. Everest is 29,029 ft high. What is the difference between these two elevations?
   a. 6668 ft   **b.** 6768 ft
   c. 64,826 ft   **d.** 65,716 ft

4. What are the coordinates of point A?

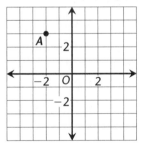

   a. $(-2, 3)$ **b.** $(-2, -3)$
   c. $(3, -2)$ **d.** $(-3, 2)$

5. Evaluate $-14 - (18 - 21)$.
   a. -11 **b.** -17
   c. -43 **d.** -53

6. David wants to buy a $1.25 sandwich and a $0.95 soda for each of his n friends. Write an equation that models the relationship between his total cost C and n.
   a. $C = n + 1.25 + 0.95$
   b. $n = \dfrac{C}{1.25} + 0.95$
   c. $C = n(1.25 + 0.95)$
   d. $C = \dfrac{n(1.25)}{0.95}$

7. Evaluate $a^2 - b + 4$ when $a = 5$ and $b = -2$.
   a. 4   **b.** 16
   c. 19   **d.** 31

8. Write an equation that models this sentence:
Eight less than three times a number y equals x .
   a. $8 - 3y = x$ **b.** $8(3 - y) = x$
   c. $3(x - 8) = y$ **d.** $3y - 8 = x$

9. Predict the cost of 5 lb of apples.

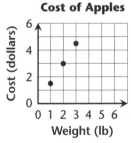

   a. $6.50   **b.** $7.00
   c. $7.50   **d.** $8.00

10. Solve $-24 = 6 - 3x$.
   a. -6 **b.** -10
   c. 10   **d.** 18

MODULE 2 — MODULE PERFORMANCE ASSESSMENT

A middle school class is thinking of two possible ways to raise money to buy new equipment for the school. One option is to sell raffle tickets for donated items. For every raffle ticket a student sells, the school will make a profit of $2. The other option is to sell $6 tickets to a fundraising performance. That performance will cost $175 (taken from the profits) to put on.

Step 1: The equation $6t - 175 = p$ describes the profit p the school makes from the fundraiser after selling t tickets. Evaluate the expression $6t - 175$ to find the value of p when $t = 15$.

Step 2: Construct a table of values to show how much profit the school would make if the class sold 10, 25, or 150 tickets for the fundraiser. What do negative values of p represent? What do positive values of p represent?

Step 3: Use the table you made in Step 2 to graph the equation $6t - 175 = p$ on a coordinate grid. Draw a line to connect the points. About how many tickets must the class sell to make a profit on the fundraiser?

Step 4: Write an equation to describe the relationship between the amount of money p the school makes after the class sells t tickets for the raffle. Construct a table of values for the equation and graph the results on the same coordinate grid you used in Step 3.

Step 5: Examine the graph. In which situation is the raffle a better idea? the fundraiser? Explain how the intersection of the lines relates to the effectiveness of each method for raising money for the school.

Step 6: Suppose the class decides to sell raffle tickets. They start with a roll of 300 tickets. After selling a certain number of tickets, 26 still remain. Write an equation to model the situation using a variable, and explain what the variable represents. Solve the equation to find how many tickets have been sold.

Answers

PRACTICE AND APPLICATIONS

Module 2, Section 1
1. ∠ARB, ∠BRS, ∠ARF
2. ∠ASE, ∠ASF, ∠ASG
3. ∠ARF, ∠RSF
4. ∠FSG; 30°
5. ∠ASE or ∠ESF
6. ∠ESG, 120°; ∠RSG, 150°; ∠BRS, 130°
7.

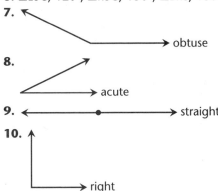

    obtuse

8.

    acute

9.   straight

10.   right

11. No. The angle for the slice shown has a measure of 105°. Since there are 360° in a circle, for three pieces to have the same size, each piece would have to have a measure of 120°.
12. 6 times
13. No.
14. 90°
15. a. 155° b. 65°
16. a. 8° b. not possible
17. a. 108° b. 18°
18. a. 90° b. not possible
19. a. 137° b. 47°
20. a. 160° b. 70°
21. a. 34° b. not possible
22. a. 72° b. not possible
23. 43°
24. about 142°

Module 2, Section 2
1. a. −8 ft b. 966 ft c. 60 mi/h d. −480 points
2. a. to the left of −2 b. −3, −2, −1 c. 1, 2, 3, 4, 5
d. −6, −5, −4, −3, −2, −1, 0, 1, 2
3. a. < b. > c. < d. > e. > f. <
4. a. 12 b. −53 c. 42 d. −26 e. 0 f. 84
5. a. 8 b. 23 c. 95 d. 95 e. 16 f. 44
6. a. < b. < c. >
7. a. J or B b. K c. vertical d. horizontal e. one
f. one
8. a. (3, −2) b. (−2, 4) c. (2, 3) d. (−5, −3)
e. (−4, 0) f. (0, −3)
9. A and G

10. H, I, and K
11.

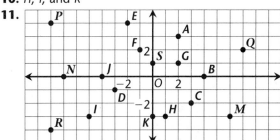

12. Sample Response: Use the lower left corner as the origin, the bottom edge of the table as the horizontal axis, and the left edge of the table as the vertical axis. You cannot do this for a mathematical plane. A mathematical plane extends endlessly in all directions. This means that you must use both positive and negative coordinates.

Module 2, Section 3
1. −4; −6 − (−2) = −4
2. −2; 4 + (−6) = −2
3. −4; 3 − 7 = −4
4. 2; −3 + 5 = 2
5.

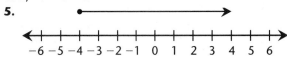

−4 + 8 = 4
6.

3 + (−5) = −2
7.

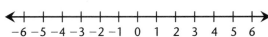

−2 + (−3) = −5
8.

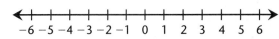

0 + (−2) = −2
9. −6
10. −5
11. −9
12. 0
13. 6
14. −4
15. 6
16. −14
17. −9
18. −3 + 12 = 9
19. −500 + 900 = 400

20. 250 + 830 + (–1080) = 0

21.

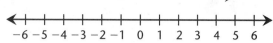

–1 – (–6) = 5

22.

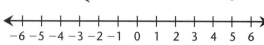

5 – 8 = –3

23.

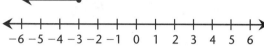

–3 – 3 = –6

24.

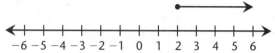

2 – (–4) = 6

25. –17 + (–2)

26. 8 + 4

27. 5 + (–10)

28. –15 + 6

29. 30 + (–42)

30. –9 + 25

31. –4

32. –11

33. 9

34. –10

35. –51

36. –14

37. –16

38. –51

39. –3

40. 23

41. 10

42. –13

43. –5952 ft

44. –18 ft

45. 650 points

Module 2, Section 4

1. a. 55 mi/h **b.**

Hours driven	Miles traveled
1	55
2	110
3	165
4	220
5	275

c. d = 55t **d.** 10 h **e.** Nita's distance from Destin after driving t hours **f.** values from 0 to 10

2. c

3. a

4. 50

5. 9

6. –8

7. 12

8. 32

9. 33

10. 27

11. –33

12. –14

13. a. Sample Response: Thomas has q quarters and wants to know how much money he has in all.

b.

q	1	2	3	4
25 q	25	50	75	100

14.

x	–2	–1	0	1	2
y	–8	–7	–6	–5	–4

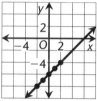

15.

x	–2	–1	0	1	2
y	2	3	4	5	6

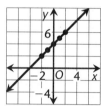

16.

x	–2	–1	0	1	2
y	9	8	7	6	5

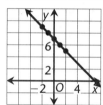

17.

x	–2	–1	0	1	2
y	3	4	5	6	7

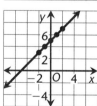

18.

19.

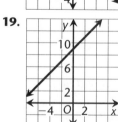

20.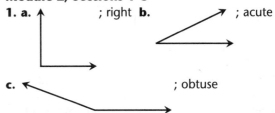

21. a. $80; The point (0, 80) is on each graph. The second coordinate represents the amount of money owed after 0 months, that is, at the time the money was borrowed. **b.** $40; The difference in the second coordinates of (0, 80) and (1, 40) is 40. **c.** $20

d.

Months	Amount Linda owes (dollars)
0	80
1	40
2	0

Months	Amount Mike owes (dollars)
0	80
1	60
2	40
3	20
4	0

e. Linda: $y = 80 - 40x$; x is the number of months since Linda borrowed the money, and y is the amount owed after x months. Mike: $y = 80 - 20x$; x is the number of months since Mike borrowed the money, and y is the amount owed after x months.

22.

x	-4	-2	0	2
y	2	0	-2	-4

; $y = -2 - x$

23.

x	-4	-2	0	2
y	6	8	10	12

; $y = x + 10$

Module 2, Section 5
1. a. $x + 5 = 12$ **b.** Remove 5 tiles from each side; 7
2. a. $m + 4 = 7$ **b.** Remove 4 tiles from each side; 3
3. $6 + x = 10$; x represents the number of problems Sharlene still has to do.
4. $m + 4 = 23$; m represents the number of mineral samples that are not clear quartz.
5. $17 - x = -3$; x represents the number of degrees the temperature dropped.
6. $p - 7 = 36$; p represents the number of patients who originally had appointments.
7. -61
8. 45
9. 55

10. 39
11. 97
12. -67
13. No.
14. Yes.
15. Yes.
16. Yes.
17. No.
18. No.
19. $x + 139 = 180$; x is the measure of the smaller angle; 41.
20. $d + 55 = -63$; d is the original elevation of the submarine; -118.
21. $85 + m = 160$; m is the additional amount of money Andrew needs to have $160; 75.

Module 2, Sections 1–5
1. a. ; right **b.** ; acute

c. ; obtuse

2. a. 105°; 5° **b.** 82°; not possible **c.** 68°; not possible
3. a. 13,804 ft **b.** 0 ft **c.** -8 ft **d.** -282 ft
4. a. 0; 0 **b.** -49; 49 **c.** 68; 68 **d.** 235; 235
e. 99; 99 **f.** -400; 400
5. a. > **b.** < **c.** < **d.** > **e.** < **f.** >
6. a. -7 **b.** -20 **c.** 20 **d.** -6 **e.** 33 **f.** 11 **g.** 0
h. -24 **I.** 34
7. a. 24 **b.** 3 **c.** 54 **d.** 44 **e.** -28 **f.** 52 **g.** 64
h. 68 **i.** 28

8. a.

x	-10	-5	0	5	10
y	-15	-10	-5	0	5

b.

x	-2	-1	0	1	2
y	-3	-1	1	3	5

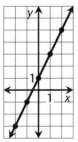

9. a.

t	0	1	2	3	4	5	6
d	0	50	100	150	200	250	300

b. $d = 50t$

10. a. Let *m* represent the number of marbles that Diana's brother has. So, the equations are $m + 38 = 75$ and $75 - m = 38$. **b.** Let *p* represent the number of points Ramon scored in the game. So, the equations are $5 + p = 23$ and $23 - p = 5$. **c.** Let *m* represent the amount of money Spring originally had. So, the equations are $8 + 9 = m$ and $m - 8 = 9$.

11. a. –12 **b.** 17 **c.** 6 **d.** 143 **e.** –75 **f.** 42 **g.** –36 **h.** 82 **i.** –54

STUDY GUIDE

Module 2, Section 1

1. $\overrightarrow{PQ}$

2. $\angle BPQ$; 33°

3. $\angle APB$, $\angle QPB$, and $\angle CPB$

4. $\angle APB$, $\angle BPQ$, $\angle QPC$, $\angle APC$, $\angle BPC$, and $\angle APQ$

5. 90°; right angle

6. $\angle APW$ and $\angle WPB$, $\angle APX$ and $\angle XPB$, $\angle APY$ and $\angle YPB$, $\angle APZ$ and $\angle ZPB$

7. $\angle APW$ and $\angle WPX$, $\angle XPY$ and $\angle YPB$, $\angle XPZ$ and $\angle ZPB$, $\angle YPB$ and $\angle WPX$, $\angle APW$ and $\angle XPY$

8. No; although the sum of the measures of the three angles is 90°, by definition complementary angles are pairs of angles.

9. Supplementary angles of equal measure are right angles.

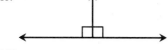

10. 45°

11.

```
          •
         • •
        • • •
       • • • •
      • • • • •
          15
```

12. $\frac{6}{10}$ or $\frac{3}{5}$

Module 2, Section 2

1. >

2. >

3. >

4. >

5. <

6. <

7. –5

8. 30

9. –588

10. 19

11. 10

12. 50

13. 2

14. 312

15. a. $A(1, 2)$, $B(2, -2)$, $C(-3, 4)$, $D(-1, -3)$, $E(3, 0)$

b, c.

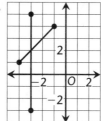

16. 53°

17. 74°

18. 21°

19.

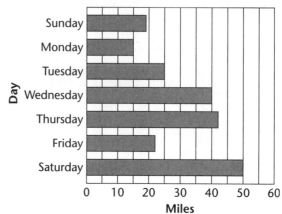

Total Miles Walked This Week by Members of The Walkers Club

20. $\frac{5}{7}$

21. $\frac{3}{9}$ or $\frac{1}{3}$

22. $\frac{1}{4}$

23. $\frac{7}{8}$

Module 2, Section 3

1. –7; $-5 + (-2) = -7$

2. –1; $3 - 4 = -1$

3. 1; $-1 + 2 = 1$

4. –6

5. –5

6. 12

7. –31

8. –7

9. 0

10. –5

11. 0

12. 8

13. –14

14. $9 + (-5)$; 4

15. $-5 + 8$; 3

16. $0 + 3$; 3

17. $8 + 2$; 10

18. –1

19.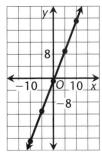

20. 2.41
21. 15.56
22. 2.98
23. 42, 47, 52
24. 56, 45, 34

Module 2, Section 4
1. B
2. $t + 2$
3. 60
4. −12
5. 15
6. −3
7. −17
8. 9
9. −4, −3, −2, −1, 0

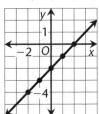

10. −21, −11, −1, 9, 19

11. Sample Response: Sarah is 4 years younger than Marcia. Marcia is x years old.

x	4	5	6	7	8
y	0	1	2	3	4

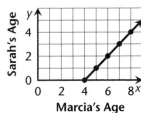

12. −43
13. −2
14. −28
15. $\frac{1}{9}$
16. 0
17. $\frac{4}{9}$
18.

Term number	1	2	3	4
Term	11	12	13	14

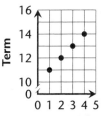

Sequence Equation: $y = x + 10$; The 100th term of the sequence is 110.

Module 2, Section 5
1. $x + 6 = 9$
2. Sample Response: During the first 5 min of an experiment, the temperature of a chemical solution dropped 4 degrees to 7°C. If x represents the temperature of the solution at the beginning of the experiment, what is the value of x?
3. ■ − ■■ = ■■■■■; $x = 7$
4. Let s represent the number of subscriptions Dorothy had sold previously. So, $s + 36 = 78$.
5. Let d represent the number of flyers David started with. So, $d − 143 = 7$.
6. −14
7. 11
8. 9
9. 23
10. 32
11. 54
12. −1
13. −4
14. 21
15. No; substituting 5 for n gives −9 + 5, or −4, on the left side, and −4 ≠ 4.
16. −4
17. 3
18. −42
19. 30 is divisible by 2, 5, and 10.
20. 130 is divisible by 2, 5, and 10.
21. 465 is divisible by 5.
22. 123 is not divisible by 2, 5, or 10.
23. James earned $48 and Andy earned $64; strategies will vary.

TECHNOLOGY

Module 2
1. 60 mi; Sample Response: At noon, Gabriel will have been traveling for 3 h. The table shows that when X is 3, the value of Y1 is 60.
2. 40 mi
3. 2.5 mi
4. 12:36 P.M.
5. 12:30 P.M.

ASSESSMENT

Mid-Module 2 Quiz
1. Any two of the following: $\overrightarrow{AX}$, $\overrightarrow{BX}$, $\overrightarrow{WX}$, $\overrightarrow{YX}$, $\overrightarrow{XA}$, $\overrightarrow{XB}$, $\overrightarrow{XW}$, $\overrightarrow{XY}$
2. Sample Response: $\angle WXB$, $\angle YXB$, $\angle XYC$, $\angle WXY$
3. 130°
4. $\angle AXY$, 50° or $\angle WXB$, 50°
5.

40°

6. 140°, 220°
7. −$48
8. 280 ft
9. −62, −92, −122
10. −9, −17, −25
11. −2, −5, −8
12. −27
13. 13
14. 199
15. −54
16. 24
17. 81
18. 35
19. 40
20. <
21. >
22. =
23.

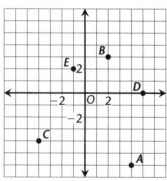

24. 11 + (−18) + 3 = −4
25. −98
26. −6
27. 46
28. −14
29. 11
30. −12

Module 2 Test (Form A)
1. $\angle AMY$, $\angle XMH$
2. $\angle AME$, $\angle EMH$, $\angle XMY$ (any two)
3. $\angle AMX$, $\angle XME$, $\angle EMY$, $\angle YMH$ (any three)
4. $\angle AMH$
5. 70°; 160°
6. −4; Positive integers indicate a river level above flood stage, negative integers indicate a river level below flood stage, and zero indicates a river level exactly at flood stage.
7. c
8. c
9. The ropes are parallel to each other. Each rope is perpendicular to the seat of the swing.
10. (1, 2)
11. (4, −1)
12. (5, 0)
13. (−5, −3)
14. (−2, 0)
15. (−3, 3)
16. 2
17. 8
18. −10
19. 3
20. −25
21. −9
22. −7
23. 0
24. 11
25. −40
26. 10
27. −9
28. 17
29. −20
30. a.

Length (feet)	Weight (pounds)	
	Steel pipe	Plastic tubing
10	50	20
20	100	40
40	200	80
50	250	100
60	300	120

b. steel pipe: $w = 5L$; plastic tubing: $w = 2L$

c.

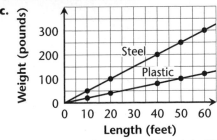

d. 45 feet of steel pipe would weigh 135 lb more than the same length of plastic tubing.

31. –7

32. 16

33. 19

34. 7

35. –7

36. –10

37. $x - 9 = 47$; x represents the number of CDs Elsa originally had; 56.

Module 2 Test (Form B)

1. ∠AMX, ∠XMC, ∠EMB (any two)

2. ∠AMC, ∠EMC

3. ∠AMB, ∠XME, ∠BMC

4. ∠BMX or ∠AME

5. 50°; 140°

6. –7 ft; Positive integers indicate a river level above flood stage, negative integers indicate a river level below flood stage, and zero indicates a river level exactly at flood stage.

7. c

8. c

9. The lines on a piece of notebook paper are parallel. The left edge and bottom edge are perpendicular.

10. (–1, –2)

11. (–4, 1)

12. (–5, 0)

13. (5, 3)

14. (2, 0)

15. (3, –3)

16. 1

17. 8

18. –10

19. 5

20. –24

21. –8

22. –9

23. –4

24. 39

25. –28

26. 11

27. –9

28. 21

29. –20

30. a.

Length (yards)	Weight (pounds)	
	Steel pipe	Plastic tubing
30	450	180
60	900	360
120	1800	720
150	2250	900
180	2700	1080

b. steel pipe: $w = 15L$; plastic tubing: $w = 6L$

c.

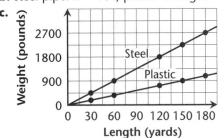

d. 45 yards of steel pipe would weigh 405 lb more than the same length of plastic tubing.

31. –3

32. 15

33. 7

34. 24

35. –23

36. –14

37. $c - 5 = 39$; c represents the number of cassettes Elsa originally had; 44.

STANDARDIZED TEST

Module 2

1. a

2. b

3. c

4. a

5. a

6. c

7. d

8. d

9. c

10. c

MODULE PERFORMANCE ASSESSMENT

Module 2

Step 1: $6(15) - 175 = -85$

Step 2:

Fundraiser Tickets ($p = 6t - 175$)	
Tickets sold (t)	Profit (p)
10	−115
25	−25
150	725

The negative values of p represent losses. The positive values of p represent profits.

Step 3: They must sell 30 or more tickets to make a profit. (See graph with answer to step 4.)

Step 4: $p = 2t$, where p = profit and t = tickets sold;

Raffle Tickets ($p = 2t$)	
Tickets sold (t)	Profit (p)
10	20
25	50
150	300

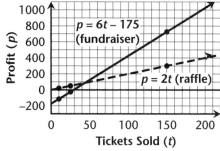

Step 5: If a lot of tickets can be sold, the fundraiser will make more money. But if the potential buying audience is small (< 45), the raffle tickets make more money. The intersection of the two line graphs shows that at 45 tickets, both events make exactly the same profit.

Step 6: $n - 26 = 300$, where n is the number of raffle tickets sold;

$$n - 26 = 300$$
$$n = 300 - 26$$
$$n = 274$$

274 tickets have been sold.

Name _____ Date _____

MODULES 1 AND 2 TEST   **CUMULATIVE**

Use the line graph for Exercises 1–3.

1. What was the average sales price of a new one-family house in 1970?

2. During what 5-year period did housing costs increase the most?

3. Predict the cost of a new one-family house in the year 2000.

Average Sale Price of a New One-Family House

4. Fourteen people were asked how many phone calls they usually receive in a day. Make a frequency table of the resulting data: 2, 3, 0, 2, 1, 5, 2, 3, 0, 5, 2, 4, 5, 2.

5. Make a table, draw a graph, and write an equation for the sequence 3, 7, 11, 15, … . Then predict the 200th term.

6. Find the volume of a cube when the length of an edge is 6 ft.

7. Sarah spun the two spinners shown at the right 80 times. Her results are shown in the frequency table. Find the experimental probability of each outcome.

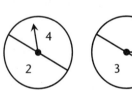

Outcome	Frequency
2, 1	18
2, 3	21
4, 1	24
4, 3	17

For Exercises 8–10, refer to the spinners. Suppose an experiment consists of spinning each of the two spinners. The resulting numbers are then added.

8. Copy and complete the table to show the sums (outcomes) that can occur.

9. Find the theoretical probability of each outcome.

10. If you spun the spinner 90 times, how many times would you expect to get either a 5 or a 7?

Spinner A Spinner B

	Spinner B		
Spinner A	2	4	6
1	?	?	?
3	?	?	?
5	?	?	?

Evaluate each expression without using a calculator.

11. $2 \cdot 4^2 - 10 \cdot 3$ 12. $150 - 30 \div 6$ 13. $20 \div 2^2 + 2 \cdot 2$

MODULES 1 AND 2 TEST   CUMULATIVE

For Exercises 14–17, use the diagram at the right.

14. Name two acute angles.

15. Name two obtuse angles.

16. Name a pair of complementary angles and a pair of supplementary angles.

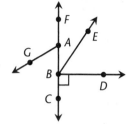

17. Find the measure of $\angle EBC$.

18. List the following integers in order from least to greatest: $-8, 7, -4, -11, 12, 5, 9, -1$.

Find the opposite and absolute value of each integer.

19. -14 **20.** 1234 **21.** 29 **22.** -8

Graph each ordered pair in the same coordinate plane.

23. $(4, 1)$ **24.** $(-2, -1)$ **25.** $(3, -4)$ **26.** $(-2, -3)$

Evaluate each expression.

27. $|-18| - (-3)$ **28.** $|8 - (-4) - 1|$

29. $-2 + 14 - 8 + (-5)$ **30.** $-25 - (-30) + (-21)$

31. The school secretary can type 60 words/min. After a year of lessons, Brian can type 35 words/min.

Time	Words Typed	
	Secretary	**Brian**
1	?	?
5	?	?
10	?	?
30	?	?

     a. Copy and complete the table shown at the right to show how many words the secretary and Brian can type in 1 min, 5 min, 10 min, and 30 min.

     b. Write an equation that shows the relationship between w, the number of words typed, and t, the time in minutes, for each typist.

     c. Graph your equations from part (b) on the same coordinate grid. Draw lines connecting the points for each typist.

     d. Use your graph or equations to find out how many more words the secretary can type than Brian in 45 min.

32. Eric sold 12 subscriptions on the last day of the school fundraiser. That brought his total number of subscriptions sold to 54. Write an equation to model the situation. Identify the variable you used.

Solve. Check each solution.

33. $32 + x = -14$ **34.** $105 = 70 + y$ **35.** $12 = z - (-4)$

Answers

CUMULATIVE TEST

Modules 1 and 2

1. Sample Response: about $25,000
2. from 1985 to 1990
3. Sample Response: about $175,000
4.

Number of calls	Tally	Frequency
0	II	2
1	I	1
2	IIIII	5
3	II	2
4	I	1
5	III	3

5.

Term number	Term
1	3
2	7
3	11
4	15
5	19
6	23

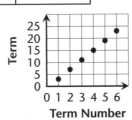

$t = 4n - 1$, where t is the term and n is the term number; 200th term = 799

6. 216 ft^3

7. $P(2, 1) = \frac{9}{40}$, $P(2, 3) = \frac{21}{80}$, $P(4, 1) = \frac{3}{10}$, $P(4, 3) = \frac{17}{80}$

8.

Spinner A	Spinner B 2	4	6
1	3	5	7
3	5	7	9
5	7	9	11

9. $P(3) = \frac{1}{9}$, $P(5) = \frac{2}{9}$, $P(7) = \frac{1}{3}$, $P(9) = \frac{2}{9}$, $P(11) = \frac{1}{9}$

10. 50 times
11. 2
12. 145
13. 9
14. Any two of the following: $\angle GAB$, $\angle ABE$, $\angle EBD$
15. $\angle CBE$, $\angle GAF$
16. $\angle ABE$ and $\angle EBD$; $\angle ABE$ and $\angle EBC$, or $\angle ABD$ and $\angle DBC$
17. 145°

18. −11, −8, −4, −1, 5, 7, 9, 12
19. 14, 14
20. −1234, 1234
21. −29, 29
22. 8, 8
23–26.

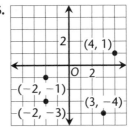

27. 21
28. 11
29. −1
30. −16
31. a.

Time	Words Typed Secretary	Brian
1	60	35
5	300	175
10	600	350
30	1800	1050

b. secretary: $w = 60t$; Brian: $w = 35t$

c.

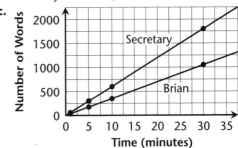

d. 1125 words
32. $m + 12 = 54$, where m is the number of subscriptions he had sold before the last day
33. −46
34. 35
35. 8